RHETORICAL INVESTIGATIONS

Rhetorical analysis of texts exposes plausible 'truths' and presumptions implied by the writer's presentation. In this book, Leslie Gardner analyses the master psychologist Jung, who claimed to be expert at uncovering personal, psychological truths. In his theoretical writings, his rhetoric reveals philosophical ramifications which bear strong similarities to those of the rhetorician of the eighteenth century, Italian philosopher Giambattista Vico.

This book is driven by an interest in arguing that it is possible to read Jung's works easily enough when you have a set of precepts to go by. The paradox of scientific discovery being set out in Jung's grotesque and arcane imagery begins to seem a startling and legitimate psychology for the twenty-first century.

It is time Jungian studies took on this most appropriate examination of analytical psychology. Bringing Vico to bear directly on Jung's thought has only been cursorily attempted before although much alluded to. We find indeed that some of Jung's ideas derive from rhetorical theory, and this book proposes to highlight Jung's innovations, and bring him into the forefront of contemporary psychological thought. *Rhetorical Investigations* will be of interest to analysts and academics, and also to those studying philosophy and psychology.

Leslie Gardner obtained a PhD at the Centre for Psychoanalytic Studies, University of Essex, and did further research at Birkbeck's Institute for the Humanities in London, and earlier at the University of Iowa's International Writers Workshop.

RHETORICAL INVESTIGATIONS

G. B. Vico and C. G. Jung

Leslie Gardner

Routledge
Taylor & Francis Group
LONDON AND NEW YORK

First published 2013
by Routledge
4 Park Square, Milton Park, Abingdon, Oxon OX14 4RN
605 Third Avenue, New York, NY 10017

Routledge is an imprint of the Taylor & Francis Group, an informa business

British Library Cataloguing in Publication Data
A catalogue record for this book is available from the British Library

Library of Congress Cataloging-in-Publication Data
Gardner, Leslie.
Rhetorical investigations : G.B. Vico and C.G. Jung / Leslie Gardner.
pages cm
Includes bibliographical references and index.
1. Jungian psychology. 2. Jung, C. G. (Carl Gustav), 1875–1961.
3. Vico, Giambattista, 1668–1744. I. Title.
BF173.J85G37 2013
150.19'54–dc23
2012039552

ISBN: 978-0-415-68603-7 (hbk)
ISBN: 978-0-415-68604-4 (pbk)
ISBN: 978-0-203-55208-7 (ebk)

Typeset in Garamond
by Keystroke, Station Road, Codsall, Wolverhampton

CONTENTS

Acknowledgements vii

Introduction 1

1 Tensions: Psychoanalysis/rhetoric/science 16

2 Jung's rhetorical stance 29

3 Topical invention and tropes – tools of the imagination: Definitions and issues 35

4 *Psychological Types* and rhetorical devices: Perspectives 57

5 Considering fantasy, fiction and Lacan 69

6 High profile representations – metaphor and metonymy: Jung, Vico and Ricoeur, phenomenological anthropology 88

7 Affinities: Vico and Jung and the themes other scholars discover 106

8 Word association tests and deliberative logic: Forensic Jung 126

9 *Pathé* and Jung's passionate agony over *Answer to Job* 149

10 Ethos, the rhetoric of *Memories, Dreams, Reflections* and perjuries of self-presentations: With two-part preamble 167

11 Concluding remarks 205

References 207
Index 219

ACKNOWLEDGEMENTS

There are many to thank in the lengthy period of my work on this book. Members of the IAJS (International Association of Jungian Scholars) have provided friendly and informed feedback at conferences, but also on the invaluable forum at www.jungianstudies.org: Michael Glock, Helena Bassil-Morozow, Liz Broderson and Mark Saban among them.

Raya Jones asked me way back 'what did I mean by "nothing"?' and has offered abiding comment and friendship over meals in Cardiff and London.

Susan Rowland's books inspired me before I knew her. A warm and brilliant teacher, she set me on her quest to persuade people that Jung is accessible. Her attachment to the wise and eloquent poet, Joel Weishaus, who shares my view about the importance of Jungian aesthetic, cannot be overlooked.

Craig Stephenson nudged me to keep thinking about Vico as Jungian; and Paul Bishop bothered to engage himself at all in my work, and reminds us all passionately of the importance of Jungian intellectual coordinates. Terence Dawson's approach to literature in considering Jungian themes has been an inspiration.

Lucy Huskinson deserves gratitude for encouragement and insistence on clarity; and thanks are also due to co-editor, Luke Hockley, who worked with me on *House: the wounded healer on television* (2010). He is an inspiration as editor, clinician and theorist.

Frances Gray's brilliant and articulate books along with discussion over shared meals at conferences and annual trips to Europe encouraged me enormously.

Nick Stratton has thrashed out ideas about our shared passion for Jungian ideas over years in valued friendship since we met at Essex.

Acknowledgement is due also to the triumvirate at University of Essex at the Centre for Psychoanalytic Studies: Andrew Samuels for reminding me of the clinical side of Jungian studies; Roderick Main for attentions to research, and listening with humour; and to Renos Papadopoulos where it all began. Kevin Lu has been a valued colleague at Essex.

Mara and Cecilia Gardner championed me; and my sons, Raffaello and Niccolo who were dumbfounded I'd do such a thing but who listened for years with unswerving support.

Gabriele Pantucci, my Italian humanist, tolerated absences in libraries or at lectures, with friends devoted to Jung, including helping me to entertain them, and propelled me forward by posing that original question from years ago, 'why don't you look into Vico?'

And we must all share in acknowledging the publishing talents of Kate Hawes, and her colleagues at Routledge/Taylor and Francis – specifically in my case thanks to Camilla Barnard – for all that they do in disseminating a vital series of books focused on Jungian studies.

INTRODUCTION

Underpinnings and propositions

Bringing Vico and Jung together first came to mind in reading James Joyce, and then, later, James Hillman. Soon I found that there were other scholars who had noted affinities between them but it had never been explored in great depth. How Vico's philosophical and technical ideas can fruitfully be brought to bear on Jung's writings and on his psychological insights reveals the impulses of communication in specific ways. Seeing each in a broader humanistic and trans-European philosophical tradition can be accomplished usefully and I propose to pursue this investigation here. And there was also a personal mission: I wanted to join other writers in the Jungian field in exploring the international popularity of his hybrid writings . . . and to analyse his prose to see why it was so engaging.

This book scrutinises the connection between Jung and Vico, and reveals an angle on Jung's work that is productive in tracing its nature and the nature of the psyche he proposed. Jung insists his work is scientific and yet he eschews the language and proofs of traditional science which he also endeavoured to challenge. His paradoxical rhetorical choices belie customary neutral, positivistic and logical 'scientific' expression. Reading Jung's work is problematic: he is overly allusive, and the line of discussion is often associative in private ways that are elusive. In some respects, his writing is about discovering those associations, and we are engaged to look in.

Examining the rhetorical forms he uses might give us clues to the energies driving the prose, and provide a way to explore his and our qualms when we read his work. Vico's subterranean and controversial rhetorical approach suits my purposes (what David Marshall calls a 'sublimation' of rhetoric); and further, Vico's work is a kind of hermeneutical anthropology, a phrase referring to Paul Ricoeur's approach, whose work has bearing on Vico and Jung's written word.

Presentation of scientific argument is often set out by Jung in visual or metaphoric ways, using also invented voices, and sarcastic or ironic discourse. How does he get from the word association tests which were praised internationally for their scientific innovation, to synchronicity and flying saucers more apparently suited to science fiction than to scientific investigation? And yet, the techniques of accessing and interpreting internal symbols, sourced in an unconscious collective, and of utilising alchemical calculations (for one example) as material and empirical evidence are the cornerstones of Jung's scientific analytical psychology. I propose that this shift in Jung's work was his discovery of an appropriate and valid scientific mode of enquiry, more than adequate to his invention of analytical psychology.

Like Vico's writings, Jung's prose is often criticised for being impenetrable and quirky. Several things have changed since both these authors put pen to paper; for one thing, there has been a shift in contemporary reader reception. In recent decades, postmodernist critics' positive response to hybrid text has made reading the mixture of symbol, allegory, logical and metaphoric styles both Jung and Vico employ more explicable. So not only is scientific or philosophical language appreciated in different layers, their innovative work is too.

For another, the shift emerged also in early twentieth-century critical discussion of Baroque prose, embellishing analysis of Vico's writing in the first place, and also indicating ways to read Jung. Vico's prose is appreciated as elaborated ornamental and layered argument, organised around central topics, *warranted* rather than ascribed to causal or 'logical' necessities. Here I refer to the shift in analysis of argument in Toulmin's work on the elaborations of logic. As will be pursued later, Walter Benjamin's discussion of the aesthetic of the German mourning play in 1928 with its new perceptions about correlations between social and political patterns makes investigation of mixed texts viable. Gilles Deleuze's seminal work 'The Fold, Liebniz and Baroque' (1993/2006) and, earlier, Morris W. Croll's work (focusing on sixteenth-century Baroque) also delve into the implications arising from prose in this elaborated style. And we bring that awareness to bear on Jung's texts.

Readers penetrate Vico's writing instinctively by grasping his poetic key, his great innovation. It is the post-modernist inclination to accommodate such ornate texts that has probably brought Vico's work back into current debates. Hermeneutic issues of rhetorical style are used as a tool for understanding theoretical work in the psychoanalytic field and this has been a theme for commentators more recently. The tension between rhetoric and the psychoanalytic project has a long history, and inherits the ancient tension of the philosopher vs. the rhetorician: the theorist vs. the practitioner. I will begin to trace this history in this chapter.

Both Jung and Vico believed they'd engaged in a revolutionary scientific way of investigating the human psyche. The discovery influenced their writing modes, and, in turn, both have had impact on several disciplines after them: literature, anthropology, sociology and psychology.

The stretch between Jung and Vico across time and space throws up anomalies and obstacles at every turn. But there are some compelling reasons that make such an enquiry irresistible.

There are particular places where Hillman and Joyce wrote about Vico that inspired my theoretic tactic: Hillman's essay, 'Vico, Ficino and Plotinus as precursors of Jung' (Hillman 1975) and James Joyce's *Finnegans Wake*. Joyce's references to Jung in his late novel, which is structured as a 'trellace' (to use Joyce's word), were based on Vico's notion of *ricorsi*[1] and the novelist exploits resonances between Jung and Vico's work to embellish the framework and the time scheme. In his personal life, Joyce sought out Jung to treat his schizophrenic daughter.

Trawling through German literature to see where Jung might have inadvertently incorporated traces of ideas directly from Vico, an eighteenth-century Italian (who had never left Naples or its vicinity), I found that Goethe accepted a copy of Vico's *The New Science* from Jacobi; Marx referred to Vico's axioms and laws of history in letters and in *Das Capital;* Dilthey was persuaded by Vico's 'poetic logic' and stylistic alignments to eras in history.

Heidegger's student, Ernesto Grassi, an Italian at University of Munich, wrote works highlighting Vico's rhetorical ontology. In the same period, Erich Auerbach, escaping Nazi Germany, translated *The New Science* which certainly influenced in turn Edward Said's cultural studies. Auerbach, whose immense importance as literary theorist for university curricula globally, along with Northrop Frye also in literary theory, specifically mention and use Jungian ideas derived from archetypes. Both acknowledge the importance of Vico's 'imaginary types' (close to Jung's archetypal figures) and rhetorical work. But Jung never mentions Vico despite being exposed to ideas deriving from his work in his readings.

But as I studied Vico's work, I realised that leaping over time and space in this way from the eighteenth century to the twentieth century is something Vico argues is possible *if* the axioms of his *The New Science* are attended to. He refers to the necessity of an appreciation of 'ideal eternal history' which leads a reader to cut across anomalous contingencies of history and to discern the similarities. Reading cultural product and history as *topics*, pivoting on warranted similarities, Vico proposes that by way of rhetoric we find a hermeneutic for discovery of 'eternal' and primal culture and language. Marshall demonstrates in his work that Vico brought his civic rhetoric underground based on this mode (Marshall 2010); and I'd suggest Jung did something very similar. I will explore how this important tenet of rhetoric functions for Vico and for Jung in related and illuminating ways.

Similarly on these grounds, I've used rhetorical theorists from throughout history, from the Greek and Roman period and the Italian Renaissance period alongside Vico, seeking justifications throughout. Apart from different emphases throughout the history of rhetoric, the coordinates remain similar – even to discussion of the gestural rhetoric of animals George Kennedy writes about (see Kennedy 1998). In my discussion, the rhetorical mode is an ontological stance stemming from a long tradition of philosophical thought. Mostly, however, I focus on referencing rhetoricians who were favourites of both Jung's and Vico's, Cicero and Longinus, for example. They both refer often to Plato, one of Vico's 'greats' which he enumerates in his *Vita.* The Roman rhetorician is, however, the most frequently referred to by both.

Broadly speaking, attitudes to time and space are similar in Jung's and Vico's work. One aspect of this affinity I'd propose that brings them very close is an approach to how the individual is placed in relation to the collective. Using those words stirs up many problems, and to clarify I will step aside to expand on this.

The universal, the personal, the impersonal/collective

In Hillman's essay he refers to what he thinks are Vico's 'imaginative universals'. In Vico's *The New Science* these universals purport to be primal pre-cognitive imaginative figures who fashion the world: Hercules, the strong hero, Ulysses, the wily leader, etc. Hillman describes them, however, as self-reflexive abstractions of common referents. But they are not quite that for Vico. In effect, by so defining them as the embodiment of a two-stepped process, i.e. the results of self-regarding activity particularising a common allusion, it is not the primal category Vico means. The distinction Hillman makes refers rather to Vico's second-level universals: 'intelligible universals'. The secondary level of 'universal' is founded on the 'imaginative universals'. 'Imaginative universals' galvanise significance, and generate the next moves but they are constituted by sensual engagement with the world. Humans generalised fears or joys as they were associated to biological reactions. These are universals which we might say are 'univocal' as Vico tried to emphasise; they are originary; they constitute the human world. 'Naming' and/or *narrativa vera* which Vico described as the first poetical communications of humankind, was expressive but also generative. I believe that Jung was pointing at the nature of such primal level or what we might say is the archetypal level.

Vico draws on Aristotle's definition of *poesis* from *Poetics* and *Rhetoric* to articulate the fashioning or naming aspect of human rhetoric. This is a distinctly human capacity; as Kennedy points out in *The rhetoric of animals*, animal gestures are *only* about communication, they are not about fashioning or creating worlds.

Here rhetoric is revealed in its ontological dimension and is exploited by Vico and Jung in distinctive ways. Using concepts from contemporary discussions of rhetoric alluded to by Vico and psychological contentions Jung proposes, I think we come up with some interesting parallels. I'd like to propose three levels that build on Vico's universals and go some way toward Jung's ideas of personality types and archetypes. These levels involve dimensions of individual and collective, mythic and personal, affective and objective: they are the personal, the universal and the impersonal.

These levels delineate elements of Vico's 'imaginative universals' figures such as Ulysses and Hercules, who share qualities with the archetypal types as Jung traced them such as the hero, the old man, the anima and also, in other ways defined by Jung, personality types, which are rather instinctive biological and affective orientations for Vico.

It is first of all important to say that, of necessity, these levels overlap. In respect to discourse, these elements have simultaneously social and civic functions; they represent or manifest the vivid interiors of the individual; and they have symbolic presence. Persons have symbolic and mythic dimension too (which Jung proposes in referring to the fable of a life), and as I argue that language and personhood (and figures) are commensurate, and accommodate archetypes, we can talk across these levels.

(1) The personal: the person has traits that cohere in particular ways and combine with a subjective interior to make a unique individual. This aspect for both Jung and Vico is the child's world. Vico equated this subjective level also with instinct – an area of irrational human drive or passion. For example, he says that humans are 'driven to human society by religion and natural instinct' (Vico 1948, 1730–44: para 555). It is a 'primitive' drive that children share with early humans. Character traits are linked to the humours in the Aristotelian sense, as his biological essays in '*Problems I*' set out: black bile indicates irritability, sexual retention, etc. But in these allusions we are as close as Vico ever gets to 'personal' in just the way Jung might express 'personal'. Personal is irrational, utterly particular and unique, applicable to humans with an interior which Vico could not articulate. Discussion of the personal is endlessly detailed and nuanced, sometimes without shape. In Vico's world, it is not an important level of consideration (in the last pages of his *Vita* there is a paradigmatic event when two groups claim his body outside his home, and disrupt the funeral – it's about the person of Vico as a notable figure in the community, and the claims the civic society has on an individual).

Irrationality is associated to the personal, and to the subjective, because it is unaccountable. In *The New Science*, Hebrews, who operated outside the world of the gentiles, respond directly to God and were an ancient and moralistic civilisation. 'The Hebrews believed in a God all mind who searches the hearts of men, and the gentiles believed in gods composed of bodies and mind who could not do so.' (Vico 1948, 1730–44: para 350) Personal qualities of the human characterise the Hebrew world, but not the gentile world where Vico occupied himself.

(2) The universal: here I use an idea derived from Perelman and Olbrechts-Tyteca's discusson of the 'universal audience' in their groundbreaking volume *The New Rhetoric* (1969). This is the world-wide audience the writer (or orator) has in mind when she prepares her work. It is assumed, as Habermas proposed too, that this universal audience is a humane and *reasonable* human group. It is a broader audience than Wayne Booth's 'implied audience' which the author or speaker works up in her imagination to address. (You might say that 'implied audience' is a combination of the personal and the universal in a fully integrated presence.) The 'implied' audience is a rather more constrained audience, conceived as a populace invented with the intentions and prejudices of the writer/speaker. In fact, 'each individual, each culture, has its own conception of the universal audience' Perelman and Olbrechts-Tyteca (1969: 33) propose,

but as they quote Sartre, 'such audience consists of the whole of mankind' (ibid.: 30). The 'primordial importance of the universal audience provides the norm for objective argumentation since the other party in the dialogue . . . can never amount to more than floating incarnations of this universal audience' (ibid.: 31) . . . there is an assumed unanimity to the universal. Paradoxically, it is 'objective' in a contingent way, imagined by the speaker in this case, but grounded in a particular audience. Perelman and Olbrechts-Tyteca cite Sartre again; '[there] is a distinction between "abstract universality" which is an imagined quality, existing in the gap between an ideal public and a real public . . . but my reference here is closer to his "concrete universality" . . . which means "the totality of men (*sic*) living in a given society".' (ibid.: 35).

The 'universal audience', and the definition of 'universal' recognises that instinctive assumptions are simply 'common sense' – a very important notion for Vico, and a cornerstone of his legal organisation of the civil world. 'Universal' is 'objective' only in an argumentative or contested way, you might say – the rhetorical and pragmatic agreements of a community who agree both reasonably but also accommodate the illogical or irrational or mythical in agreements about certain strictures. These common agreements allow them in deep-seated ways to converse with each other. The individual's subjective perceptions may or may not coincide with the common sense of the community. And this is what distinguishes the personal from the universal despite the strong element of those qualities in the universal (as we are defining it here). This is the category in which I suggest both Jung and Vico most commonly share ground.

(3) The 'impersonal': communication is outside time and space; cold, and cut off from contingency and from history. It is objective in a rational and determined way, determined by ideal or transcendent precepts that are agreed on sometimes by dedicated other-worldly avowal. You might call this as I believe Nancy Struever means to in her essay about Vico and the impersonal, the 'classical' – appealing at an esoteric level, these are objective and civic forms that aspire to metaphysical status. Does this impersonal level converge with the mystical? Vico's 'intellectual universals' have correlations here. They are the abstract and reflective categories that philosophers refer to. Other-worldly and *certain* only by virtue of the utter conviction of the speaker or writer (and an audience's adherence to them), the extremes of subjectivity converge here with the impersonal. We come full circle.

Keeping in mind that these divisions overlap with each other, we begin to see the rhetorical dimension of what Jung refers to as the 'archetypes', and his notions of mytho-poetic time: similar to Vico's idea of primal time, pre-conscious time. Ideas, images, entities and personalities manifest in a visual or audio presence, or a language, that is immediately understood by humankind. Jung experiences himself as a figure in his own fable, a figure in a specific time and place coinciding with primal time and space. Farther on in this book, when we look at his memoir in contrast to Vico's, the implications emerge that make his discussion in his earlier volume, *Psychological Types* and its appeal to a discussion of Abélard's ideas of nominalism significant.

Ars topica and probabilities – the enthymeme

Similarly, it is a commonplace in our time that language and culture are inseparable, and it was Vico who was one of the first to explore this connection and seek its laws. He proposed the use of *ars topica* as instrumental in making *and* investigating the ways of the human world. Language and culture are correlative themes. As practised by Cicero, one of Vico's central figures (as he sets out in his *Vita*), the practice of engaging in *ars topica*, relies on the instinctive, common sense of the *gente* (a broad appellation of a specific community as a civic world) which uses what we find are very contemporary applications of *inference*.[2]

The fundamental strategy of *inventio*, a canon of ancient rhetoric, Vico interprets as a means of finding argument by discerning patterns imaginatively recognised through memory and *fantasia.* It is a stratagem not only for persuasion but also for the means of constituting the world. In other words, at the same time as it is a strategy of *inventio* it is also a 'discovery' embedded in memory and psyche revealed or made manifest by way of inference that is an enthymeme, the paradoxically 'necessary' logic of *probabilities*. In Aristotle's *Rhetoric* 'probabilities' are a kind of *warranted* certainty founded in the concrete and contingent world. Propositions are asserted, and they may or may not be 'truth'. Jung's psychic world, on these grounds, are as viable as any scientific or empirical assessment of what is certain and/or 'true'. In this way, inferences are the tools of a topical logic, exploited by Jung in his science and recommended by Vico's strategy of 'poetic logic'.

Cognitive German scientist Walter B. Weimer in the 1970s and 1980s explored the psychology of inference and demonstrated the impact of the collective psyche on the individual, and vice versa. Inferences for him are measurable (and therefore scientific) associations. He refutes Burke's ideas of identification as basis for adherence since they are not communal axioms. Harking back to Wundt, which he has in common with Jung, Weimer recalls the influential experimental model relying on inferential experimentation that Wundt engaged in that we know influenced Jung's early work (also see Shamdasani 2003). Jung found this inadequate. Vico's and Jung's use of inference in their psychological and philosophical work went in a different direction, I'd suggest. Inference accommodates not only cognitive psychological and individual terms, but also figural and collective (mythic) association. The tension between psychological treatment and rhetoric has a long history. The 'talking cure' is a rhetorical endeavour *par excellence*, having persuasive and transformative visceral effect. Entralgo (1970) specifically explored this interaction, starting with early Homeric days when disturbed people were urged to talk in order to release bad air pent up inside as a route to healing. There are other dimensions to talking and communication that must be acknowledged even in this presentation of a rhetorical investigation.

Other languages, translation

In this volume, I am entirely working on Jung's material in English translation (except in those cases where Jung wrote in English). Patrick J. Mahony's work on Freud's rhetoric (1987a) was based on English translations, although he complains when those translations go awry. While I hope in future work to look at the fact that translations of Jung, especially Baynes' translations, tend frequently to make adverbial forms of nouns (and this theme has been examined before, if not specifically about Jung – see Samuel Weber's book on Benjamin which explores this anomaly in translation of Benjamin's work from German (2010)), and I'd propose that Jung's frequent use of *heimlich* in the opening chapter of his *Memoirs, Dreams, Reflections* is a conscious rebuttal and gloss to Freud's use of *Heimlich/umheimlich* in his essay on the 'Uncanny' (as other commentators have noted), but I am not taking this up further here.

Walter Benjamin, alongside Ricoeur, another background figure in this book, informs much contemporary discussion of translation based on his reading of Nietzsche. But to bring this theme closer to our topic of Vico and Jung's rhetoric, which Benjamin did not specifically do (he was dismissive of Jung whom he perceived as a mystic), Samuel Jaffé, writing about Freud's work in his essay 'Freud as Rhetorician: *Elocutio* and the Dream-Work' (1980) comments that '"translation" may be used as a metaphor either for "interpretation" as in the passage from Plato's *Ion* or for "expression" as in Blass's paraphrase of Thucydides' (Jaffé 1980: 106).

Translation itself is a transfer of meanings, a metaphor of originary significance in the ways that all communications are representations. It not so much that they are approximations of original meaning (whether translation from the interior, or from another language) but that they transport meanings between cultures, subjective interiors, other persons and teleology as analogies. 'Metaphor's' first definition in Greek is ' transport' after all. In the transference, the baggage of new locations and persons takes on different associations. Commentators since Nietzsche, Benjamin and Derrida discussed translation in contemporary times, and as it is comprehensively expounded in Ricoeur's work on metaphor, this definition of metaphor has become a truism. And it is for my work in this investigation too.

Vico's translators of *The New Science* into English, Thomas G. Bergin and Max Frisch, whose work I use here, are much praised internationally; Italians have commented that their work makes Vico clearer to them than the ancient and overly elaborate Italian Vico used. Translations of his other works come with useful glosses and notes; the *Art of Rhetoric* is actually a compilation of students' notes from his lectures and classes, but they certainly have the authentic rhythms and clear-headedness of Vico's works. And I have also quoted him a good deal – people interested in him and in Jung's ideas might find that reading him here will inspire them to look at his completed works directly. He is not as difficult as he is made out to be.

Although I am not a clinician, I observe that engaging with a patient's personal material as Jung or any clinician does, requires the same kind of hermeneutical activity on the part of the analyst as a translator engages in when she works with original text. If a translator gets a close and approximate idea of the arrangement, grammatical construction and vocabulary of a text, a rhetorical reading will be able to steer fairly close to the direction of the writer's creative intention.

I am aware, however, that while this is a fairly accurate way of analysis, it is not the full picture. I am engaged in analysing a kind of paraphrase of Jung's propositions, a technique, however, that is not only ancient, but was also a favourite practice of Jung's. Vico paraphrased too; it is a legitimate form of commentary after all. He is also notable for making errors but made his point anyway, and nearly always got it right (one famous example of an error is his mistaking which Zeno he meant). But as Mahony reminds us in another of his volumes, *Psychoanalysis and Discourse,* in the chapter entitled 'Toward the understanding of translation in psychoanalysis' (1987, 3–15), 'intra-lingual translation or rewording within the same language, in short paraphrase' is similar to the 'inter-lingual translation or rendering via another language; [although] this [paraphrase] is the most common use of the word'. Translation of interior meanings that coincide with common meanings is a parlous and rhetorical enterprise making a negotiable weave of significance.

Reference to one's self; becoming more who you are

What can I manage to establish on these grounds? Is it that we can leap across the great gap between an eighteenth-century philosopher in a time when there was no real language for the personal interior, and a twentieth-century psychologist absorbed in using newly devised terms for personal dynamics – images and feelings? In the last chapters of this book, an investigation of their books about themselves will begin to provide comparison.

Vico referred to his autobiography as the 'story of himself', the *Vita,* and referred to himself in the third person throughout. Integrating how things come into being with their becoming more themselves as Vico proposes, we have a mixture of aspects we call the 'personal' and the 'impersonal'. This is classic, civic individuality in Vico's schema of what an individual is. Without the terminology of psychology, the individual when referred to at all is seen in the context of a cultural style, language and civilisation. Personality is linked to qualities that refer to types, to use Jungian terminology.

Jung refers to his memoirs as a story of the fable of his life; he creates a kind of mythopoetic individual evolving from coincidence of a specific (conscious and unconscious) psyche in time and space: the synchronous personality is about individuating into the 'fabulous' type you always were. Does this mean eschewing extraneous traits you retain only to shore up a persona out of sync with the fable of *you* in its time? Is the goal of a 'fabulous' individual to become 'universal'?

Vico aims at an 'impersonal' self, a classical discussion of a life within precepts of the laws of history in his autobiography. Jung's inclination is toward a universal, 'fabulist' notion of the individual in similar vein but perhaps without the civic dimension. The personal in both cases is put low in the pecking order of references to a life story. In both cases this has been considered unusual. In Vico's time, autobiography apart from Augustine's *Confession* was unknown; and Jung's memoirs are criticised for lacking the personal details of life – a memoir that does not say much about the daily life of its subject.

Despite these obstructions to comparing Jung and Vico, investigating Vico – in another language, also in translation, from another century and country – we can find clues about how to enquire into the nature of the integration of cognition and style in Jung's analytical psychology. How things come into being, Vico proposes, has all to do with their becoming more themselves. In future, another road which I do not take in this book, is the exploration of Vico and Jung's letters which comprises another rhetorical form, *the epistolary*. The interweave of personal, impersonal and community (mythic or societal, or civic) and their recommendations about these dimensions provide another ground for contrasting the three levels outlined above.

Recognition of something like these distinctions appears in Jung's writings in a personally important way to me: 'there exists a [second] psychic system of a collective, universal and impersonal nature which is identical in all individuals' (Jung CW9 para 89). The personality develops and also instantiates a collective type. Vico asserts this notion as an adage.

In axiom XIV of *The New Science* (1948, 1730/44: para 147), Vico states that 'the nature of things [*natura di cose*] is nothing but their coming into being [*Nascimento di esse*] at certain times and in certain guises'. And in the following axiom XV, he adds that 'the inseparable properties of things [*cose*] must be due to the modifications or guises with which they are born. By these properties we may therefore verify that the nature or birth [*natura e nascimento*] was thus and not otherwise.'

Extrapolating from these conjectures about types, there are several directions to take. We propose that the 'type' is generative; it is a dynamic idea about creating or fashioning: both psychologist and philosopher discuss the vital coalescence of personal and universal.

Hillman discusses distinctions of interpretation of Vico's poetic characters (related to his 'imaginative universals' in providing mythical figures of the imagination), and claims they are compatible with his new approach to Jung's work: 'archetypal psychology'. Hillman uses the fable of Apollo and Daphne, which Vico also used as an example. But Hillman alters Vico's gloss on their story in a revealing way. Later on, I will investigate how each theorist uses this story.

(Another instance of this mythopoetic key can be seen in how Vico discusses establishment of the concept of identity. To build a burial mound to hold the body of a dead person marks a specific piece of property, a place: the ground is identified with that individual in concrete ways. She is buried there; it is her place. It establishes her identity in coordination with property. The elements of the civic world evolve from birth, marriage and burial, Vico states: property, family and identity.)

Oscillations of identity and metaphor

While Vico's ideas of the 'intelligible genus' are a secondary, abstracted development in his commentary, they reflect also the move to the next period of humankind's development toward philosophy. The move is from a mythopoetic world toward a logical world. Here authority is mythologised to a higher reality, for example by the Egyptians, the same precursor referred to by Vico and Jung, Hermes. The wise exemplar of human thought, Hermes presided over logic and wisdom as interaction between god and man. We negotiate meaning, learning skills from Hermes.

Vico insists that these poetic universals are not meanings at a remove, by analogy: 'poetic genera' or 'true poetic allegories' give fables 'univocal' meaning. These fables are an 'imaginative class principle' (Vico 1948, 1730/44: para 403) insofar as they make meaning, Vico says, by

> identity not of proportion but of predictability, allegories signify the diverse species of the diverse individuals comprised under these genera. So that they must have a univocal signification connoting a quality common to all their species and individuals (as Achilles connotes an idea of valour common to all strong men) . . . such that these allegories must be the etymologies of the poetic languages, which would make their origins all univocal . . . *fable* was defined as *vera narratio.*
>
> (Vico1976/1730–44: para 403)

How you mean and what you mean are inextricably involved: you might say Vico uses extrapolation by metaphorical 'thought' to express his point in the axiom quoted above. Catechising these precepts originated with Vico in elaborated form. And, also, just as the matters of which the 'poetic genera' are treated become 'certainties' it is impossible to establish that certainty by way of logical and rational methods, and this proves (for Vico) that nature is fundamentally inaccessible to humans. Original poetic language is impossible to 'explain' (except by 'translation'). Our natures (and nature itself) is a given at inception, and as a species we cannot parse out human nature either since we did not create human nature. We may perceive sequences but we cannot know nature or ourselves from the inside as we know a human creation such as mathematics, or the dialectic. We did not make nature. In fact, questions of 'how' are matters of probability, to be argued out inferentially to achieve 'certainties' or 'probabilities'.

In fact, 'imaginative genera' are nearly impossible for us to grasp at such a remove in time. Later in *The New Science* Vico expands on the autonomous and inexplicable nature of 'imaginative universals':

> the origin of poetry is finally confirmed by this external property of it; that its proper material is the *credible impossibility* [my italics]. It is impossible that the bodies should be minds, yet it was believed that the thundering sky was Jove.
>
> (Vico 1976/1730–44: para 383)

The world is first encountered as a mix of inexplicable and unshaped emotions and forces. Forced by necessity, those first humans created imaginative entities to contain and adapt nature. The 'imaginative universals' are 'more "real" than the individual, and the individual derives his reality from it' (Verene 1981:74). Further in this discussion, the proportions of nominalist and realist positions which Jung discussed in *Psychological Types* will be applied. Those arguments are presented in psychological ways that correlate with Vico's ideas. The privileging of the imagination and of metaphor are equally emphatic in Vico and Jung's work.

From imagination to abstraction; individuation

Ernesto Grassi, a student of Heidegger, compares the use of metaphor in Vico's *The New Science* to Ovid's *Metamorphoses*, and it is useful to set out his explanations of how material Vico's idea of metaphor is, and thereby its concrete impact on human psychology and history:

> Preminenza quindi per Vico del problema della metamorfosi in luogo di una ontologia? . . . Siamo completamente nell'ambito di una metafora che implica la *critica di un linguiaggio astratto* nel quale il significato delle parole non viene riconosciutto concreto in funzione della necessità, del qui e dell'ora della concreta situazione. . . .
>
> La passione come fonte della trasformazione delle varie tappe della via, problema fondamentale del divenire dei fenomeni: la metamorfosi in luogo dell'ontologia, la metamorfosi come originario problema filosofico – uno dei problemi vichiani fondamentali
>
> (Grassi 1990: 176)
>
> [Primary for Vico is the problematic of metamorphosis supplanting ontology . . . We are in the field of metaphor which entails a *critique*

> *of abstract language* in which the significance of a word is not denoted in concrete form as a function of necessity [Vico's primary motivational force in creating meaning] but as the concrete situation . . . Passion is the source of transformation at the various stages of life, and involves the fundamental problem of phenomena: becoming: metamorphosis in place of ontology, metamorphosis as the fundamental philosophical problem – [this is] one of Vico's basic predicaments. [*my translation*]

Using increasingly idealised portraits of imaginative types, the process is that individuals identify with them by finding similarities, and begin to abstract themselves, and to know themselves as separate entities.

For Vico, accustomed as a professor of rhetoric to arguing both sides of an issue, a rhetorician appreciates that a *premise*, the underlying assumption, directs the finally proposed outcome of an enquiry. And so the move from 'imaginative universals' to 'intelligible universals' follows the trajectory of the inferences available in the community. (Is this persona in Jungian terminology?)

> the human mind does not understand anything of which it has had no previous impression . . . from the senses. Now the mind uses the intellect when, from something it senses, it gathers something which does not fall under the senses . . .
>
> (Vico: 1976/1730–44: para 363)

This movement of individual separation from unconscious complexes, reflects Jung's ideas of individuation. In many respects, archetypes function in generating identities and the processing of human mentality at source too.

> Individuation means precisely the better and more complete fulfillment of the collective qualities of the human being, since adequate consideration of the peculiarity of the individual is more conducive to a better social performance . . . the idiosyncrasies of an individual are not to be understood as any strangeness in his substance or in his components, but rather a unique combination of already existent universal elements.
>
> (Jung CW7: para 257)

While Vico felt progression of the individual's separation from mythic world was a step toward barbarism in the long run, there are many similarities in their ideas of human progression: 'In purely psychological terms this means that mankind has common instincts of ideation and action. All conscious ideation and action have developed on the basis of these unconscious archetypal patterns and always remain dependent on them . . .' (Jung CW13: para 12).

Metaphor is the cornerstone of rhetoric, especially in its modal aspect; conditional and subjective, a sophistical rhetoric is probably the most appropriate means of discerning significance in the subjective arena of psychology. Warrants for probable explanation, topics as a means of categorical definitions and hierarchies, abduction (a means of inference based on best explanations), underlie our communications and the negotiated belief in the world.

Etymological associations infer 'narratives' about a word and its associations in the world. Metaphors, for Vico, are 'little fables'. New words are metaphors derived from things we are already certain of. And the feeling and sense of the primary material stays with the transfer of meaning. (This has been catechised by many theorists, not only (or even first) by Vico: see Aristotle, Max Black, Paul Ricoeur, and other writers on metaphor who agree). Resting on this understanding of metaphor, the concept of *narratio* comes to have important meaning for a psychologist especially in case studies. (And as I will develop later on too, it is important for legal cases presented in court.) *Narratio* becomes an 'intentional' representation of meanings. These fables of meaning have broader ramifications; and they take on autonomous life.

Amplification and decorum

Considerations of 'fables' and tales deriving from the interior world offer other means of significance. In dreams, Jung applies associations that amplify out to 'a significance [that is] quite apart from subjective impressions – by their plastic form, which often has a poetical force . . . their chief significance lies in their intrinsic meaning and not in any personal experience and its associations' (Jung CW8: para 554-–5).

A sample of this probabilistic approach is evident in Jung's technique of amplification. (Later I will fit this into the 'topical logic' Jung deploys habitually.) Amplification is not only a technique the Jungian analyst uses, it is also a form of argumentative 'proof', in this case, arguing out based on an elaboration of dreams, or visions to reveal (or discover) significance.

The technique of amplification depends on the rhetorician's (or analyst's) ability to bring appropriate personal and cultural components to bear on a patient's images and dreams. These are integrally related to what that image might mean, and the 'proof' is found in the probability of the connections. But also, the 'feel' of the connections (as Ricoeur points out) has to be right.

The recognition of the importance of 'decorum' is crucial: as it is to Neo-Platonists of all kinds from Isocrates to Augustine, to Vico and Jung; what language is appropriate to the content and to the audience. *Decorum* acknowledges that a hierarchy of alignment is central to a view of the world as emanations from a central god 'zone'. Augustine famously designated low, middle and high style in Book 4 of *The Confessions*, using 'low style' deliberately and incongruously in his sermons to bring sublime ideas to ordinary people in his congregation. Augustine sought to mimic Jesus's parable style; this is contrary to Aristotle's dicta in *Rhetoric* that sublime style is appropriate to sublime spiritual material.

Neo-Platonists like Vico and, I'd say, Jung, look at allegory and analogy as heuristic devices to be shown a way to find original, essential meaning. Attention to arrangement (*dispositio*) displaying levels of significance, and etymological discussion and use of allegory to exemplify hidden meaning is also typical. We need only consider Jung's alchemical and Gnostic writings for his argumentative attention.

Perelman concurs with Augustine, and proposes further, in a next step, that each philosophy has its appropriate style: 'NeoPlatonism would be inclined to use hierarchical poetics – i.e. etymological definitions revealing derivation of words from earlier time; it would focus on "discovery" and on *revelation* of meanings not on constructed argument' (Perelman 1982: 45).

The alignment of style, rhetor and contexts, and era is a fundamental precept of Vico's poetic history.

Other rhetorical tools Vico favours are the pre-eminence of *topics* as a fundamental organising strategy of communication, embedded by reciprocal inferences in the culture and in the psyche. 'Necessary' associations and sequences stem from patterns of connections, organised around the axes of appearance/reality or up/down, opposites etc. These are pivotal *topics* in Jung's writing and thinking. Later in this book, *topics*, *topical logic* and *topical proofs* will be discussed as a common argumentative organisation of analytical psychology.

Rhetorical enquiry looks at an event or a congruence of events to find what's set it off, or what's brought events together, based on contingent premises of perception and action along with idealist, 'impersonal', eternal significance. As I will elaborate further on in discussion of Leo Bitzer's *The Rhetorical Situation* (1968), the exigency of the rhetorical moment impacts on the premise of the strategy of the discussion.

Before getting to specific samples and analysis of Jung's work, however, I will first review that battle to establish these themes in psychoanalysis, and analytical psychology.

Notes

1 *Ricorsi* is the re-appearance of an event, the same as last time with a longer view. This definition is much debated by Vichian scholars and I have put it crudely here.

2 To add to the list of their affinities Cicero is not only one of Vico's core authors but he is the rhetorician Jung most frequently references in his work (see the index of Jung, *The Collected Works,* by C. G. Jung, Gerhard Adler and R. F. C. Hull 1977).

1

TENSIONS

Psychoanalysis/rhetoric/science

> All things are potent with unfathomed codes. We pass by without attending to them, without being even aware of them.
>
> (Ernst Curtius, *Franzosischer Geist in neuen Europa* 1925 in Gelley 1966)

In a more recent work, *The Rhetoric of Rhetoric* (2004), Booth complains about the prevailing suspicion of rhetoric. When it is used as an adjective in ordinary language, it has pejorative connotations. 'Rhetoric' means deceptive and 'empty words' to many contemporary scholars and to the general public (Booth 2004: vii–xv).

To bring the discipline of rhetoric to bear on a discussion of psychoanalytic theory doubles up the anomalies. Psychoanalytic theory is regarded suspiciously when it claims to be scientific, as we have seen. And even worse than Freud's science, Jungian analytic psychology appears more extreme: it privileges 'ornamental' or figural expression. Both Freud and Jung's 'science' rests on unreliable reports 'directly' from patients' psyches to provide proof: dreams and visions are cited from often mentally unstable patients. Arcane and obscure mythical characters and events, Gnostics, and alchemists are also hauled in as evidence in Jungian spheres. This combination of data provides the bulk of proof. But even psychology is anomalous. Kuhn's paradigm-shifting analysis of scientific disciplines did not include psychology. As is well known, he contended that science was an argumentative rather than an objective and logical endeavour, depending on agreed-upon ideologies or dogmas. 'Necessity' was redefined to be about 'certainty' and not about 'truth'. In Kuhn's book, *The Structure of Scientific Revolutions,* science emerges as a rhetorical enterprise. But psychology and psychoanalysis are not mentioned.

There are two threads that weave this theme together that I will track, sometimes each on its own, and sometimes together: (1) the impact or presence of 'ornamentation' or 'excessive' language, or 'figural' language in supposedly neutral scientific prose and (2) the underlying suspicion of argumentative rhetoric as a solid basis of science, despite the latest critiques of science. This unease is especially the case with psychoanalysis: the 'talking' cure. But it is figural or ornamental elements that make rhetoric problematic, and this has been so since Plato's day. Discourse is underhand when it makes emotional appeals. These formulations – anger; 'narratio' – stories of misery or grief; dazzling beautiful charms of prose or persona – provide lures which are subjective and irrational supplications, not to be trusted. The commentators I use in tracing the issue of rhetorician and scientist, often mean extraneous ornamentation when they refer to rhetoric, its hollowness or premeditated status.

Freeing science from its chains of logical, rational hide-bound theorising, allowed advances in technique and visions of a new world. To bring such insights to bear on psychoanalysis and psychology itself must open up further awareness of human nature and capacity. But there has long been resistance and tension. I will start with the most extreme claims.

In *Modern Occult Rhetoric,* Gunn claims that psychoanalysis is an occultist practice so recognised by its secret and indirect language and proofs. A thrilling secrecy for the initiated is created by indirection and by metaphorical, 'rhetorical' terminology. The jargon's appeal is compelling just as its language designs and intends it to be. Evidence in psychoanalytic theory is culled from unreliable personal testimony and its interpretations are shaped into 'case studies', made convincing by the writings of such master rhetoricians as Freud (Gunn 2005: 1–25).

Gunn proposes that its authors' writing capacities are its downfall: 'To understand something as "rhetorical" is to understand it as negotiable, as a contingent and protean object that can only be discerned partially – indirectly through case studies' (ibid.: xxiii).

Like case studies of hysteria and their investigation and cure, the language of the occult is a magical, persuasive language, whose allure is hard to resist. And, particularly early on, it seems a sphere for women with contact in abstruse places which mingles with strange hysteria. Like Freud's analyses and Jung's, references in the occultist's world are of titillating hidden potent and sexy deities and appealingly intricate beliefs.

Further, the case studies work up into good narratives. Occultist writers like Alistair Crowley (*The Book of the Law: Centennial Edition*; *The Book of Thoth* and *The Goetia* among many other titles which are constantly in print), or Scientology's L. Ron Hubbard (with titles like *Dianetics* or *Scientology*) are gripping and popular reads, full of the same paranoiac introspection, and excessive heated prose. Public reception of Freud's publications was initially taken in similar ways by many readers. His books were bestsellers in their time, even after a slow start – particularly his publication about the Dora case, and *The Interpretation of Dreams.* These books have gone on selling steadily since their first publications in 1900 and, in the case of the Dora case, in 1905. It might be that now they have found other serious audiences, but originally they sold also because they were intimate and robust narratives, with startling interpretations.

As an example, a sympathetic review of Freud's *Delusion and Dream* (1921) reprinted in the *Guardian* (6 October 2008) newspaper from an earlier issue dated 6 October 1921 demonstrates contemporary response:

> In this remarkable book there lies at least a double interest. There is, firstly, a longish short story of unusual merit and charm . . . and secondly, Professor Freud's commentary on it from the psycho-analytic standpoint, a brilliant and ingenious treatment of the story as a narrative of real happenings . . .

The *Guardian*'s headline more recently in the 16 October 2007 issue reads: 'Dr Freud's new treatment of fiction'.

A less sensationalist writer about psychoanalytic writing, Donald Spence, starts from a premise related to Gunn's in *The Rhetorical Voice of Psychoanalysis*. There he is disparaging of psychoanalytic theory because it relies on language that is hollow because it *is* rhetoric, and such language is unscientific:

> rhetoric displaces evidence; we lose the ability to reach what Jurgen Habermas has called an 'uncompelled consensus'. Protected by its use of secrecy, arcane language, and unprincipled rhetoric from the challenges of the disbeliever, alchemy and the occult in general became even more fallible and reached a dead end around the time of the Renaissance. Is psychoanalysis headed the same way?
>
> (Spence 1994: 3)

Spence's book is a clarion call to jettison rhetoric from psychoanalytic theory. Why? Because rhetorical language is always contingent. It is not only that he understands rhetoric to mean language that is provisional and florid but that he thinks psychoanalytic writing relies on opportunistic rhetorical concepts to prove a point. This is damaging and unscientific: 'The time has come to call attention to the rhetorical voice of psychoanalysis before it can do further damage and before more evidence is displaced by unsupported assumptions' (ibid.: 5).

Classical rhetoric language which aims at being 'pleasing' and 'persuasive' contributes to a psychoanalytic language that creates shadows, arcane and specialised words which disguise and obfuscate meaning, with made-up language, like the neologisms of the occult. Such rhetorical language is fustian, and excessive ornamentation. It promises significant and powerful truth, but it is a hollow undertaking. Spence claims that in the same ways as occult language is deceptive so is the language of psychoanalysis.

Earlier in the twentieth century, I'd contend that Stephen Toulmin raised more profound issues. He also contemplates the rhetorical/argumentative position of psychoanalytic language, and also tries to come to terms with the nature of its scientific posture. Psychoanalysis is a 'half-fledged science' he claims (Toulmin 1948: 132) seeking desperately to reinforce its own status. But since it is the 'logical status' of a discipline that is the measure of its being scientific, a language that employs figural arguments and proofs will have great difficulties, according to Toulmin, in proving its bona fides.

Freud and his followers, Toulmin says, only appear to focus on Aristotelian logical analysis by tracking cause to effect. They do so in order to fall into line with what they think is certain and logical and therefore, scientific. In their theoretical writings, Freud and his colleagues present and prove their proposals in this way. (Toulmin does not mention Jung's ideas.)

But Toulmin thinks that they confuse their endeavour, and it is not the traditional underpinnings of 'mechanical' causality that is their proof. Toulmin notices that in the reports of the face-to-face case work, Freud actually focuses on analysing *motivations*. And, curiously, it is when the theories are written up, in order to conform to a traditional view of how science should be proven and expressed, that theoreticians use the explanations of causality but not in their practice. This misconception has caused damage to psychoanalysis' reputation, he claims.

Toulmin presumes that psychoanalytic language is rhetorical (Toulmin 1948, Flew 1949, Madden 1966). But, as I am arguing, although he spots that it is a subjective construct, which involves motivation, he focuses only on the *logic* of motivation. There are other constraints on motivation – repressed desires, unconscious associations, emotions – the subjective and irrational range of human experience, etc. Demonstrations, i.e. extrinsic and deductive justifications, in Aristotle's *Rhetoric*, are usually, but not always, logical deductions leading to action. Toulmin's ideas are based on his definitions of 'warrants' for action which are his supports for argumentation (Toulmin 1958). Motivation is cast as a logical coordinate so that psychoanalysis might achieve scientific status. Motivation can be isolated and quantified. Scientific proofs must be extrinsic, based on unconditional support, not dependent on shades of definition in terms, and so forth (Toulmin 1948, 1958).

But on the other hand, there is an aspect of motivation that is distinctly contingent and subjective. And, in fact, argumentative analysis of discourse is the most effective means by which a commentator can assess motivation. But, as for his premise, Toulmin's argumentation turns on a belief in extrinsic *logical* underpinnings, and this pulls him up short from committing himself to consideration of the figurative level of scientific discourse. Jeanne Fahrenstock pursues the idea that figurative language is distinctly at the basis of all scientific endeavour. Therefore figurative language is totally the language of science. Fahrenstock demonstrates underlying ornamental ploys of scientific writings, discussing inference and gradation, for example, to prove its ubiquity.

Paul Ricoeur supports the discussion of Freud's 'proof' in psychoanalysis; argumentation clearly includes motivation as a persuasive element, and he demonstrates that its triangulation with subjective elements to achieve proven healing transformation makes the process quantifiable and verifiable and therefore, a scientific project.

At the same time, Roy Shafer in *A New Language for Psychoanalysis* (1976) recommended making certain that psychoanalytic language is 'action language'; he advises authors of psychoanalytic texts to 'eschew mixed physiochemical and evolutionary biological language' (Shafer 1976: 3). Such metaphors are 'inappropriate [when] elevated to status of theoretical terms'. Verbs, and in circumspect times, adverbs, should be used instead of adjectives and analogies. He wants to prohibit psychoanalytical terminology and theories from use of the figural realm, i.e. its use of analogy and indirect reference. The metaphorical edifice of the mechanistic language Freud uses undermines psychoanalysis' status as a science. Like Spence, his concern is use of what is deemed irrational formulae as proof.

Psychoanalytic theory should reform itself to become less 'rhetorical'.

Rhetoric is traditionally closely associated to logic, and of course to argumentation. But Aristotle's 'demonstrations' are two kinds of proofs. They are on the one hand syllogistic, rigid verification in which contradictions are honoured as outside contingent event. But they can also be extrinsic proof that are agreed-on conclusions by an audience not subject to logical deduction (Aristotle *Topics,* Warnick 2002, Perelman and Olbrechts-Tyteca 1969, Nichols 1987, Stocks 1933).

By using the coordinates of argumentation to reckon motivation, a form of human purpose that combines external and internal, personal drive, Ricoeur and Toulmin are able to bring psychoanalysis into line with scientific argument. Motivation can be discerned and analysed and verified. In this way, by considering psychoanalytic theory in the light of argumentative language, and raising its status, Toulmin only challenges Spence's dismissal of the power of rhetoric in part. He uses the underpinnings of logical language to 'prove' that basically the subjective element of motivation is really 'logical' and not contingent or irrational. Therefore, it meets the criteria of irrefutable and verifiable science which is its nature.

Equally persuaded about the value of using rhetorical language to discuss psychological concepts is Michael Billig (Billig 1987, 1996, 2002). Billig develops another aspect of psychoanalytic language that moves it toward appreciation of it as a fully subjective and yet still valid rhetoric. Billig defends the earliest rhetoricians, Gorgias and Protagorus, despite their bad reputation. Plato condemned them as ethically anomalous because they were adept at arguing both sides of a case (Plato, *Gorgias*, *Symposium*). Billig revives admiration for the Sophistical proposition that examination of all sides of a dispute is valuable. Both the anticipated and the reactive response to the audience is a useful means to investigate psychological theory, and the sophists had to take that on board. He proposes that psychological theory is a form of dialogical thinking, and sophistical rhetoricians devised the most appropriate technical idiom to theorise about psychology. He links dialogism to rhetorical strategy, and especially to the sophistical tradition. However, he does not address the ornamental or figural devices of rhetoric, staying close to sociological communication theory and argumentation.

John Shotter, a socio-psychologist, reveals that despite appearances, his arguments are based on the extrinsic objective proofs of rhetoric. In *Conversational Realities* (1993), he applies rhetorical terminology to psychological discussion, citing Vico as a principal. Shotter uses Vico's idea that historical eras have a distinctive and specific style. This notion supports his proposition that conversational exchange 'constructs' realities.

> [Genres are] . . . form-producing ideologies, that is, the 'imaginary worlds' they embody. Indeed, the study of writers' practices, rather than their content, can be expected to extend to a study of the *tone* in which they write, for the different dialogical opportunities for relationship (and being) offered to readers by authors will become important.
>
> (Shotter 1993: 63)

In both Billig's and Shotter's case their considerations reflect sociologically orientated hypotheses. While psycho-sociologists do often use discourse analysis, the aesthetic and ornamental aspect of rhetoric is not addressed. This element is crucial to Vico's approach to rhetoric – he is looking to the persuasive and alluring side of rhetoric.

So far, I have been demonstrating that psychology and psychological analysis has been accruing increasing status as a science despite its reliance on variable human talk. But this is not broad enough scope for our purposes.

Psychoanalysis gained status by reference to logical discourse. Spence and Gunn are challenged in at least one of their assumptions, i.e. that psychoanalytic talk is hollow rhetoric. Toulmin, Ricoeur, Billig, Shotter, Shafer, *et al.* point out that scientific talk can be rhetorical and still have scientific status. But, there is still a way to go. It is particularly vital to discuss figural/poetic language in a study of Jungian stylistic. There are rhetoricians and literary theorists who make links to expression and scientific endeavour.

Booth recalls Susanne Langer's work that points at the necessity of considering a broader emotional and figural scope in thinking about all communication, not only psychoanalytic discourse:

> A philosophy that knows only deductive or inductive logic as reason, and classes all other human functions as 'emotive', irrational, and animalism, can see only regression to a pre-logical state in the present passionate and unscientific ideologies . . . All other things are dismissed as irrelevant to intellectual progress; they are residues, emotional disturbances, or thowbacks to animal estate.
>
> (Langer (1942) cited in Booth 2004: 65)

And, by following work by such commentators as Alan Gross (2002), Arthur Fine (1986), Walter B. Weimer (1973) and Jeanne Fahnestock (1998, 2002), among others, we trace the demonstrable notion that scientific argumentation relies heavily on ideas pre-formulated in analogy or metonymy. Fine proposes that Einstein's mode of thinking was not only entirely conditional and based on motivational (which he directly links to the rhetorical) propositions, but was formulated in the realm of metaphor.

In discussing Freud's work, another critic who directly cites rhetoric, Patrick J. Mahony, investigates the rhetorical devices Freud uses in all their complexities, also bringing to bear ideas of dialogism. As we will discuss further, sociological commentators like John Shotter (see above), Nan Johnson (1988) or Norman O Brown (1973), argue that writers and speakers often include anticipation of audience reaction in their message. In Brown's case, for example, the fact that he was reading Poe's stories in a musty old paperback created associations to Poe that he maintains greatly influenced his reception of the story (see Brown 1973).

Mahony does not go quite as far as including his personal response as a reader ('reader-response' theorists focus on this dimension of rhetorical study which I do not include here either), but he does explore the contexts of Freud's writings, and his personal education in rhetoric.

Mahony also glosses the difficulties of Strachey's translations into English which he claims miss important nuances of tone and allusion. He recognises that his own study of Freud's style falls short of a full investigation. But, as a devotee of continental structuralism, he also is not inclined to look outside the 'conscious, active enterprise' he assumes psychoanalysis is (Mahony 1987: 65). He cites Lacan's recommendation that analysts have a 'rhetorical education so they can understand the patient's rhetorical strategy' (Lacan 1955: 352): 'C'est ainsi en effet que procède le discours pour *convaincre*, mot qui implique la stratégie dans le procès de l'accord . . . Ce procès s'accomplit dans la mauvaise foi du sujet, gouvernant son discours entre la tromperie, l'ambiguité et l'erreur' (Lacan cited in Mahony 1966: 65).

He does not pursue Lacan's claim that there is a language and rhetoric of the unconscious (see Lacan 1981). Recalling from his readings of Entralgo (1970), Mahony reminds us that Greek rhetorical tradition refers to a form of verbo-therapy to cure patients from Homeric times. He learns about magical word charms, or 'persuasive and strengthening conversation [which] were believed to have powers to cure' (Mahony 1987: 66 and Nussbaum 1994). In fact, as Fortenbaugh (1975) suggests, it was Plato's fears about the diabolical powers of enchanting rhetoric and its magical influence that led him to ban poetry from his Republic. Its appeals were dangerously irrational and potent.

Mahony admires Freud's explorations of the rhetorical function in psychotherapy. Freud's scrutiny of literature and his recommendation that an analyst have thorough literary grounding attest to Freud's sagacity (Mahony 1987: 67).

After readings of Barthès, Lacan and Derrida, Mahony notes that unlike these commentators' views, the popular understanding of rhetoric is limited. The opinion that rhetoric is all hollow style persists.

Lacan moved the underlying metaphor of Freudian psychoanalysis from biology to discourse, he points out. Mahony itemises the divisions of rhetorical argumentation, logic, ethos, pathos and the five canons, invention, arrangement, style, memory and delivery, to begin his demonstration of its value. In Mahony's opinion, '[a]ccordingly the ethical and pathetic arguments in rhetoric help bear the burden issuing from a weak logic' (Mahony 1987: 67).

In *Psychoanalysis and Discourse* (1987b) and in *Freud as a Writer* (1987a) he discloses Freud's devices, citing letters in which Freud recounts how he would focus on one person to address in a lecture hall, or in his mind when he was writing, so he could concentrate on individual communication. Mahony scans Freud's provisional and tentative style, mostly lost, he says, in Strachey's translation. The integrity of Freud's endeavour is further revealed, he tells us, because Freud let his unconscious organise his writings and lecturing. Kenneth Burke's idea that rhetoric is about 'identification' comes into play here (Burke 1969) in his very Freud-inflected discussions of rhetoric. The effort of rhetoric is to induce adherence by using empathy to achieve identification and so your argument is more effective. As Mahony says, '[t]o a large degree the transference relationship entails a patient trying to persuade *an audience that he himself has created* [my italics]. By contrast the therapeutic alliance, a cooperative effort with a real audience, is eminently dialectical' (1987a: 69).

Despite his recognition of Freud's adeptness using metaphor, analogy and allusive, audience-reflecting writing, Mahony, like Billig and Toulmin, focuses primarily on the dialectical aspect of Freud's rhetoric.

And, further, as theorists proposing structuralist analysis recommend (see Culler 1997) Mahony monitors the semantic and the semiotic composition of the text to follow the energy driving the writing. Unlike other semiologists, he adds a contextualising element to this mix which is outside their scope. He alludes to the writer's intentions, and the writer's own assessment of success in achieving those intentions.

But, as Booth points out, in addition to assessing the writer's intentions, and tracking semantic and semiotic coordinates (which Mahony, and Lacan, of course, do in examining Freud's writings), it is equally valuable to analyse the product noting conscious and unconscious effects. Who the writer thinks she is, and who she thinks the audience is, which may well not be who she appears to herself or to them to be, is revealed unwittingly in a close reading of the material: 'tackling individual poems to discover their true (and usually ironic) center, [the critic] openly reject[s) the *flesh-and-blood* author's intentions, [and]

. . . always emphasiz[es] . . . the *implied* author's rhetorical intention' (Booth 2004: 70).

Booth seeks to find 'the persuasive vitality implanted in every successful poetic invention . . . ' (Booth 2004: 71).

Noting metaphoric allusions and distinctive associations in the text's referencing is not interesting to Mahony. He does not make the distinction of an *implied* author from the real author. This means that Mahony is not tackling the implications of Freud's choice of argumentation. While it is not entirely his stated project to do so, in fact a rhetorical reading is not fully realised. His approach, as we will explore further in discussing Lacan's seminar on Poe's story in Chapter 5, assumes that rhetoric is dialectical and its deductions are more or less incontrovertible.

The incontrovertible value of figural rhetoric and its universality as a discourse which could assure certainty were established in the earliest days of rhetoric. But over time, there were divisions in rhetoric, and ornamentation and/or eloquence was split away from logical, dialectical argument. Philosophy was separated off too, leaving empty poetical verbiage behind to mean 'rhetoric'. And this hollowness is what 'rhetoric' has meant until the last century. This history is tracked in Vickers (1988), Ong (1958), Wardy (1996) and Sloane (1997) among many other works.

In the eighteenth century, as a counter-Enlightenment move, Vico weighed up the issues of dialectic vs. eloquence and deduction vs. a topical nature of argument in his orations and published essays, especially *On the study methods of our time* (Vico 1708–9, 1990). 'Certainty' does not necessarily rest on logical 'incontrovertibility', he argued (Vico 1708–9, 1990). And many contemporary rhetoricians like Michael Leff (2005), Barbara Warnick (2000) and Chaim Perelman and L. Olbrechts-Tyteca (1969), also point out that an alternative form of argumentation, topical invention, is potentially even more meaningful in establishing certainty in an audience.

Topical invention deploys metaphoric association (and other figural devices like 'copiousness' which sets out numerous links of words, and 'notation' which attends to definitions, etc.) as its strategy, rather than relying on critical, logical deduction and dialectic. While these rhetoricians named do not always address psychoanalytic thinking directly (although Perelman does discuss Freud in *The New Rhetoric*, 1969), the pertinent implications of this mode and its coming to be recognisable scientific discourse for Jungian psychology is evident.

Its form of 'demonstration' is based on proofs in common sense and in the fitting or appropriate topical links the rhetor discovers. We might call this common sense the 'collective unconscious' in Jung's system.

Vico proposes that the common sense of the *gente* expressed in maxims or in unwittingly held beliefs is 'incontrovertible' and extrinsic proof which would succeed in persuading an audience should a rhetor decide to refer to it (Vico 1711–12, 1988). Proof is expressed deploying his 'key', 'poetic logic': this is the incontrovertible, yet poetical, logic of the devices of metaphor, metonymy, synecdoche and irony.

> Vico had a great insight: the customs and laws of the ancients were not in the 'language' of modern times. Instead the ancients spoke in a different tongue, whose words could not be accepted literally; their meaning lay hidden behind a secret door. A key was needed. And the key which Vico called 'the master key of this science' was simply that early people 'were poets who spoke in poetic characters'.
>
> (Mazlish 1966: 30–1)

This is Vico's 'true narrative' (Verene 1992, Grassi 1980, Vico 1990: para 338, Mooney 1985: 240) and it is a mode of speaking that relies on this imaginative or 'poetic logic':

> For in worshipping their Jove, the ancestors do not wish merely to note the experience . . . but seek to contain it imaginatively, to grasp it truly in a name. Born of a nature that at once craves the universal and is bound to particulars Jove is an image that survives the moment, and becomes a statement of what the brutes now are . . . ; and the action undertaken in consequence, divination and the practice of auspices, are referred back to Jove as are all similar experiences of being watched over or otherwise directed. Jove becomes thereby an imaginative class concept in which their lives have standing, and a poetic statement in which their history is told.
>
> (Mooney 1985: 240–1)

Topical invention located true narrative 'logically' and causally in a discussion of myth, for example, because the community agree consciously and unconsciously on its significance, and further, they know how to talk about its significance. This insight opened history up for Vico. Shifting or exploring associations of poetical figures 'moved' history. Vico's certainty of this correlation is not shared by other critics on the relations of history and discourse.

Jungian commentator Paul Kugler in his two volumes, *The Alchemy of Discourse* (1982) and *Raids on the Unthinkable* (2005), puts the concept in postmodern terms:

> certain terms . . . will be literalised and given a privileged ontological position around which the other elements . . . will revolve and to which they will refer . . . [as] the 'origin' of all the others . . . language has subtly trapped us inside the logic of the 'origins' metaphor, unconsciously elevating the term to a transcendental status . . . to account for all the other terms.
>
> (Kugler 2005: 34)

Kugler worries that since our language references are trapped inside the language itself, we can never find 'a ground, only a mediator' (Kugler 2005: 36). Figural language is instrumental in constructing a world, and trapping us in it with its incontrovertible meanings. Figural and literal are both extrinsic discourse. He finds that the 'ultimate ground' is 'the unconscious itself. And this is the absolute ground which gives authority to all schools of depth psychology' (ibid.: 38).

Yet, I think Jungian rhetoric proves otherwise.

The proofs and arguments in Jung's works rest in his extensive 'copious' philological references and imaginal associations. In Hillman's works, such as *Senex and Puer* (1985) and *Re-inventing Psychology* (1992), *Anima* (1985) and his discussions of archetypal psychology (1983), which argue by extending associations, or in works that are poetical discussions of transference and psychology by Aldo Carotenuto such as *Eros and Pathos* (1989), the tendency is to collapse distinctions between the metaphoric and the literal, either by means of irony or negation, or by other forms of mediation. These styles refute Kugler's position.

The copious allusions that topical invention relies on, as we will explore further on, use metaphoric association as poetical/logical proofs. In some senses, only in the certainties gained by the reading experience, i.e. by finding the links in the argumentation significant, can adherence be achieved. We arrive at a psychology that relies on analogy, metaphor and copiousness, the devices of 'ornamentation' with books like *Women who run with the wolves* by C. P. Estés (1992) whose underlying message is that narratives convey literally 'real messages' and that they are healing.

Coming at the opposite end of Spence's position, is Hillman's plea for an appreciation of the 'eloquence' of rhetoric's argumentative power even though he does not delve fully into the value of its dynamic, as I will hope to explore in this book. Our difference is partially to do with his focus on an approach to therapy which my enquiry is not:

> Therapy turns back either to Cartesian structuralism which abstracts speech into unutterable root units, or to pietistic revivalism . . . and the inchoate sound of feeling is all. Neither . . . can carry psychology toward giving words to the full size of soul, for they lack the main mark of rhetoric: *eloquence*. We need . . . belief in the verbal imagination and the therapeutic incantational power of words. Besides [others] . . . there is the Mediterranean of the imagination, an island sea of rhetoric from whose froth Venus rises.
>
> (Hillman 1976: 214)

In this regard, Kugler's anxieties can be dispelled when we revert to the contingent form of incontrovertibility Vico's rhetorical position suggests. Writers on ancient Greek and eighteenth-century rhetorical themes resort to equivocal talk: and Nancy Struever suggests it is Vico's language that displays possibilities.

> Ambiguity, the *tropic* quality of language, dominates – man is the oblique animal; but the structure of ambiguity is atemporal and accessible, it forms a 'poetic logic' of figurative techniques . . . Vico believes in the omnipresence of rhetoric, and therefore the omnicompetence of rhetoric as a heuristic tool.
>
> (Streuver 1974: 523)

It is the purpose of this book to suggest that Jung has a deep and similar engagement with rhetoric. Jung's 'incontrovertible contingency', you might say, is his fondness for the argumentative possibilities of paradox and his association with that of the figural means of communication.

We will move toward summary, but first there are other devices to consider. Apart from a predominant commitment to *topics* rather than to critical, logical enquiry there are other rhetorical techniques which they both favour.

- Analogy (correlation of representations by claims of similarity: metaphor, synecdoche, metonymy, allegory, or irony);
- Paradox (fundamental to Vico's outlook, and Jung's favoured 'shock' tactic with readers and patients) and irony;
- Amplification (based on etymological associations as well as oppositions, including definition, etc.);
- Exemplum (specific symbolic or literal representations);
- Narrative (contiguous, inferred or other sequential organisations of event); and
- Dialectic, an idea that attributes and events in life flower from the psyche of each personality (or rhetor in Vico's case) into a receptive world that is always reciprocal and inter-active.

These pivotal techniques permeate consciousness as well as verbal or written poetics, and also (presumably) the unconscious. These arise in Vico's rhetorical and philosophical theories, and Jung's world of psychic healing. To a great degree which I want to investigate, this packed listing of technique characterises both Vico's and Jung's work.

This book is organised in a specific way that is influenced by these two writers except that I do not resort to images. Its structure is not set out as thesis, proposal and counter-proposal. It is not always argued in a linear or logical order in which evidence is lined up to prove conclusions. It is set out as a series of links between Jung's stylistic and the rhetorical precepts as characterised by Vico's particular orientation. But it has been a long road from the earliest days of suspicion about rhetoric to present day reception in psychoanalytic and analytical psychological fields of study. Using poetical or mythical approaches, both these writers claimed to be putting forward a scientific approach. Only in contemporary times, ever since discussions among Kuhn, Lakatos and Popper, Jeanne Fahnestock, Alfred Fine, Chaim Perelman and many others, has the metaphoric/argumentative nature of the scientific enterprise been validated. This only a part of the story.

2

JUNG'S RHETORICAL STANCE

Jung was sensitive to the requirements of his audience, and wrote with persuasion of them in mind. His aims in writing were educative, or transformative, and he was also aware of formal rhetoric which we gather from known school curricula in Switzerland at the time. As for Vico, Cicero is a favourite source; he wrote about him and quoted him more than any other rhetorician.

Jung manipulated effects for the three levels of audience referred to earlier: the impersonal (universal, theoretical writings aimed at scholars and his scientific, medical professional readers alike), and then the collective addressee (primal, culturally embedded, readers) and then individual (personal) readers we find in his letters (although many of his letters which I am not referring to in this book, were written for public dissemination).

In fact, from his attention to these tiers of addressees he derives a rhetoric that also acts as an instrumental part of his performative, transformational purpose. In one example, we see in his analysis of a dream how he inculcates his communicative strategies as forms of technique in dream interpretation. In *Psychology and Alchemy* he looks at a particular dream. For him, dreams are like mini-dramas, he says, organised in phases, and Jung applies traditional rhetorical language to define them.

> A dream begins with a **statement of place** . . . ; next comes a statement about the **protagonists**; statements of time are rarer . . . this phase of the dream is ***Exposition*** – the scene of action, the people involved, and often the initial situation of the dreamer.
>
> In the second phase comes the ***Development*** of the plot . . . the situation is somehow becoming complicated, and a definite tension develops because one does not know what will happen.
>
> The third phase brings the ***culmination*** or *peripeteia* – here something decisive happens or something changes completely;
>
> . . . The fourth phase and last phase is the ***lysis,*** the ***solution*** or ***result*** produced by the dream-work. (There are certain dreams in

> which the fourth phase is lacking, and this can present a special problem . . .)
>
> . . . The last phase shows the final situation, which is at the same time the solution 'sought' by the dreamer.
>
> (Jung CW9 1949: para 561–4)

The strategy of using rhetorical terms follows in a long tradition of using such terms as a *topos.* Ernst Robert Curtius discusses this motif in several appendices of his work entitled 'Grammatical and rhetorical technical terms as metaphors' and 'Etymology as a category of thought' appended to *European Literature and the Latin Middle Ages* (1979). In his discussion of the *topos* 'jest and earnest', for example, he mentions that the technical grammatical term, *coniunctiones* is playfully used erotically to suggest copulation. Jung borrowed the term in talking about his alchemical motifs. I would suggest Jung knew that there were those sensual inferences too. The visual images of alchemical *coniunctiones* are certainly erotically charged.

In this passage, the rhetorical terminology Jung uses is traditionally applied to a discussion of *narratio*, i.e. the expository aspect of argument, located, in classic forensic argumentative order, just after the *premise* is set out. He plays with arrangements.

Underlying forensic argument sets out evidence in the narrative as if it were suspect. The exposition is presented as proof in the narrative. Hence, Jung sets the dream in a defensive context, striving to uphold the plausibility of meaning that the dreamer imparts. The dream is an argument. The terms of the argument are held up to scrutiny. They are used to embellish Jung's commentary on narrative use of evidence as proof.

I will track Jung's use of several terms in this analysis to see how they impact independently on his interpretations.

The label 'expositio', which Jung proposes as the opening phase of the dream, is a controversial term. Both Lanham (1991) and Vico in his *Oratoriae* (Vico 1984/1711–41) point to several meanings for this term which Lanham finds 'confusing'.

1 It is a setting out of the points to be *disputed* (which is 'divisio'); and/or
2 It is 'a setting forth, an exposition', i.e. a general *setting forth* of a topic.

The distinction is between (a) isolating items for conflict, or, on the other hand (b) giving an overview of fact. By his rearrangement Jung has shifted significance. (We will also return to this important notion of 'setting forth' further on in application to presentation of the subject of an autobiography when we come to talk about Jung's and Vico's memoirs.)

But now to return to the dream: Jung means 'divisio' to apply to the development section of the dream, not to the 'expositio' opening section. It is more standard for these phases to be the other way around. In other words definition (a) above is assigned later to the development phase. Traditionally, 'divisio' is the location of the 'tensions' in an argument; but within Vico's scheme, however, the conflicts are located in the 'expositio'.

In other words, Jung moves the location of 'tension' away from the original situation, the people and location, of the dream. Another psychologist would find the population and place where the dream takes place the crucial scene, rather than locating the ongoing 'play' as the crucial focus. Jung designates the *peripeteia* (from Aristotle's *Poetics*), i.e. the dramatic reversal, as the crucial points of interpretation, picking up his notion that dreams are mini-dramas. Freud provides a refutation: the 'primal scene' is important as a symbol of what is core for him, the oedipal complex. However it is the underlying, base-line point of tension, i.e. the original situation of reference. Any dream refers to this set up and the analyst finds out how. But for Jung, the setting of the action in a dream is significant only as the start-up for the process of interpretation, not its end purpose.

And, in fact, deciding what the 'reversal' is and when it occurs in the dream is a form of 'amplification' or commentary in Jung's scheme, i.e. the designation of a specific moment(s) being the reversal expands/embellishes dream meanings. Subjecting definitions to amplification brings Jung into other dimensions of significance. It's here an appreciation of copiousness comes into play. The more words it takes to flesh out a meaning, the better.

And, finally, the last phase, *lysis,* which means 'conclusion', i.e. closing down, but which also denotes 'decomposition' – and thereby indicates the dissolution of the dream's power.

Along with these terms, Jung provides us with a series of short *exempla* to demonstrate meanings. There is ideological significance in his choice of *exempla*, or narrative samples. We find this in the nature of amplification as it is applied to the specific dream. Trenchant amplification and links in meaning move outwards to a collectivity according to Jung and not to personal dimensions. As any rhetorician would know, a piece of written or spoken work is 'compromised' by its intention. When Jung glosses the segments of dreams as he does, he fleshes out the crisis of the dreamer in the dream imagery. But he does not want us to think he's planting his ideas even though his interpretation seems strikingly apt. To waylay our suspicions of contrivance, he adds this statement:

> Naturally, these statements are not an interpretation of the dream; they merely outline the initial situation. This division into four phases can be applied without much difficulty to the majority of dreams met with in practice – an indication that dreams generally have a 'dramatic' structure.
> (Jung CW9: para 565)

Jung claims he knows the argumentative/intentional underpinnings of the psyche's representations in the personal and collective realms. Dreams cannot be explained as if they were rational references to other meanings; they have their own style of communicating. Dreams are a distinctive mode of communication and he is able to codify them within their own realm.

In his lecture, he sets out synopses of the dreams which I summarise here: first of all, the first dream: it is among theatrical houses, with signs in German and English above the stage that feel like ads – warning people it's a Catholic church. The dreamer beckons his friend in who is against the communal nature of religions – but, his friend says, as a Protestant, you would not understand; nearby a woman nods vigorously. Before entering they see rules against approaching the Lord, and they go in.

Then Jung synopsises the second dream, set in a mosque with a large space full of texts from the Koran; the same nodding woman from the earlier dream is upset at admonishments 'not to flatter' – and she leaves ('Then there's nothing left [to do]') – the dreamer agrees but remains, joining the crowd who are celebrating their joyful belief. The organ plays a Bach fugue and the party escalates with good food and drink; a priest assures him such trivial style of socialising is fine – Americans are less ascetic. At this point, Jung recounts, the dreamer, relieved, now wakes.

He defends his summary and his deductions about the dreams, not only in their particulars, but in his general point that dreams have their own ways of communicating.

Dreams are not representative of some secret 'other' meaning: he sets aside Freud's interpretive methods: 'I doubt whether we can assume that a dream is something other than it appears to be . . . I do not make assumptions about its possible cunning or its tendency to deceive' (Jung CW9 para: 567).

But there are ambiguities he sets out to resolve in his analysis and they are in Jungian terms:

1 Is there coherence in this psychic event? And what is it?
2 Is the female agent in the dream significant for the male dreamer?
3 Is there collective, important significance to the dream?
4 Is it a religious attitude of a particular kind – a distinction about the 'numinous' the dreamer makes?

Posing questions such as these sets the interpretation on a specific course. In addition, framing the dream as a dramatic structure, he seeks out and finds 'peripeteia'. His technique is to look for the turning points in dreams to illuminate the meaning for the dreamer, and further to show its compensatory purpose. He looks for the patient's affect as the markings of turning points.

Instinctively colluding with Jung, the dreamer too fixes on designated moments helping to identify them. The 'peripeteia' is a transfiguring moment, and, in this case, Jung seizes on the religious themes of the dream where affect is running high. The dreamer has reported an 'incomprehensible' but distinct 'numinous character to his experience' that has disturbed this dreamer by his own report. Jung nominates the moment, defends his decision, and explicates its significance for the dreamer (and for us).

Could the 'peripeteia' have been any other events in the dream than those he fixes on? Is it opportunistic that he chooses this or that event as a turning point? Why isn't the decision to enter through the door to this Catholic Church the turning point rather than the departure of the female figure?

But Jung insists that the moment of reversal is when the disappointed and distressed female figure leaves the room. He chooses this 'turning point' for several reasons. He knows about the dreamer's other dreams and claims they fit into a longer sequence. The female figure's unhappiness is a piece of dramatic action for the dreamer that marks a shift in the mood and the location of the dream. So it is not incorrect to nominate this 'turn'.

Once he has established the shape, he explores the dream's 'real' source in the very 'real' collective unconscious with its shared common imagery. He points out too that the intrepid 'complexes' act in dreams.

Jung tells us that this sequence of dreams was reported by letter from a scientist undergoing a painful breakdown. We assume that Jung is quoting him directly. Jung proceeds to his amplification from references in the scientist's language that are his evidence.

His interpretations 'could be no other', Jung claims. The dreamer loves wine (possibly too much) and he has suffered loss of meaning in his life. To rectify this, the dreamer had wilfully turned to religion. It had not helped; his associations to religion seemed to alienate him from the over-riding sense of the numinous. The evidence is supported by a preoccupation with religious matters that shows up in the dream's imagery.

Jung's interpretation lies in the contradictions of the scientist's personality, he claims. The incongruous social setting and the overwhelming sense of numinosity are at odds. Jung reassures us he is not altering meanings to fit his theories: 'the dream I am going to relate has not been tampered with at all. They represent an entirely uninfluenced natural sequence of events. The patient had never read any psychology much less any analytical psychology' (ibid.: para 560).

And, he adds in a footnote: 'Although the dreams cited here are mentioned in *Psychology and Alchemy*, they are examined from a different standpoint. Since dreams have many aspects they can be studied from various angles' (ibid.: fn 2: para 560).

In fact, when we look at the dreams in this sequence in *Psychology and Alchemy*, which Jung directs us to contrast, we discover his purpose there is not to reveal the emergence of religious feeling but to explicate elements of alchemical imagery. We conclude that there are different analyses according to Jung's purpose. How are we to reconcile this? I think the solution rests in the nature of his psychology which accommodates multiple narratives.

Jung addresses this issue as he defends his selections of reversal points, setting out the tenets of his psychology as he does so. For example, he justifies that despite its female aspect, the 'anima' – the female figure in the dream – is integral to a male dreamer's psyche. He specifically refers to her powers of transformation in the dream. That is the focal point. The tension she creates leaving the room is the male dreamer's tension.

Jung's theory of the compensatory function of male and female and the anima's bridging and symbolic task in making meaning is argued out. Combining these facets, and applying what he knows of the dreamer's background along with his collaboration with the dreamer assures him that he's got it right.

Jung engages in 'amplification' to get to his collective themes here. He works outward from what imagery he finds in this dream to explore the figure of the hermaphrodite, an ancient religious figure, with proof provided him by the male/female figure in the dream at hand. Collective imagery is empirically available. He associates the imagery to what this religious event is. It is a public event for this dreamer, with unresolved *numinosity*. And it includes themes that he earlier set out to the audience of this lecture in his discussion of creeds: he distinguishes between Protestantism, with its lack of religious symbolism, and Catholicism. He contrasts pagan elements to Christian elements to discover a common religious impulse.

The pay-off is that the dreamer thought Jung's interpretations were 'correct'. This is proof located in extrinsic reality, and the fact it worked has made it a convincing argument. And, it makes sense in a way that it might never have done for any other dreamer; except that Jung might have construed it for another dreamer in just the way he did here to amplify to collective meaning but by using different routes.

We note that Hillman, acting as an advocate and elaborator of Jung's work, goes a long way, but not entirely, to associate Vico's poetic characters are compatible with his own development of Jung's work: 'archetypal psychology'.

3

TOPICAL INVENTION AND TROPES – TOOLS OF THE IMAGINATION

Definitions and issues

> Providence gave good guidance to human affairs when it aroused human minds first to topics rather than to criticism, for acquaintance with things must come before judgment of them. Topics have the function of making minds inventive, as criticism has of making them exact.
>
> (Vico 1976/1730–44: para 498)

The most fruitful form of argumentation is topical invention – so Vico recommends, and so Jung comes to choose as a scientist, in my estimation. Descartes' insistence that extreme scepticism would reveal 'clear and certain truths' by dialectical logic was the prevailing pedagogic and epistemic view at the time. Vico's counter moves begin with revealing definitions and purposes.

Vico's handbook *Institutiones oratoriae* (Vico 1996/1711–41) begins with a brief discussion of the etymology of the word *rhetorica.* It comes from a Greek term, he is reported as saying (the handbook is a collection of verified student notes from his lectures) that has not been translated accurately into Latin as 'rhetorica'. But, even so, when this word *rhetorica* (or 'eloquence') is transformed and/or translated into Latin, it retains important associations embedded in the Greek word.

Rhetorica would be, from the Greek, more accurately translated as deriving from:

> *fluentia* (words that flow) and *dicentia* (words that speak). . . . Fluency is indeed a peculiar view of speech from which the things that are said without prior preparation or reflection emerge by their very nature, not so much from the speaker, but seem to be speaking forth themselves.
>
> (Vico 1996/1711–41:3–4)

In its later, Latin denotation, as the name of the 'discipline' of persuasion, the definition retains this regard for fluency:

> fluency is the most difficult skill of this art, and therefore it is the last to be achieved, and is acquired more by practice than by precept. . . . Eloquence does not encompass all of the power of oratory even though it is the other virtue of speech and of equal importance by means of which issues are spelled out freely and with clarity . . . Rhetoric, or eloquence, however is [also] the faculty of speaking appropriate to the purpose of persuading.
>
> (Ibid.: 4)

Wise *eloquence* and appropriateness (*decorum*) require training and knowledge of the soul as well as skill. Vico's definitions are different in emphasis than other theorists' definitions and reflect his priorities. 'Eloquent' strategies are closer to *poesis* which has a generative as well as an ornamental dimension in Vico's conception – *poesis* is about 'making', creating or fashioning. Vico intends, as Struever says, that impersonality or formalism applies to the civic/political person: poetic processes are generic, not literary – '"making" is a range of inventive interactions in historical development' (Struever 2005: 332). This is a broader concept of *inventio* which for Vico is an argument relying on a radical constructionist purpose of discernment from memory, imagination as well as from deduction.

In this chapter, I want to explore two inter-related ideas that derive from and inform Vico's and Jung's writings and technique. This will involve exploring several traditional aspects of Western rhetoric. But also, and here I invoke the broader and original meaning of *techné* which Frascari defines: it 'belongs to the notion of *poesis* which reveals or discloses . . . the truth . . . and goes hand in hand with *episteme* or *scientia* [wisdom]' (Frascari 1990: 11); *techné* includes an instrumental dimension, as *poesis* includes an ornamental dimension, 'eloquence'. The imagination in its manifestations in image or speech/written form is both generative and discerning, and these functions imbricate to form new symbols and action.

The aspects of topical invention that I want to investigate in respect to Jung's works rely on the affinities between the psychologist and the philosopher. Setting out these principles orients specific discussions for the remainder of the book.

It is utterly feasible to discuss Jung's writing in contexts of Western rhetoric – he is steeped in it, as were the alchemists and astrologers he studied. Rhetorical code has magical force, as Plato complained, so the power of the word in material and symbolic dimensions has long been recognised. Since it could not be countermanded without great skill in undoing the 'charm', Plato advised banning it.

Jung exploited this mingling of dimensions and in turn this intermingling animated his theories. As is well known, the precepts of rhetoric are as follows: the five canons: *inventio*, seeking premises for argument; *disposition*, arrangement; *expositio*, style; *memoria*, memory; and *action/pronunciato* and then the three divisions of rhetoric: *juridical* or 'forensic' which focuses on past action: we may apply this to Jung's word association tests, and to writings on the infrequent times he assisted in court cases; *deliberative*, an enquiry into future action – 'demonstrative' analyses predicting probable outcome by submitting proofs, artificial and natural, dialectical or rhetorical, to an audience: we may consider Jung's function as a healer and interpreter of dreams; and *epidiectic*, ascribing praise or blame – weighing up individual lives based on communal values – serving pedagogic purpose as well as celebratory purpose: we may consider Jung's memoirs in this regard; these were well known to him as core subjects in the curricula as Jaffé sets out (1980) in assessing Freud's similar schooling.

The trivium was a pedagogic requirement: including grammar (structure of language), rhetoric (the effects of language), and dialectic (the logic of language) (see Veltman 2002). Steeped in Western tradition, Jung felt that he could only claim therefore dim insight into those works of the East he read – the Upanishads or the Tibetan Book of the Dead – constrained by Western forms of knowing. He was aware of the limitation. This is an important precept for Vico as he understood history and radically differing values of language in time and place.

Jung knew well the triad of the rhetorical event too: the rhetor, the message and the audience. He was intensely aware of methods of persuasion, since it was his work, and it was salient to his message that he openly integrate the audience he was targeting and be transparent about underlying premises. Evidence abounds in his letters, lectures and writings. Awareness of audience as crucial component of the triad is a relatively new attitude. Early pedagogic handbooks primarily addressed the rhetor's function, following Aristotle's lead. Recognition of the audience in its own right (not simply as passive respondent, willingly manipulated by the adept rhetor) and of the message – without its articulator or its audience figured in (à la Derrida or Barthès) occurred late in rhetoric's history. Jung was adept at playing an audience both instinctively and intentionally to his ends. Merging the instrumental and the symbolic did not frighten him and in fact it is the source, like it is for Vico in his discovery of the poetic key, of his innovative psychology.

All cultures and all persons use rhetoric that is distinctive – this is George Kennedy's broad definition of rhetoric (Kennedy 1988) and it was Vico's – although 'personal' meant a kind of 'impersonal' type of axiomatic presence for the eighteenth-century philosopher. Vico's ironic recounting of historical event as it pivoted on the *topos* of appearance/reality is a favourite *topos* also for Jung as I will be exploring. Commenting in *Archetypes and the Collective Unconscious* (CW9i), Jung complains about the way meaning insistently foists itself on experience, causing us to seek pathetic metaphysical significance:

> only when all props and crutches are broken, and no cover from the rear offers us the slightest hope of security, does it become possible for us to experience an archetype that up till then had lain hidden behind the meaningful nonsense played out by the anima. This is the *archetype of meaning,* just as the anima is the *archetype of life itself.*
>
> (Jung CW9i 1934/1954: para 66)

He continues in a Vichean vein:

> Interpretations make use of certain linguistic matrices that are themselves derived from primordial images. From whatever side we approach this question, everywhere we find ourselves confronted with the history of language, with images and motifs that lead straight back to the primitive wonder-world.
>
> (Ibid.: para 67)

I'd suggest he implies the collective unconscious here. In his essay 'Flying Saucers' (Jung CW10 1958/1964), later in his career, as I will look into further, he investigates the 'viability' or otherwise 'probable reality' of an after life and of UFOs. His proofs rely on assessment of the common public psyche and assumptions. These are distinctly topical approaches to argument.

Vico matches these startling attitudes. In book 2, 'Poetic wisdom', of *The New Science* he explores the reality of the poet Homer and he relies on assessment of the conflicting community mores he finds in the *Odyssey* and the *Iliad* – as many scholars before and after had noted. Homer becomes a heroic poetical figure, the embodiment of the Greek people: 'real' in a rhetorical way. He is a 'type' embodying features of the founding poet, a composite of all the itinerant poeticising beggars of the community; 'blind' since they did not have personal features but replaced each other nationally and historically. In fact being a heroic type he is more real than he appears to be (Vico 1976/1730: para 412–17). Vico notes the disingenuousness of scholars when they assess the past and he points out their obtuseness in the case of Homer. Seen only through their own eyes, they cannot separate projections of current situations to the past (Vico, 1976/1730: para 500). The interplay of appearance/reality generates meaning in his discussion here, and he resorts to irony to distinguish past from present.

Looking back more closely at Vico's work and rhetorical tradition, we find more affinities but also recognition of the similar sources of innovation in the philosopher and the psychologist.

Part 1 *Topos* and *inventio*: truth and certainty: persuasions

Although he was an earlier supporter of Descartes, like most European scholars at the time, soon Vico became a critic opposed to the Cartesian stance of privileging of dialectical invention as the best all-purpose probe to discover 'true' knowledge. A more worldly and probabilistic approach is topical invention. Topical invention turns on themes, and dispositions of audience and writer/speaker. Dialectical invention relies on a deductive form of logic to create 'necessity'. The rhetor appeals to rational deduction to convince. In topical invention, commonplaces or maxims, common sense, and clusters of argument are among the persuasive components. The debate between dialectical invention and topical invention was central to contemporary debates of epistemology and ontology.

Vico's core idea of *poesis* and his allegiance to topical invention function together deeply in his work; communication/language has instrumental and symbolic dimensions – language is generative and transformative. Rhetoric through its *techné* functions as epistemology and as ontology and instantiates a world for humankind. Vico's claims originate from his rhetorical studies of Aristotle and Plato.

Aristotle's definition of rhetoric in *Rhetoric* (books 1 and 2), or in his later volume, *Topics* (book 3) (and its appendices, *Sophistical refutations*) simply says that rhetoric is the 'art of persuasion by any means'. It is this last phrase 'by any means' that has prompted much commentary in the centuries since he wrote it. Methods of persuasion range from blunt verbal force, just short of physical blows, verbal or written. Force ranges from the imperatives of deductive logic, and imposition of authority, to soft insinuation and charm (which Plato feared).

In my reading, Aristotle's 'demonstration' and 'proof' in *Rhetoric* depends on a belief in a human cognition that is predisposed to conscious and rational processing: *logos (Rhetoric* book 1, 1). Following Vico's discovery, I'd place rationality as a belief that is secondary to imaginal cognition. And although Aristotle divided the first canon of rhetoric, *inventio* (location and creation of the argument) into *logos*, *pathos* and *ethos*, it seems clear he favoured *logos.*

Logos is deductive and rational *reasoning*. And for Vico (and other commentators) as he understands it from Aristotle, the word also means the *concept* of reasoning (Vico 1996/1911–41: 47–8). By using the same word for the process and for the thought, Aristotle opened up the issue of logic and dialectic vs. rhetoric.

To parse out the confusion in simple terms: 'thinking rationally' is a phrase of action, or a verb, and 'thought' is a word of agency, a nominative. Because they operate in different speech registers, an important complication arises. The *rational* 'thinking' of *logos*, which implies logical deductive activity, is not inclusive of all 'thought' which can also partake of irrational and ornamental or figural ways. Syllogisms are the formula of logical necessity, Aristotle sets out, and (what Vico considered a defective form of necessary reasoning) the *enthymeme*, with its dependence on common sense inference, seemed more appropriate to designate the creation of figural or irrational forms of necessity. The *enthymeme,* Aristotle points out, is the *syllogism* of rhetoric. I will return to this later.

> Things are 'true' and 'primary' which are believed on the strength not of anything else but of themselves: . . . On the other hand, those opinions are 'generally accepted' which are accepted by every one or by the majority . . . or by philosophers of merit.
>
> (Aristotle 1954, book 1, 2)

This last avers to a topical approach by means of inference to argumentation, and to general common sense, or communal agreement. Inference applies to the third term, as a communicative bridging mechanism, I would propose, in the *enthymeme* (rhetorical syllogism) which works on common psychological ground as instinctive reference. Weimer points out its psychological dimension: the human nervous system is oriented to pick up common necessary reactions to environment for survival purposes. A given orientation to find these ways makes symbolic communications a matter of universal orientation. The 'reality' or the 'truth' is a plausible conjecture or proposition that humans call empirical 'fact'. As I will try to develop in a discussion of Jung's writing about Abélard in *Psychological Types* this inferential dimension is a primal manoeuvre that informs his psychology.

There were 'contentions' that might be founded on opinion and on irrational or fallacious argumentation that might nevertheless be persuasive. They might well conform to universal symbols of communication. (But, either route – irrational or fallacious argument – might easily be turned to the disadvantage of an opponent.) Deploying these forms of persuasion is even more important than arguing from self-evident logical proofs, is what he means. Self-evident truths are not a solid basis for adherence or for certainty.

While Aristotle considers *pathos*, the affective means of persuasion, and *ethos*, an appeal to authority, to be important rhetorical techniques as well, they are lower down the hierarchy of the means of persuasion. What kind of 'truth' does Aristotle generally think such means lead to even if they achieve adhesion or certainty?

Generally, irrationality is related to use of the figural and to the imagination, i.e. images and arguments deriving from the hyper-personal sensual experience and fantasies – metaphor, visual images, etc. On one side of the debate, these are questionable forms that rely on the imponderables of cultural or communal cliché that are unreliable in debate although they are accepted. Religious visions may not be accepted as proof in one culture while they are entirely persuasive in another. And, another strike against the persuasive power of imagination is that it incorporates memory, an unreliable instrument. But, despite its unreliability, Aristotle allowed it, and called it 'natural proof' although it was lower in the hierarchy of 'necessary' proof.

Part 2 Topical invention and topical logic, modes of argumentation

Unlike Aristotle's inclination to privilege logic and rationality, Vico's distinctive idea of language's role in cognition favoured *elocutio* (expressivity) and *narratio*, imaginative and plausible links in chains of association. *Inventio* – the establishment of grounds for argument – was Vico's starting point in contrast to Descartes (and probably Aristotle's but that is beyond my scope here). Descartes starts from an attitude of critiquing a proposition – a dialectical mode of enquiry, analysing a statement for its certainties, its unquestionable impersonal core of truth. Descartes asserts he does not trust the hyperboles and tricks of rhetoric but it is, I suggest, along with many others, that he simply advocates a different tradition of rhetoric.

Unlike his approach, *inventio* is a strategy of searching for the means and grounds of joining in discussion and uses topical rhetoric as its mode to achieve plausible and viable certainties. Dialectical logic is contrasted to topical logic, seeking a good-enough 'truth'.

Vico cites Cicero's *Topics* frequently, along with Aristotle's *Topics,* which included extensive lists of themes or motifs to win a case. Primarily the discussion pivots on legal or juridical cases. This tradition extends right through rhetoric's history originating probably with the Stoics whose rhetoricians (explored in Plato's *Gorgias* among other places) explored contentions from both sides. Although they suffered a bad reputation in the nineteenth and early twentieth centuries because their commitment to seeing both sides of an issue appeared problematic, their imaginative insight into the legitimacy of varying points of view has come to seem more sophisticated. Nevertheless, they were important authority for philosophers/ rhetoricians throughout medieval and Renaissance times. They deployed dialectical logic but within the framework of topics in what contemporary rhetorician Perelman might call 'quasi-logical' arguments.

Boethius, an important source for Vico, wrote an important work on topical argumentation analysing 'hypothetical propositions' which he suggested provided valid-enough strategies of proof. Abélard built on Boethius's influential work, and analysed it further in ways congenial to Jung's discussion of him which I will pursue farther on.

In this event, 'topics' are first resort for forming an argument – these universal categories of meaning generally arose from *common sense* – the meanings of a community and patterns of thought deeply embedded in humans. There are close associations to patterns of the 'collective unconscious' as Jung designated this layer – instinctive and communal. Critical analysis and discovery of logical cause-and-effect sequences did not always create powerful emotional and unfailing certainty which was claimed. They are representations of a hypothesis about reality rather than a true instance of phenomena, as Weimer avers. A further discussion of the rhetorical syllogism, the *enthymeme,* might be salient here.

A *syllogism* is A equals B, and if B = C, then it follows A = C. The syllogism is founded not only on the conclusions, but also, in this case, on a premise that a sequence is stable. This premise is deemed logical and incontrovertible and therefore the conclusions are true and certain.

However, in terms of the rhetorical syllogism, the *enthymeme*, the bridge is by *inference* to a conclusion; it is debatable: i.e. the premise follows on to a conclusion, but the premise is implied. A must be C because our premise is that identity and sequence are stable ideas. In this case, B is the third element, let's say. (She says she sees things; people who say they see things are visionaries; she must be a visionary. Our common understanding is not questioned; and also our collective agreement is that we believe that certain people who say they see things actually can, and that it's unusual, and that they are a special sort of person, a visionary.) You might say that the collective unconscious in Jungian terms which is engaged with primal complexes such as attachment to mother, is the missing third element influencing action: the shared inference creates the significance and the truth. More on *enthymeme* and its part in my discussion below.

Other themes of rhetoric provide useful strands to follow in exploring topical invention, and I will pursue each further below:

1 *Enthymeme* as an argumentative manoeuvre
2 *Authority:* Vico and Jung invoke authority of Cicero, high in status, along with Horatio and Longinus' ideas of rhetorical importance of 'ornamentation' – assertion of belief of highly important sources
3 *Inventio* – exploration of the distinctions of ways, and how ways correlate to circumstance, are at the core of topical invention – unlike the purportedly neutral and contingency-free ways of dialectical invention.
4 *Arguments of ornamentation* – *copia*, *narratio*, *amplificatio*, *elocution*, *decorum*, and personification
5 'Probability' and proofs: *testimony*.

To state this in another form: Jung and Vico use commonalities, and passion (*pathos* – emotion and feeling) as well as logic to persuade based on *topical invention* which is a trawl through 'places' to find appropriate argumentation rather than analysis by critical ratiocination. As Crowley and Hawhee (1999: 102) suggest in their discussion of the *kairos* ('the right or opportune moment') of a situation, the art of invention is the ability to frame a critical approach that suits your point. *Topics* are also a ready-to-hand way.

By most accounts, *topics* are the most natural and common form of invention. Aristotle lists many categories in *Rhetoric* and *Topics*: opposition; genus and species; appearance/reality; higher/lower, etc. These categories function as *a priori* means of organisation and construction generated by human modes of cognition. Hauser sets out three important aspects of topical invention, and I paraphrase him here:

1 Topics provide '*given*' mental perspectives, built into their definition; but, in fact,
2 They are also '*containers*' holding the content within their orientation,
3 And, thirdly, they function as a *discovery* of new things we might say.

Hauser elaborates his metaphor to a vessel of meaning:

> A place for topical reasoning is like a cistern in that it also has no content of its own. It is able to accommodate some contents better than others . . . but the place is not changed by the material placed in it . . . a place is also a *heuristic* because it helps us to discover what can be said about anything put in its place.
>
> (Hauser 1986: 64–5)

The particular application of the *topos* of appearance/reality, for instance, is salutary: Vico exploits the contradiction of the phrase 'poetical wisdom' in application to history (and also to science). 'Wisdom' is cold, logical and self-evident 'fact'. 'Poetry' is a crafted, passional expression. Vico argues paradoxically that the laws of history rather rely on the wisdom of the imagination, an unreliable faculty. 'Wisdom' is put into suspension by its association, however, here to poetry. The mingling of functional and instrumental elements with the conceptual dimension galvanises Vico's ideas and discloses the nature of the cognitive power of *topical logic*, a tool of topical invention. This is the *locus* for me of the birth of Vico's great discovery, *poetical logic*.

To retrace: topical logic was an important development in rhetorical thought just previous to the enlightenment (Ong 1958), and it seemed to theorists to be self-contradictory in ways I mention above. 'Topical argumentation' might engage in what seems to be methodical, objective connections, as it too is in its way 'logical' or self-evident. But, at its core, its strategies rely on common sense and cultural mores. What could be more irrational than that? The parameters of 'opposition' or definitions of genus and species, for example, can differ in contexts. Aristotle points out that 'topics' were motifs that encapsulated the *content* of an argument but also *shaped* the argument (*Topics* book 1, 1, i).

Topical invention stimulates topical logic. Proponents claim the high status of dialectical logic for topical logic. Vico's 'poetical logic' aspires to similar status (Vico 1976/1730–44: para 495–7). He makes claims for the imaginal mode that affirm the same 'certainty' and 'truth' values that deductive logic claims. We know only what we make, and the imaginal cognition we engage in as humans in our earliest times both as a species and as individuals means we engage in 'poetical' logic which is both symbolic and instrumental. (Jung makes an analogous argument in much of his work, perhaps most overtly in the 'Flying Saucer' or 'Synchronicity' essays, for such truth claims about psychic reality.) Tropes are the cogs of 'poetical logic' just as the elements of deduction are for logic. Tropes are metaphor, metonymy and synecdoche, and finally also irony which Vico sets out in full in *The New Science*. In Vico's philosophical system, they play out in the same way as axioms of self-evident logical propositions do (Vico 1976/1730–44: para 400–11).

Related to Hauser's clarifications set out above, Lanham also points out that a confusion of aims (topical motifs as *either* shaping mechanisms or as content – performative or nominative – as Aristotle claimed) opens up one of the important issues of rhetoric (Lanham 1991: 110); he emphasises one particular aspect of the theme in the specific context of communication. We will use a familiar example from Jung's work to demonstrate this overlap and also to demonstrate affinities in his modes of significance as both representations of meanings and instantiations of meaning: transformative and generative.

Is the coincidental appearance of a scarab beetle just when a woman describes her dream to Jung about such a beetle as significant as he says it is? Is it an instance of 'synchronicity', demonstrating the laws of the universe and their convergence on this woman's psyche? Or is that incident a manipulation of imagery and meaning by the rhetor, Jung, in order to deceive the dreamer albeit with presumably good intent? This story appears in volume 8 of the collected works, published in 1952 (para 843 ff.). Is the universal 'law' of coincidence/synchronicity playing in this individual woman's life?

Jung discovers convergence of universal law with the woman's specific event. This specific human's time converges with the beetle's natural timing and flight plan. The overlap impacted directly on Jung's patient's hard-core rational approach to life, he tells us. The shock of the shadow side of rationality, a coincidental irrational occurrence, broke through her personal hard shell. He tells us that this is apt 'argument' on many levels. It's persuasive since, for one thing, it serves his purpose in breaking through to her, on the way to healing (and so, also, he is exonerated from opportunism). 'Synchronicity' is a form of significant coincidence (in Jung's definition), and that's what happened here, a transcendent coincidence. In fact, Jung claims axiomatic status for his notion of synchronicity, and he arrives at this claim through the workings of *topical logic,* ascribing symbolic meaning to transformative significance. In discussing this special form of coincidence, Verene applauds the notion of self deployed by Jung. The psychic reality encompasses image and concept in a unique way resolved in the notion of paradox. I will explore this further below in discussion of the 'Flying Saucers' essay.

Genus/species: the rhetor reshapes the definition of *genus* and thereby transforms a *species* for argument's sake – *genus* manifests itself in *species* therefore by redefining the nature of the *species*, *genus* is repositioned. The discovery of a *species* of inorganic protein matter, the 'prion', which embeds itself into organic matter and redefines the *genus* 'virus'. Scientific investigation of the human form of mad cow's disease was totally altered. *Topos* here is both a device as a 'container' of significance, and also instrumental in shifting meanings.

Topical logic is an elaboration of the argumentative use of *topics* and it effectively establishes certainties. There are irrational and pathetic elements that come to be applied in this form of logic that are out of sync with classical definitions of *topics* and of *logic.* Traditionally, *topics* do not include predication or judgement. They are pivots, or foci of argument. There are no extensions and no feelings attached. (In another context, however, Ricoeur extends the definition of metaphor to contain predication, as we will explore later (see Ricoeur 1976) and which we can see applies here overturning the classical definitions.)

But 'topical logic' includes intentionality. In the 'synchronous' event of the scarab beetle, Jung reads the situation just as it occurs but as he intends it too. And this is the anomaly. 'Intentionality' is established by predication and judgement, but as we recall from Hauser's definitions, *topics* are content-less designations, applicable to *any* argument, suitable to the purpose, chosen by the rhetor. No opinion and no contingency are designated. 'Topical logic' is a deviation from this. It is an extension of *topics.*

To restate this in its original Aristotelian context, *topics* are the static place of an argument which also refers to a processing function. The 'topic' as a source of a specific kind of topical argumentation has the capacity to galvanise an argument when rhetors take advantage of the 'embedded' judgemental aspect, mingling agency and action. Predication and judgement come to attach themselves to specific *topics* so that they are more than simply locations of neutral argument. They have an attitude, although in time we may have forgotten there is an embedded judgement at all. Here is where 'topical logic' emerges.

In our exploration of Jung's topical logic (as I am contending), it is important to investigate the association of feeling and judgement since it is an important hinge in his psychology (as it is in Vico's philosophy – like Hobbes' noting that fear is a primal force in creation of human natural law, so does Vico ascribe fear as the drive to create a god from the loud 'voice' of thunder).

In his discussion of the medieval humanist, Rodolphus Agricola, Ong (1958) recounts the history of the application of judgement to *topics*. Exploitation of *topics* in this application generated a dynamic and/or contentious proposition. For example, 'he opposed his brother': judgement is implied (in our culture) which makes the oppositional pair a motivation to action. Brothers are not commonly thought to be in opposition. This exploitation of *topics* is unlike the 'scientific demonstration' Aristotle would require of logical invention. Opposition puts as a scientific or neutral hypothesis simply sets black against white, a 'natural' and irrefutable opposition. Both demonstration and logical argument are uninflected (Vickers 1988: chapter 3). In this proposition, topical logic evolves categories of invention that lead to compromised 'artificial' propositions, i.e. brother opposing each other, an axiom is overturned. It is the only kind of certainty and truth we have.

Jung's reasoning based on imaginative association is just this kind of 'scientific demonstration', a rhetorical proposition, in fact, a demonstration of 'topical logic', and he refers confidently to extrinsic reality, i.e. truthful propositions by inference particularised in a common culture.

Enthymeme

Introduced above, Ong has more to say that explores the rhetorical *syllogism* that leads us into further investigation of Vico's innovations: '*enthymeme* primarily signifies something within one's soul, mind, heart, feelings, hence something not uttered or "outered" [*sic*] and to this extent not a fully conscious argument, legitimate though it may be' (Ong 1982: 85) . . . and their parallels to Jung's.

Why is the primacy of *inventio* crucial to Vico's topical logic? And how does this relate to the form of rhetorical syllogism I mention here? The deployment of inferential rhetoric, and its use of the *enthymeme*, relies on the first moves in an argument (see Vico 1984/1711–41: para 29 ff.). It is possible to conceive a rhetorical strategy built on 'memory' or 'delivery', the other canons of rhetoric. The rhetor might determine that loud and dominant talk ('delivery') rather than arrangement or inception of the argument is the most successful way to persuade. Vico proposes that *inventio* (inception of the argument – where you start your case, the ground you choose) specifically as it utilises *topics* and other quasi-logical ploys (as defined in Perelman and Olbrechts-Tyteca, *The New Rhetoric)* such as the *enthymeme* are most effective. How topical and related ornamental strategies obtain proof derives from Aristotle's precepts.

The *syllogism* in its logical form – all people are mortal, Socrates is a person, and therefore Socrates is mortal. [(1) all persons are mortal; (2) Socrates is a person; (3) therefore Socrates is mortal.] This sequence purports to be a series of incontrovertible steps to arrive at its conclusion. The implication is that there is nothing to dispute.

However, to return to the *enthymeme*, as an elaboration of the *syllogism,* Aristotle proposes:

> It is clear . . . that rhetorical study is concerned with modes of persuasion. Persuasion is clearly a sort of demonstration, since we are most fully persuaded when we consider a thing to have been demonstrated. The orator's demonstration is an *enthymeme* and this is, in general, the most effective . . . [it] is a sort of *syllogism* . . . but it differs from the *syllogism* of strict logic . . . men have a sufficient natural instinct

> for what is true, and usually do arrive at the truth. Hence the man who makes a good guess at truth is likely to make a good guess at probabilities.
>
> (Aristotle 1954 I,1,5)

Aristotle's 'demonstration' is his proposition that rhetoric is a counterpart to dialectic: 'demonstration' is a scientific and objective deduction in this case, it holds high status as proof. Using this language to refer to *enthymemes* carries over from the discourse of deductive logic.

Enthymeme is a 'defective' syllogism for Vico and others; it is a deductive argument based on 'probabilities' and inference. Lionel Bitzer notes that *enthymemes* have a distinctive place among the repertoire of types of *logical* proof. In this way, they are not 'defective' since they are a kind of logic. In the rhetor's discussion, contingencies are accommodated, specifically located incontestably in the participants' contexts, which is what the *enthymeme* accomplishes. It is a strategic and well-formed device. Vico called it 'defective' in order to bring it into closer proximity to the *syllogism* rather than its being a separate manipulation. This raises its status from a secondary proposition, and keeps it within Cicero and Aristotle's authoritative demonstrations. As a proponent of poetical logic, and topical logic, *enthymeme* is an essential logical manoeuvre and he wants to assert its prominence. The *enthymeme* relies on the missing third term, unlike the *syllogism* and this is fundamental (Bitzer 1959).

It is possible to use 'fallacious argumentation' successfully to persuade (Aristotle sets out lists of examples – as does Vico) even if it is dishonest. Like *enthymemes*, 'fallacious argument' relies on probabilities (*Rhetoric*, book 2, 24, 1401a) – that is that they are rhetorical formulae rather than logical formulae. How is it that we are persuaded by less than perfectly formed logical deductions? And it is not only a matter of status.

For one thing, logical deduction though apparently self-evident does not always achieve adherence. As Perelman and Olbrechts-Tyteca point out in their volume, *The New Rhetoric,* and as Vico would agree, there is a distinction between an argument's logical inevitability and its persuasiveness. (We can know smoking cigarettes will damage our lungs, and hear it set out to us as a logical deduction that we should not smoke, but we are not persuaded to stop. A striking and fearful image of a diseased lung, or black smoke permeating a room may do the trick, however.)

In *Gorgias* Plato argues, as I will too, that logic is based on opinion (*doxia*) which I will pursue further in discussion of Jung's definitions of scientific psychology. In that case, certainty is founded on conviction that is *already* in place. Jung's often repeated assertion that he knows of God's existence, it is already, he does not 'believe' it, relates to this assertion.

Vico's *enthymeme*, the imperfect syllogism (Vico 1984/1711: 41 para 89) is what Perelman and Olbrechts-Tyteca would call a *quasi-logical* proposition (Perelman and Olbrechts-Tyteca 1969). It is 'imperfect' in that it leaves out the 'middle term' which, despite its suppression, is clearly implied. It is not that it is based on 'probability' but that the middle term is not there. We shift analysis away from uncertainties implied in the term 'probability'. This missing third term is generally understood and the rhetor underscores it to make the point. The *enthymeme* relies on assumptions of common knowledge embedded in *topics* and in what is peculiar to a culture. These are you might say actually shared 'certainties'.

An often-used example of an *enthymeme* or the *quasi-logical* proposition too (which has the added advantage of giving appearance of logical deduction) is the speech Marc Anthony gives to the crowd over Caesar's dead body in Shakespeare's play (Perelman and Olbrechts-Tyteca site this too): 'Mark'd ye his words? He would not take the crown. Therefore 'tis certain he was not ambitious' (Shakespeare, *Julius Ceasar*, III.ii).

We note the speaker's assumptions, assuming the crowd's agreement, about what a crown represents, and about what ambition is, and that to decline the crown is to be unambitious, etc. These are attractive qualities, they all agree, he implies, for a ruler determined not to be a tyrant, and that's the irony. The audience gets it.

Vico's handbook points out Aristotle's precept that as a form of invention, *enthymeme* is 'artificial' or 'artistic' proof, as opposed to 'natural' proof (Aristotle, *Rhetoric*, book 1, 1, 1356b; book 2, 23). 'Natural' proof includes the logical deductive formula of the syllogism because it is incontrovertible like nature's laws are, and impervious to the rhetor's disposition or to cultural disparities, etc. Other evidence like eyewitness testimony and documentation is also 'natural'. Unlike the *enthymeme* these natural proofs are given and indisputable certainties (Aristotle, *Rhetoric*, book 2, 22). The skill of the rhetor is in creating the artificial and probable proofs of the *enthymeme.*

Jung relies on this rhetorical strategy in his writing by establishing by inference the certainties of his new psychology, as Vico does in his writings. Jung amplified meanings by referring to 'complexes' or compelling and strongly felt (and unexpressed) 'middle terms' in his propositions to explain motivation and action. His alchemical, etymological and mythic examinations purport to be symbolic representations of a missing term, 'contingent' or 'variable' as they erupt from the collective unconscious. This 'missing term' draws on underlying customary and archaic meanings.

As Aristotle and Vico agree, generally men (*sic*) know the 'truth' although 'truth' needs some qualification. Effective and wise rhetors 'quickly penetrate to the very core of a matter. . . . Discernment follows by which he should know and love all things which are proper; further, an unbridled fantasy by which he can make customs and emotions of others his own' (Vico 1984/1711–41: 15).

Aristotle recommended the *enthymeme* to speakers, not to writers (book 3, 17). It was easier to control references by voice and gesture in response to audience on the spot. *Acuity* or discernment plays a large part in interpreting raw material cogently and with intent. This faculty can be abused, and Vico disparages the clever-clever conceits of some rhetoricians (Vico 1990/1709: 9).

Authorities

Appeal to authority is crucial to a writer seeking a place in a tradition. Choice of predecessors positions those writers not only by who they choose but also generally by the fact that they are willing to refer to past authority at all. Referring to authority is a powerful rhetorical ploy, often invoking cultural maximal figures, even if they are used in illicit ways, and it can make an argument successful.

Descartes, for example, felt that he was making a new departure entirely from the past; he did not want to stand on the past which was old and worthless now, but looked to the future. In his first *Meditations* he says 'it was necessary, once in the course of my life, to demolish everything completely and start again right from the foundations if I wanted to establish anything at all in the sciences that was stable and likely to last'. He disowned predecessors (see Lachterman 1983). Descartes' attitude to history was entirely different to Vico's for whom memory and discovery were the foundations of cognition and meaning. But apart from my (and others') thinking Descartes overstated his position on this issue, as I will elaborate farther on, Vico and Jung felt distinctly differently about history even though they had different reasons at times. It gave them legitimacy for their innovative positions, although it is clear that in some cases, especially for Jung, this was an ironic posture.

Vico and Jung shared reference to several antecedents: Cicero, Longinus and Horace were the most important. And while Jung hardly ever mentions Descartes, Jung and Vico shared an antipathy to precepts that the seventeenth-century Frenchman proposed. How they spoke about their predecessors is an important aspect of their work, and gives me another opportunity to demonstrate their affinities. Pro-Cicero (and Longinus and Horace) and anti-Descartes represents a mix of national pride and a bid for legitimacy in Vico's case; for Jung it is more clearly an attempt to lay claim to legitimacy.

A brief example of Jung's and Vico's use of Cicero's work will highlight their sympathies by comparing how they used the Roman's ideas. Vico begins his comment in his philological work *On the wisdom of the ancient Italians* (177x, 1988/1711):

> it is my view that poets and painters are called 'divine' because of [a] faculty for feigning. Just as the divine facility in creation is 'nature' so what we call 'naturalness' is a rare and excellent virtue . . . and Cicero would render it as 'a genius flowing spontaneously and, somehow after a fashion, natural. (Vico cites Cicero, *De Oratore*, II.15.77)
>
> (Vico 1988/1711: 106)

Vico had begun the paragraph quoting Plutarch's admiration for Homer's 'divine' *and* 'natural' art. The best art seems to 'grow spontaneously'. This statement is paradoxical. How can something 'fashioned' be 'natural' – nature is chaos; and isn't 'fashioning' artifice? 'Growing' is a faculty of natural entities, not artificial entities. Vico cites Cicero's gloss on style here to propose what Vico thinks eloquence or artifice to be: it is a coincidence of 'natural' shape and the rhetorician's art in shaping that meaning. The semblance of an easy flow of the natural into the artificial which Vico calls 'fluency' is a priority in persuasion of an audience. As mentioned in opening this chapter, fluency denotes authenticity because it appears as if speech emerges unplanned from a sensibility that the rhetor shares instinctively with the collective. It brings adherence by agreement with the audience. Since they sense a sharing of the certainties, rhetor and audience are as one, and the audience is convinced. (For Perelman and Olbrechts-Tyteca, this is the pivotal aim of rhetoric, to achieve agreement through sameness.)

Vico is attentive to the paradoxical naturalness of the artifice of rhetoric if it is done adeptly. In fact, the most effective 'naturalness' is achieved or fashioned by artifice. He plays on the *topos* of artifice/reality – art vs. nature – and Jung does too.

Jung talks about Cicero and he refers not only to 'natural artifice', but also about the effects of 'fluency'. The reference appears in *Symbols of Transformation* when Jung quotes Cicero's broad explanation of libido in part of his own discussion refuting Freud's narrower sex-related definition: 'will is a rational desire, but when it is divorced from reason and is too violently aroused, that is "libido", or unbridled desire, which is found in all fools' (Cicero, *Tusculan Disputations*, book 4, vi.12) (Jung CW5: para 185 ff.).

Here Jung uses Cicero's idea of the imposition of natural 'will' on spontaneous irruption to create 'wise meaning'. Without this imposition, there is no meaning, just the chaos of intense longing, or 'libido'. Jung goes on to say that '*libido* means a "want" or a "wish" . . . Cicero uses it in this sense when he says "Gerere rem aliquam libidine non ratione" – (to do something from wilful desire and not from reason)' (ibid.: para 186).

Both Vico and Jung use Cicero here as a philosophical authority. Vico also cites Cicero as a stylist throughout his works, using examples to illustrate rhetorical technique. Although he does not mention it directly, Jung knows the value of Cicero's rhetorical principles by pointedly using them. We refer again to copiousness in his own work, and its central position in Cicero's style; both Jung and Vico expand on words and associations they use in order to bring out their originary purpose and extensions.

The close awareness of the association of style and meaning is a notable element in Vico's philosophy of rhetoric (see Berlin, White, Frye). When Vico comments on Cicero's renowned prose style, especially the 'periodic sentence'; it is a gloss on the fluency of the best kind of rhetorical 'shaping'. Cicero's stylistic decisions about the 'periodic sentence' rest on a belief in the integrity of the determined coincidence of will *and* free expression, i.e. rational fashioning coincides with spontaneous significance.

Vico scoffs at his colleagues who criticise Cicero's 'periodic style' for its artificiality, by which they mean its evident lack of authenticity (Vico 1998/1774: 60). Yet, Cicero's style substantiates the coincidence of form and content. The prose is styled in sequential layers which elaborate reasoning in such a way that arguments appear to grow from each other spontaneously. An adept rhetorician or poet (or painter) replicates meaningful form in just this way. Vico set his argument in contexts of the interplay of the *topos* for persuasive purpose and also to entertain and thereby engage us.

Longius' and Horatio's devotion to 'ornamentation' along with their suggestions about the hierarchy of styles ('appropriateness'), and their appreciation of passion are elements of great importance to Vico and to Jung in their communications. But these elements are effective not only as embellishment but as core pieces of significance that cannot be achieved as well without them. The rhetor develops his skills as a discerner of meanings ('acuity'), and as a creator of meanings which are discovered by him by practising his art.

Spontaneity is an instinctive unconscious irruption and the good rhetor locates it. Vico calls this faculty *acutezza* (acuity) (see Vico's handbook of rhetoric) and it is the element of a movement outwards, consciously deployed to meet irrational 'irruption'. 'Acuity' engages conscious recognition of underlying unconscious collective significance (see Vico in his autobiography). Underlying cultural meanings function in this way, autonomously, and are expressed unwittingly in affect, and/or in images or behaviour (Vico, poetic logic section, new science). The words and associations used incorporate specific spontaneous meaning, but they irrupt from a pool of previously unavailable images and ideas. Their *definitions* extend back to source, and amplify significance out from that source (Vico 1788).

Jung traces a similar movement in his discussion of archetype, whose impact irrupts of necessity, described in an overwrought passage of *Archetypes and the Collective Unconscious*:

> Only when all props and crutches are broken, and no cover from the rear offers us the slightest hope of security, does it become possible for us to experience an archetype that up till then had lain hidden behind the meaningful nonsense played out by the anima. This is the *archetype of meaning,* just as the anima is the *archetype of life itself.*
>
> (Jung CW9i: para 66)

Establishing argumentative possibilities ('invention') by means of *topics* is a first resort for both Vico and Jung. It prepares the ground for embellishment and connections. This priority is a different one from finding critical argument in logical, deductive reasoning.

Before turning to Descartes' anti-authority stance, a quick mention of one other form of authority is warranted that also plays a crucial role, which was alluded to earlier.

Apart from testimony of the un-extraordinary person, the rhetorician points to *chreia,* testimony of famous figures. The use of those authority figures, like the use of maxims, adages of importance to the community, appeals to a fixed ethos of the community and is the ground the audience and rhetor meet on. As a famous figure, Jung encounters the double-edged nature of this ploy in his memoirs by walking a fine line to respect the community, leaving out experiences with the Nazi party in Germany at the time of World War II, and leaving out affairs with mistresses as a married man. Testimony is a 'natural proof' in its naïve form; *chreia,* the fixed and elaborated words of famous men or women designed to reflect the ethos of a community is an 'artful' proof. Jung's encounter with these forms of testimony will be explored in examination of his *Memories, Dreams, Reflections,* in later chapters.

Before expanding on other elements of the rhetorical repertoire to show affinities, examination of Descartes' anti-authority posture offers an opportunity to flesh out other elements of Vico and Jung's orientations.

Authorities – Descartes, part 2

It is clear from Vico's earlier writings that he was an admirer of Descartes, a revolutionary figure in his time, but he soon discovered that Cartesian aims were irrelevant and also pedagogically unsound.

Vico's 'poetic' and topical logic is an insight into an underlying interweave of 'fantasy', judgement and so-called truth as 'fact' as I have been arguing. Vico dismissed the mechanistic knock-on deductive logic of Descartes which assumed the absolute validity of self-evident truths. Although self-evident proof is an aspect of Aristotelian discussion in *Rhetoric* and *Poetics* (see Ong 1958: chapter 5), the motif Descartes dwelled on: 'cause and effect's logical irreducible sequence', was not. Cartesian assumption that there is objective 'truth' to find is contestable. Vico seeks rhetorical truth, since as he proposes, humans construct reality (if that is what 'truth' is) within the constraints of Providence and Nature. 'Reality' is a belief, after all, or a 'complex' perhaps as Jung might call it (Einstein referred to reality as a type of religious belief). 'Truth' pure and objective is external to humans. Not only is 'truth' outside human range, it is not a useful goal. Like Vico, Jung wanted to confirm and prioritise 'probability' as a kind of 'certainty', we might say the 'truth' of the psyche. In a discussion of Abélard, which I will pick up later, Jung comments on the discourse of this problematic:

> Reality is simply what works in a human soul and not what is assumed by certain people to work there, and about which prejudicial generalisations are wont to be made. Even when this is done in a scientific

> spirit, it should not be forgotten that science is not the *summa* of life, that it is actually only one of the psychological attitudes, only one form of human thought. . . . The psyche creates reality every day.
>
> (Jung CW6: para 60 and 78)

Dismissing previous authority so he could have a clear field, Descartes also disparaged rhetoric. Of course, this was another overstatement since he was a master stylist (see Gaukroger 1997). He not only uses topical invention, but he uses ornamentation frequently to make his argument.

Ernst Robert Curtius' book *European Literature and the Latin Middle Ages* explores important scholarly topical motifs and many obviously appear in Descartes' work. At the opening of *Discours*, the writer sits alone in a room and makes a momentous discovery. This is the traditional *topos* of the solitary scholar studying in isolation, stumbling onto a great insight – from St Jerome, the hermit in his cave, to St Augustine, studying alone in his rooms.

Descartes' disparagement of rhetoric is itself an age-old theme from pre-Socratic times. Curtius discusses the history and elaboration of this theme: authenticity vs. artifice, copiousness vs. simple dialectic, fluency vs. strict transparent deduction.

Holding to the idea of the purity of philosophy, which is to 'loosen the restraints' of rhetoric for Descartes, he maintained that 'clear and distinct' ideas exist *independently* of who says them or how they are said.

> I greatly esteemed eloquence and was in love with poetry, but I thought both were gifts of the mind rather than the fruit of study. Those with the most powerful reasoning, and who best ordered their thoughts to make them clear and intelligible, can always persuade us best of what they put forward even though they speak the dialect of Lower Brittany and have never learnt rhetoric; and those who have the most pleasing conceits and know how to express them the most decoratively and harmoniously would always be the best poets, even though they knew nothing of [Horace's] *Ars poetica.*
>
> (Descartes 1637/1968: 45)

In this extract we note another classical theme: the truthfulness of spontaneity, a *topos* going back to the Greek poets which we explored earlier. Curtius cites references as early as Hesiod's *Theogony* in its celebration of eloquence 'as a natural gift of the gods' (Curtius 1953, 64). In fact, to display spontaneity of expression makes a strong impression of sincerity; it is the 'fluency' a rhetor aims to achieve. (This important issue in the psychology of courtroom testimony and lying comes under scrutiny by William Stern and by Jung in the chapter below on forensic rhetoric.)

Descartes relies on the traditional *schema* academics and humanists use; they refer to the overwhelming power of *logos*: self-evident thought which overpowers its listeners, who become impotent in its presence. Gorgias set this theme out, to name one of the first precedents: in his *Encomium on Helen*. It is an apologia: Helen is blameless in leaving her husband since she had been confronted with the full power of Paris's persuasive *logos*. And Paris claimed he was possessed by a god's will.

The power of Descartes' 'clear and distinct' ideas sweeps away challenge. Minds trained to strip away excess are controlling and compel agreement. Rational thought carries us away.

Descartes announces in the opening chapter of the *Discours* that he will use fable to make his rational meanings clearer. Fables are analogies for the 'clear and distinct' truths he wants to convey, i.e. he will use 'artificial' means to persuade us of objective truth. In the end, rhetorical formulations took over Descartes' work.

Vico deplored the limiting, deceptive method Descartes had proposed. It leads to cynical and ironic critique that does not take on the earthly realities of a situation. Wise 'eloquence' depends on experience, and is best suited to a grounding in *topics*. The 'poetic logic' of metaphor, metonymy, synecdoche and irony were founded in the laws of history, and therefore they have the gloss of timeless incontrovertibility.

In any case, Vico did not agree that the basis of conviction was its logical truth. The appeal is to the pre-verbal, in fact to imagination and 'fantasy' as he called it (Vico, *The New Science*, book 2).

> Every opinion has about it a certain shadow of the truth that the wilfulness at work in our souls lays hold of as truth itself; thus each man has his own sense of things are there are, as the saying goes, as many opinions as heads.
>
> (Vico 1965/1709: 58)

Vico's rhetoric was a cognitive and social construct and relied on convictions about opinion, about poetics, about philosophy and psychology. Communication is both generative and referential.

Verene's seminal work on Vico's poetic science (Verene 1966) explores the ironic juxtaposition of these concepts. Vico aimed to analyse imagination as a kind of 'science' with its own laws. The problematic was equally vital for Jung who used archetypal figures as exempla of scientific data about the psyche. Necessity focuses cognition, and those impulses remain embedded in meaning. The world is processed and articulated with the goal of grounded survival in mind (Vico). Rhetoric is concerned with all aspects of motivating people to act, and is fundamentally driven by this urge.

To appreciate how their rhetoric accommodated an audience, we will focus on one strategy that both Vico and Jung used: *elocutio:* etymology as an instance of expression. I propose that Jung looked to this interactive style to formulate his theories and communicative style.

First I will tackle a major objection to Vico's (and Jung's) use of etymology. To say the least, Vico's etymologies are controversial. He used definitions to open up a word's associative links rather than to contain a word. He made errors – he did not know Greek, for example, but also he followed tracings-back in a word's life with his own ends in mind – and he seemed to make errors. One of the important themes of etymological definition (which we will explore further in discussing a passage from Jung's *Mysterium coniunctiones* below) is accuracy. Accuracy becomes a point of tension for communicator and recipient.

The historian of rhetoric, Brian Vickers, has disparaged Vico's speculative and reductive correlations of history and stylistic modes which are almost entirely based on his etymological researches, on those grounds (Vickers 1988).

But many important scholars excused Vico's etymological errors. Erich Auerbach's defence is characteristic. In the introductory discussion about forms of imitation in literature (Auerbach 1953), he tells us that since words participate in a kind of linking of signification, manipulation of associated meanings can achieve the goals of an argument better than deploying some fixed definition. And this is a legitimate ploy, he feels. In a later volume, Auerbach feels it is a legitimate ploy (1973). In fact, he claims Vico used this ploy successfully. Vico's ideas about cognition meant that the etymological associations – or, as Nancy Struever calls them, 'narratives' (1983) – are intentionally arranged to make his points. So, there are no errors ever, you could say, since associations embedded in the word, once retrieved, are always valid.

Facts are *probable* solutions to tensions rather than 'true' solutions. Definitions and narratives belong to their own time and place, and are deployed consciously or unconsciously. As Vico commentator John Schaeffer points out, 'The cognitivist view has become familiar enough: figures of speech are really conceptual structures, crucial both to cognition and culture' (Schaeffer and Eubanks 2004: 28).

Tropes as heuristic devices

Following on from this, Vico's correlation of style and historical moment is proper in his analysis of the cognitive power of metaphor. Metaphorical thinking is a kind of allegory of etymological thinking. Vico agrees with Aristotle that the greatest art of language is metaphor – its creative use to express resemblances by identity, and to generate new words, new things and new ideas. Not only did metaphor represent a certain originating moment in history, i.e. the age of the gods, but it was the creative act of the discerning and acute rhetor.

Vico's conception of metaphor is based on identity, not resemblance. Vico's *fantasia* is a kind of 'real' thinking, what Grassi calls, as we will explore, 'vera narrativa' – and it is the common sense of the human race. Later we will discuss this in relationship to Jung's two kinds of thinking. Verene comments on this Vichean conception:

> the genius of *ingenio* required for finding what is common between things is possible only because of the primordial power of transference between particular and universal which is accomplished within *fantasia* within the unit of *universale fantastici*.
>
> (Verene 1981: 174)

Commencing with identification, based on the immediate, incontrovertible experience of the senses, humans project human-ness onto events and things in nature. Initially, humans signified by grunts that later were elaborated into linked words, phrases and sentences (grammar was last) – primordial associations remained embedded in the linked communications. Hence etymology is a primary heuristic. This is Vico's discovery:

> The poetic characters of which we speak were certain imaginative genera (images for the most part of animate substances, of gods or heroes, formed by their imagination) to which they reduced all species or all the particular appertaining to each genus; exactly as the fables of human times. . . . These . . . were true fables or myths, and their allegories are found to contain meanings not analogical but univocal, not philosophical by historical.
>
> (Ibid.: 207)

4

PSYCHOLOGICAL TYPES AND RHETORICAL DEVICES

Perspectives

In his discussion of Abélard and Luther in *Psychological Types*, Jung focuses on distinctions between nominalism – which he properly ascribes to medievalist Abélard – and realism/sensualism which he attributes in contrast to Luther's position. It is the book's major theme that personal type and philosophical inclination are deeply intertwined. In fact, they refer to archetypal approaches. Is this a reductive view of personality and of philosophy? I'd propose that it grows from an understanding of rhetoric that ascribes drives to philosophical positions. I propose here to investigate Jung's argument and the rhetorical strategies that accommodate both the personality and the philosophy of the figures Jung appraises. His is an innovative viewpoint, and he starts by setting out the dilemma. I propose that he manages to avoid psychologising the philosophy, and over-stating a metaphysical scope for the drives.

He enquires into how symbols are regarded in argumentation and into considerations about their nature. And to extend this to our theme, Jung investigates how philosophies impact on humans as communicators, and what they mean in his own analytical psychological schema. Since the background 'glue' of ideology and personal orientation are essential to the concrete linguistic and stylistic representations manifest in the world, how does application to personal types influence his rhetoric?

Later than *Psychological Types*, but certainly during Jung's career, discussion about nominalism was paramount in academic circles. Norman Goodman's work on nominalism inspired much vigorous response from ethical pragmatists and linguists, like Hilary Putnam and Quine. Reconsiderations of Abélard's 'propositional attitudes' by German and Italian philosophers also propped up and contrasted to Goodman's work on nominalism and helps to orient Jung's discussion.

First, I will set out Goodman's ideas in an abbreviated form, showing how they differ from Jung's (and Vico's) philosophies, and then I will critique nominalism as described by Goodman to draw out the problems, and bring in Paul Ricoeur's resolution – all using Vico's rhetorical precepts of invention as a guide.

Goodman's volume *Ways of Worldmaking* (1978) followed on from his *Languages of Art: a theory of symbols* (1976) and discussed the relationship of representation to reality. As Walter Benjamin comments in the opening of his book on German baroque drama, the problem of representation is the core issue to contemporary aesthetic and ontological (not to speak of epistemological) philosophy.

As a 'radical nominalist', to use his own phrase about himself, Goodman equates artistic and scientific disciplines; they are equally viable as explanation about the world, he says. He contrasts paintings and poetry to scientific papers. Both forms, to a greater or lesser degree, intend not only to give pleasure in imaginal and/or linguistic embellishment, but also to succeed in effecting change, through their communications. Kuhn's work proposes different avenues for scientific communication since he focuses rather on a community of shared-linguistic commitment. But for Goodman, symbols of a variety of kinds may be used in different ways but they are equally valid as persuasive and normative communication. He feels comfortable in talking about their equivalent truth value.

> Truth moreover pertains solely to what is said and literal truth solely to what is said literally. We have seen though, that worlds are made not only by what is said literally but also by what is said metaphorically, and not only by what is said either literally or metaphorically but also by what is exemplified and expressed – by what is shown as by what is said.
>
> (Goodman 1978: 18)

This broad attitude stems from Goodman's relativist stance. He proposes that construction of meanings may well derive from individuals and/or from disciplines. But while he is aware of individual perspectives as they are reflected in the presentation of an end product, cultural or scientific, he thinks these specific standpoints are trivial and irrelevant, unlike Vico and others. Style is a minor element in consideration of a work for Goodman: 'Stylistics . . . is confined to features of what and how the works symbolise, and still further to such of these features as are characteristic of a given author, period, region, school, etc.' (ibid.: 38).

He avers that 'discernment of style is an integral aspect of the understanding of works of art and the worlds they represent' (ibid. 40), but the author's specific intentions are not a core element in deciphering such products. The cognitive awakening that a work of art or a piece of writing may afford its listener, observer, or reader by stretching imaginal domains is important enough in itself.

His solution to reconciling multi-perspective versions of 'reality' is to see them as simply exemplifications of 'reality'. Metaphor is only ever a form of example since there is never one over-all ideal 'reality' it refers to. In some ways, everything is exemplification. Expressivity reflects 'mood' and predication reflects attitudinal orientation. He is neutral and unconcerned about how content and message interweave except to say they do.

For him, fictional representations are 'exemplificational [*sic*] relations between predicates with empty extensions and descriptions of those predicates' (Dempster 1989: 394). No overall world view encompasses all constructions of world and trying to find the world by stripping away versions of 'reality' strips 'reality' away. And there is nothing left. Goodman avoids any assumption about what 'reality' is since there are so many, to put it crudely. His idea is to exclude, as a nominalist, 'intensional [*sic*] entities, such as meanings, senses, or concepts from his ontology' (ibid.: 395).

Representations of centaurs are of beings that do not exist by common agreement, and yet we find meaning in certain ways from their representation. The literal interpretation is that they are false creatures, and representations of them are, by extension, false. This is resolved, as he thinks, in his discussion of links between 'extensions in predications . . . [as in] two predicates have the same meaning just in case they have the same primary and secondary extensions . . . and everything denoted in a primary extension is incorporated into its secondary extension' (ibid.: 395). And so, the link to a kind of symbolic significance is integrated into how a centaur will mean.

Referring to the problem of abstract, non-representational art, music or writing, Goodman insists that they can still be absorbed into his epistemology eventually on the same grounds as fictive representations can be as primary extensions. 'Styles of saying – as of painting or composing or performing – may often be compared and contrasted irrespective of what the subjects are and even of whether there are any' (Goodman 1978: 25).

In Dempster's critique, he goes on to find that Goodman's idea of exemplification contradicts the philosopher's strict nominalism. Predication for Goodman is 'partly a matter of the systematic influence it has on the meaning of linguistic environments into which it can be inserted' (Dempster 1989: 396). The difficulty Dempster finds is in Goodman's relativism – how does one extension of predication firmly apply, and not another. (It is close to Jung's problematic explored in the discussion of the 'Enigma of Bologna': i.e. the difference between nonsense and sense is hard to detect.) It is not only in personal contexts and other variables that such matters can be assessed, Jung points out, but it is a matter finally of judgement, which issue, in a footnote, Goodman not only defers but limits: '"Judgement" as used here must be freed of exclusive association with statements; it includes, for example, apprehension of the fit of a design, and the decisions a pool-player takes in aiming his shots' (Goodman 1978: 139).

Hilary Putnam takes him up on this point in a critique on Goodman's work, positing that judgement has definite contributions to make in assessing meaning, and finds this a shortcoming in Goodman's argument as any rhetorician too must find. How we judge the authority of the representation is integral to finding significance – is it a virtual presence, a full presentation, an aspect of a video game, the result of legitimate trials, etc. (Putman 1979).

Ricoeur points out a different problem in thinking about ideas Jung imputes to nominalism. He says that Goodman sees metaphoric expression in a confined way, as taxonomy – metaphor has meaning only based on predication, i.e. a resemblance is categorised either in one field of reference or another. There is no particular element of transformation, or transposition involved in shifting domain – meanings are just reassigned. In the same way as Putnam objects to the deferral of judgement that Goodman resorts to, Ricoeur complains that Goodman is not acknowledging that we also have a sense of 'rightness' about a metaphor, about its aptness in joining elements that has to do less with a re-categorisation of resemblance than to do with recognition of a transfer of meaning. After all, some metaphors are meaningless and inept, 'flat'.

Goodman's notion of shifting nomenclatures within 'schemata' is not quite enough. Ricoeur objects that Goodman leaves out viable considerations of the effectiveness of fictive representations which have 'null connotation' (Goodman's phrase). As we referred to above, Goodman explains them by calling them 'exemplifications' and by consigning them to secondary streams of predication. They gain 'realness' by borrowing from primary predications to which they are associated. Like Dempster, Ricoeur complains that this undermines the nominalist position, because it relies on an underlying connection based on assertion of a general metaphysical principle about the prominence of precedent extensions, in this case. But it also so aligns literal and metaphoric functions so closely as to do away with the distinction.

The notion, therefore, of what metaphor is as a 'trope' is obliterated and it seems only to have a functional and conceptual movement. Here, we have already seen, Vico would disagree. Anything that diminishes a metaphor to less than its capacity is problematic for Ricoeur too.

> Metaphor's power of reorganising our perception of things develops from transposition of an entire 'realm' . . . . [In Goodman's scheme] the well-worn notion of 'transporting' becomes a conceptual migration . . . the organisation brought about in the adopted region is *guided* by the use of the entire network in the region of origin. This means that even if the territory to be invaded is chosen arbitrarily . . . the usage of the labels in the new field of application is governed by the previous practice. . . . The use of *schemata* is governed by the law of 'precedence'.
> (Ricoeur 1975: 236)

Further, Goodman's governing idea of 'precedence' brings embedded unspecified applications – a metaphysical dimension. And, as Ricouer explains, to reiterate – and to extend the discussion – Goodman evolves a theory that equates literal and figurative and short-changes what figure is, and what metaphor is.

> Does not the fittingness, the appropriateness, of certain verbal and non-verbal predicates, indicate that language not only has organised reality in a different way, but also made manifest a way of being of things, which is brought to language thanks to semantic innovation? It would seem that the enigma of metaphorical discourse is that it 'invents' in both sense of the word: what it creates, it discovers: and what it finds, it invents.
>
> (Ibid.: 239)

We arrive at a rhetorical resolution of the anomalies of the nominalist position. While I cannot delve more into all Ricoeur's (or Goodman's) ideas on nominalism and its bearing on the ontology of figural language here (which is Ricoeur's goal and Goodman's target), I have tried to extract pertinent arguments for my purpose in briefly exploring what representation for a nominalist might amount to.

In Jung's discussion, he traces the problematic from pre-Socratic times and on through Abélard. He hopes to establish that nominalism is a matter of the disposition of a personality and also to say that this is empirical fact (although this has its own dilemmas), and that this insight does not diminish the value of philosophy. He does not agree it opens up vulnerability to *ad hominem* fallacy which Goodman seems to think it does (see Goodman 1978).

Pronouncements of philosophy or science are as much somatic or sensual argument (and he cites Anatole France on the universal and perennial sensual aspect of the word, see Jung 1967: para 40) as the application of attitude or systematic logical thought are valid argument. These attributes are part of our sensual makeup as humankind and each is specific to the individual. In fact, to neglect the sensual dimension is to leave out a principal aspect of human interpretive capacity.

> Reverence for the great mysteries of nature . . . will not suffer from the extension of psychology to this domain to which science has hitherto found no access. We only shift the symbols back a little, shedding a little light on their darker reaches, but without succumbing to the erroneous notion that we have created anything more than merely a new symbol of the same enigma that perplexed all ages before us. Our science is a language of metaphor too, but in practice it works better than the old mythological hypothesis, which used concretisms as a means of expression, and not, as we do, concept.
>
> (Jung CW6: para 428, p. 257)

Jung finds that Abélard makes this distinction as an extension of his predisposition to the world. Jung opens this discussion of the 'conflict' by highlighting a core idea. A pivotal set of opposites is most coherently investigated within the framework of the personality, he says. To prepare the way to talk about Luther and Abélard, he first focuses on two representative players: Antisthenes and Origen. He analyses their philosophical positions in the context of their dispositions and personal circumstance, as far as he knows it.

'Characteristically', he says, Antisthenes 'through the time-honoured method of projection, delicately suggests what cause he is defending against Plato'. Antisthenes mocks Plato, accusing him of having a 'wilting penis'. Jung informs us that in common parlance, this phrase refers to someone who is 'mentally poverty-stricken'. Fortuitously, for Jung's point, Origen, the 'realist' plays out dissatisfaction with his member in real life taking the metaphor literally. Origen so loved Plato's ideas, he 'sought to lay low by means of self-castration, in order to pass without hindrance into the richly furnished world of ideas' (ibid.: para). Manifestation of philosophical ideas here has material representation in a cruel way.

There is another dichotomy playing out too, which Jung embellishes: Antisthenes is engaging in envy; he perceives himself an outsider. A nominalist position is taken up by outsiders, he says: i.e. 'the whole school was composed of proletarians or at least of people on the fringe, all of whom indulged in corrosive criticism of traditional values' (Jung 1921, 1971: para 42). Antisthenes draws broad conclusions based on his envious feeling – his conclusion is closer to sensation than it is to conceptual analysis. He won't universalise; each school is not the aggregate of a communal disposition, but composed of individuals whose points of view are added on together amounting to corrupt 'agreement'. The sensual element draws him and he uses concrete references to establish concept. Inevitably, this includes attack on the collective establishment for Antisthenes and for other thinkers with a disposition to nominalism.

> generic concepts are without reality and objective validity. Anyone, therefore, who speaks of 'man' speaks of nobody, because he is designating Oύτε αυτό Oύτε ώστε (neither this nor that) . . . . The denial of the substantiality of generic concepts follows directly . . .
>
> (Ibid.: para 44)

Antisthenes is bound by his personality which plays out in the philosophical content. However, Jung argues that taste and smell, and the tangibility of abstract concepts linger both for nominalist and for the realist.

Jung focuses on elements of the nominalist argument for most of his discussion which I will do too; in fact, he seems to prefer the arguments of the rather more earthy, sensible 'types' whom he designates as nominalists: 'The manifest and fundamental opposition was clearly conceived by Gomperez {Jung says} as the problem of *inherence* and *predication*' (ibid.: para 45).

Jung seizes on the argument of predication vs. inherence, a central distinction for the nominalist whether Abélard (and discussion about him, among others, by Martin Lenz 2005) or twentieth-century figures like Nelson Goodman, or commentators on the nominalist position, Nino B. Cocchiarella

(Cocchiarella 1986), whom I will discuss below. Other nominalist thinkers, like Quine, however, believe there are truly abstract, independent, non-concrete propositions with no predicates. (This is a much contested view, but I will not pursue Quine's formalist logical distinctions here.)

What is sensual about ideas manifests itself in the disposition of an individual, or, otherwise, in a collection of individuals, who react according to their differing sensibilities. For example, 'warmth' is perceived by touch, and even though for some it is hotter than for others, the quality rests in the thing itself. Jung explains:

> From the plurality of perceptions, we derive the concept 'warmth' and . . . we immediately connect in our thoughts with something concrete, thing-like. Thus 'warmth' and 'coldness' are thing-like for us because of the reverberation of sense-perception in the abstraction.
>
> (Ibid.: para 45)

Jung refers here to the age-old dilemma of predication, i.e. whether an emotive or sensual quality is attributed to the material object or to the perceptions of the observing psyche. Ricoeur comments, sensibly enough, in response to Goodman's attribution of emotion to a painting, for example, that it is not the picture representing an emotion of sadness which 'feels' sad; it is the observer viewing it who feels sad – to reiterate: the sadness is in our psychic connection to the object (see Ricoeur 1975: 240).

Predication is extended in personal attitude (intentionality) and in personal linguistic dynamic (verbs, adverbs *and* nouns). It is the *locum* of concreteness in Jung's discussion. In early psychic life, in historic times among 'primitives', and in early individual human life, among children, thing-ness predominates. Vico remarked on a 'poor soul's' inability to use verbs due to mental and psychological inadequacies in *The New Science,* and drew similar conclusions – to be pursued elsewhere.

Predication orients the experience, closely following on from material presence. Jung equates mental images which are extraordinarily sensual for the primitive and the child, with the mental images of even the most sophisticated mind. As abstraction takes hold, the images are 'de-sensualised' and the psychic image becomes idealised. The tremors of mystification fall away from words: 'even "educated" European patients constantly need reminding that thinking is not doing – one patient because he believes that to think something is enough, another because he feels he must not think something or he would immediately have to go and do it' (Jung CW9: para 46).

Jung knew the struggle between concrete and ideal – nominalism/concrete vs. 'realism'/abstraction – from personal experience. He had suffered, we learn in *Memoirs, Dreams, Reflections*, from a similar confusion of the magic of psychic imagery in his dream life. As a boy, he'd been afraid to allow the psychically anguished dream of the giant turd falling on the cathedral to play out, for fear of some indescribable punishment that awaited him. The anguish of his parent's difficult marriage played out in his illness we surmise along with him; his fainting fits play out from his reaction to school.

Jung elaborates on how a personality disposed to introversion and to logical thinking, might perceive an argument each in her own way – even while the same coordinates are analysed similarly or differently by another extraverted, feeling philosopher (because sometimes people *do* agree with each other, introvert and extravert, sensationalist and conceptualist): Tertullian with his dazzling ratiocinations, subverting his passions (see Jung CW9: para 75), or Diogenes with concrete downright methodical plodding forward.

> since the two types of thinking [introvert and extravert] depend on a displacement of the accent of value, it is of course equally possible that in the case of the introverted personal feeling may, for various reasons, be pushed into the foreground and will subordinate thinking, so that his thinking becomes negatively critical . . . . we have therefore to class the particular conflict between the principles of inherence and predication as a special case . . . the special nature of this case lies in the positive and negative parts played by personal feeling.
>
> (Ibid.: para 45)

At the primary level of grammar, predication involves the interconnection of extrinsic and psychic, a weave that implicates the persona. Like Abélard, whose thinking I will come to below, Ricoeur turns to grammatical exposition to demonstrate the close interconnection of the concrete and the abstract (this is related to discussion of personal/impersonal and universal from earlier material in this book too):

> Reference is itself a dialectical phenomenon to the extent that discourse refers to a reality, to the world, in sum to the extra-linguistic; it also refers to its own speakers by means of procedures that belong essentially to discourse not to language.
>
> (Ricoeur 1975: 75)

The personal pronoun 'I', has no significance in itself but takes on meaning in referring to the speaker; and verb tenses – past and future – are anchored by reference to the present. The 'present discourse itself qualifies itself temporally', what Ricoeur calls 'auto-designative'. Adverbs and demonstratives too are connected to an instance of discourse and obtain meaning in that way (ibid.: 77). Personality is implicated. 'I' is no one other one than the tangible speaker with all her inclinations, emotions, skin textures and economic status, etc. 'I' accumulates significance from the speaker. We apply this notion to Abélard's intellectual reconciliation which we will see, however, is not quite adequate for Jung.

Abélard proposes to accommodate the contraries between individual response to the broader category of genus and species. 'It is precisely because he considered none of the accepted standpoints right, but always sought to comprehend and conciliate the contrary view' (ibid.: para 68). Jung's admiration for him is evident.

Abélard's 'conceptualism' weds the concretizing inclinations of the nominalist position to the realist's position, by stressing the act of generalising in reference to a 'plurality of perceptions' we might perform.

> For him the intermediate position was *conceptualism*. This is . . . a function which apprehends the individual objects perceived, classifies them in their genera and species by reasons of their similarities, and thus reduces their absolute multiplicity to a relative unity. . . . For anyone who is psychologically so constituted as to perceive chiefly the similarity of things, the inclusive concept is . . . given from the start; it forcibly obtrudes itself with the undeniable actuality of sense-perception . . . but for one so . . . constituted as to perceive chiefly the diversity of things, their similarity is not clearly given; what he sees is their difference.
>
> (Jung CW6: para 70)

In rhetorical terms, medievalist topical logic has prevailed in Abélard's strategy. Cocchiarella's commentary on Abélard's 'conceptualism' underscores the medieval philosopher's analysis and corroborates Jung's reading, both based on the biography of Abélard by the French biographer, De Rémusat:

> conceptualism [is] concerned with the notion of a mental construction . . . and with the construction of concepts . . . . concepts are anything but objects. Conceptualism differs from nominalism insofar as it posits universals, namely, concepts, as the semantic grounds for the correct or incorrect application of predicate expressions . . . . and it differs from logical realism, on the other hand, insofar as the universals it posits are not assumed to exist independently of the human capacity for thought and representation . . . . concepts are rather cognitive capacities. . . . Concepts, in other words, are inter-subjectively releasable cognitive abilities which may be exercised by different persons at the same time as well as by the same person at different times.
>
> (Cocchiarella 1986: 75)

Abélard's theories are attractive even though they suffer from logical one-sidedness, Jung thinks. And it is this quality which makes Abélard"s 'conceptualism' finally inadequate for Jung.

> He sought the mediatory position in the *sermo*, by which he meant not so much a 'discourse' as a formal proposition joined to a definite meaning – in fact, a definition requiring several words for its meaning to be established . . . . in the *sermo* [a definite fixed meaning Jung claims Abélard intends] the universal lived, and there alone.
>
> (Ibid.: para 74)

He is not really a nominalist, inasmuch as *sermo,* the 'word', contains the universal by implication. *Sermo* derives from the Latin *sermonem* (nom. *sermo)* 'discourse, speech, talk' originally 'a stringing together of words' (OED). If anything, this must allude to the formal trope, the synecdoche, in which the part is subsumed by, but also instantiates, and represents, the whole. But Abélard never quite made it to the stage of figural resolution which is where Jung wants him to go. Jung is sympathetic but objects to Abélard's concluding paradoxical formulation: 'a one-sided logical-intellectual formulation . . . : "Thus both man and no man are rightly called species"' (ibid.: para 76). The vitality of the proposition is stripped away and becomes a scholastic quibble.

While the achievement of the scholastics to rid the *word* of its endangering magical power was considerable, medievalists lacked the psychology to reconcile opposites, which cannot be mediated except on the psychological plane, Jung thought. Abélard does not appreciate the imaginary dimension, since he is locked into the intellectual coordinates. But Abélard's notion of 'propositional attitudes' comes very close to incorporating predisposition of argument and convincing hypothetical surmises about reality that Jung (and Vico) find appealing (see Lenz 2005).

Jung finds the solution in the crucial role of *fantasy* in making 'reality'. This theme recurs throughout my discussion of Jung's work, and its appeal is enormous. In line with this thinking of personality and philosophical approach, we see that 'reality' is not an absolute or extra-sensory place; it is a *topos* and/or also an attitude toward viewing life. The psychic activity of *fantasy* is a distinct human capacity with its own ways of cognition. *Fantasy* informs the two points of view, playing over against the introverted or extraverted inclinations of a personality. This 'autonomous activity' is a constructive activity that is as much 'feeling as thinking; as much intuition as sensation' (ibid.: para 78).

> Fantasy it was and ever is which fashions the bridge between the irreconcilable claims of subject and object, introversion and extraversion. In fantasy alone both mechanisms are united . . . Fantasy is for the most part a product of the unconscious.
>
> (Ibid.: para 78, 79)

After a long discussion by means of parable, and demonstration of the rigidities of the scientific outlook at the religious outlook expressed in the Catholic

Church, Jung arrives at a practical, essentially rhetorical view that accommodates his ideas about *fantasy.* It is a revitalising element in psychic life, from the unconscious. He is stretching towards the romantics as he will discuss in the next chapter of *Psychological Types.*

As quoted from Benjamin, 'Truth is a programme to be fulfilled' and it is only in practical, psychological terms that 'truth' is ever useful to us. Exploring the vagaries of Adler and Freud's depth psychology, he determines that they err for being one-sided.: 'Both theories reject the principle of imagination since they reduce fantasies to something else, and treat them merely as a semiotic experience' (ibid.: para 93).

In a footnote, Jung glosses his use of 'semiotic' here; he uses it

> in contradistinction to 'symbolic'. What Freud terms symbols is no more than *signs* for elementary instinctive processes. But a *symbol* is the best possible expression for something that cannot be expressed otherwise than by a more or less close analogy.
>
> (Ibid.: para 63, n. 44)

The trope of paradox sums up the 'union of opposites' Jung seeks; strategically in his argumentation, he is a great investigator of domain shifts. For example, in using the parable, he performs a mythologizing effect on narrative. In fact, he explicitly praises Christ's choice of dissemination of the word by this means. Using dreams and stories as parable is a frequent construct in his prose. But overall, personality is the key to transformations of meaning into new significant fusions. Personality becomes a species of metaphor, indeed a kind of domain, when it manifests itself in discourse. The various solutions Jung found to express himself not only were intellectual decisions, like the sarcasm in *Job*, or the ironies of *Flying Saucer* essays, but also internally irrupting formulations of emotion or intuition at the other extreme – *The Sermones of the Dead.*

The symbol for Jung is by its nature a *topos* of paradox. It is dynamic, yet fixed, personal yet also collective; it substantiates its meanings and is an instantiation of meaning. It holds opposites in tension but contained. In his final discussion of transubstantiation in *Psychological Types*, Jung demonstrates some of the various aspects. Luther clung to the sensual experience of the Communion in the consumption of bread, locating Christ as material presence. The sensual is an essential component of the sacrament for Luther. The spiritual is an incidental. On the other hand, Jung points out that Zwingli's adherence to the spiritual component and, in his case, the bread was incidental to its spiritual potency. In the end, the Communion host is a symbol and while it is impervious to intellectual understanding, it is meaningful in other ways. Vico makes a telling remark about paradoxical comment:

> as rational metaphysics teaches that man becomes all things by understanding them (*homo intelligendo fit omnia*), this imaginative

> metaphysics [his poetic wisdom] shows that man becomes all things by *not* understanding them (*homo non intelligendo fit omnia)*; and perhaps the latter proposition is truer than the former, for when man understands he extends his mind and takes in the things, but when he does not understand he makes the things out of himself and becomes them by transforming himself into them.
>
> (Vico 1976/1730–44: para 405)

This is surely a sentiment that Jung might enthusiastically subscribe to.

5

CONSIDERING FANTASY, FICTION AND LACAN

To explore more closely Jung's attitude toward reality and its impact on his submerged rhetoric, I want to take a side step to highlight Lacan's very different rhetorical strategies after Vico provides us an opening *exegesis* (after Baudrillard!) and then return to a text of Jung's, 'The Enigma of Bologna' and explore further themes too in his 'Flying Saucer' essay with considerations of 'Synchronicity'.

Jean Baudrillard paraphrases Ecclesiastes in his book, *Simulacrum and Simulation* (1994): 'The simulacrum is never what hides the truth – it is truth that hides the fact that there is none. The simulacrum is true' (Baudrillard 1994: 1).

Excavating the rhetoric underlying the themes two psychologists (Lacan and Jung) take reveals core values and orientations as I strive to follow Jung's precepts, and Vico's, about the close integration of personality, culture and communication. As Gérard Gennette comments: 'first concentrate on the relation of the subject of the enunciation . . . to the narrative [content], or on the manner or aspect I which the narrator perceives the derivation plot' (cited in Struever 1983: 108–27).

While the structuralist critic tackles the first stage, tracking formal relations in a piece of writing, there is a deeper level. Judgement, deviancies and irrationalities, personal assessments intrude in crucial and telling ways. Jung's psychology especially directs us to include external coordinates.

Vico relates knowing and kinds of testimony and evidence to argumentation of the writer or speaker. Articulation of empirical evidence of knowing is, at best, an argumentative strategy: 'the domain of argumentation is that of the likely, the plausible, the probable to the extent that the latter escapes mathematical certitude' (Perelman 1963: 110). Such contemporary comment refers back to the rhetoric of Gorgias pulling the thread from past to present.

Our theme in the pieces I will be examining is 'nothing': starting way back and corroborating signs across history is achieved through etymology in its anthropological aspect. For Jung and Vico it is a favourite strategy. Etymology links words by association to their origins. Implicit in such an endeavour is the belief that contemporary definitions were founded on the authority of primordial language where it all began. Tracing a word back through layers of time and overlaid meanings accumulated in time, we get to what it *really* signifies. Etymology brims over with ideological choice, and Jung and Vico knowingly exploit that quality under guise of asserting authentic meaning at origin. Kenneth Burke notes this ideological necessity: "'facts' of an historical assertion are but a strategy of inducement (apparently describing the *scene* for the action of a drama, they are themselves a dramatic act *prodding to a further dramatic act*)' (Burke 1941: 6).

Early in Vico's book *On the most ancient wisdom of the Italians unearthed from the origins of the Latin Language*, the translator explores Vico's choice of the word 'effigy' in association with archetypal concepts – Vico complains these ideas are misconstrued by historians and artists. His discussion will serve as an introduction to our comparisons about writing about 'nothing' or representations of fictions in Jung and Lacan.

Vico has been attacking historians and poets for their mindless 'distortions' – historians and poets narrate event, and justify how they order them by:

> hunting out the ultimately distinctive circumstances of the situations [to] . . . uncover the causes peculiar to them . . . they thrive on imitation [painting, ceramics, poetry] and embellish an archetype taken from common nature with traits that are *not* common . . . or they set off an archetype first expressed by another artist, with better features of their own. . . . Some of these archetypes can be better *feigned in effigy* than others, because the models always surpass their *copies*.
>
> (Vico 1988/1710: 61)

This is the familiar complaint of the Platonist who decries false imitation. But Vico goes on to establish that the imitations lead 'upwards eventually' to 'the supreme, best, and greatest God'. They do so by common agreement. Vico's point is that the laws of history were based *not* on cause but on common sense ideas determined by the prudent observer. Human cognition functions in these imitative ways. To impute any other explanation to our human way is ignorant.

Let us focus more closely on Vico's usage of the words 'feigned' and 'effigy'. The translator (L. M. Palmer) explains Vico's choice etymologically. The choice of the word 'effigy' aligns the word in common with the related word from Latin 'feign': it is from the Latin *configi,* past participle of the verb *confingere:*

> the mathematician [says Vico] *feigns* intellectual elements of God's spiritual activity; the artist only feigns the phenomenal things of ordinary natural consciousness. If imitating God's creative activity is feigning, then it seems appropriate to call copying God's created works 'feigning in effigy.
>
> (Ibid.: 61, n. 8)

'Feigning', 'effigy' and 'fiction' all share one source in the old Latin. Looking at the definition and derivations of the word 'fiction' in the OED, we note it comes from the Latin, originally, via Old English, and Old French Provencal:

> Fiction: from M.L. *fictitus,* a misspelling of L. *ficticius* 'artificial, counterfeit,' from *fictus,* pp of *fingere* . . . something invented,' from L. *fictionem* (nom. *fictio)* 'a fashioning or feigning', from *fingere* 'to shape, form, devise, feign,' originally 'to knead, form our of clay, from proto-indo-european *dheigh* – (cf. O.E. *dag* 'dough').
>
> (from the online etymological dictionary © November 2001 – Douglas Harper and the Oxford English Dictionary [accessed April 2006])

'Fiction' associates to narrative remnants. 'Devising' is the human way, and as the words become more distant from their source, i.e. copies of copies, they devolve into effigies. But always *fingere* remains embedded in that word 'effigy'. Lifeless statuary is related to the original, creative 'shaping' that fiction is. 'Feigning', 'effigy' and 'fiction' with their abiding connectedness stands revealed. Vico harks back to the ideas of one of his four acknowledged great writers, as he sets out in his *Autobiography:* Francis Bacon wrote important material on 'false idols' or 'statuary'.

The next step is the move to connect 'fiction' and Jung's hollow, hoax memorial text of an 'effigy' in his essay on the enigma of Bologna, and Lacan's examination of a missing letter. Their approach to 'nothing' is revealed in Jung's text and logically set out in Lacan's and what is at stake in both enquiries paradoxically is the nature of what we would like to call 'the external' or reality.

Lacan wholeheartedly found that discourse (if not classical rhetoric per se) was at the foundation of considerations of psychoanalysis. We might say he legitimised the semiotic approach, and pursued it in his own way. His use is a step away from full submersion into discourse, however. Jung submerges communications deeply into his strategies of analysis and has a similar underlying belief in discourse.

Lacan's opening seminar in *Ecrits* is the often-used example of Lacan's method of analysis. It concerns the story of detective Dupin in Poe's 'The Purloined Letter'. The fiction is a 'nothing' since it is a creation or a shaping of what was not previously there, an imitation – a secondary or tertiary level in Vico's Neo-Platonic hierarchy as he sets it out in *The New Science.* Lacan uses Poe's story which has a further fictive complication – there is a deliberately missing text at its core. We never learn the dangerous content of the queen's letter, which is the pivotal object. The story, then, is an imitation of an imitation of nothing. 'Nothing' is as close as we get to the origin of fictive reality in this case. Jung's discussion of a hoax text critiques centuries of commentary on an anomalous passage putatively said to have appeared on a memorial stone. This text is anomalous for several reasons: first, the text is a riddle; and second it was a hoax, a joke by an ancient writer in medieval times. It is 'nothing' – and there is reason to doubt it ever existed in fact. It exists as hearsay.

Jung takes his places among nearly countless earlier commentators since medieval times to add his remarks. In the case of Lacan's analysis, numerous commentators have followed on from his work, including followers like Anthony Wilden and critiques by Derrida and Barbara Johnson not to speak of Zizek.

Adding further to this commentary, in a small way, highlights of Lacan's essay enable talk about Jung's approaches to texts that has not been opened up before.

Hidden in plain sight

Here is the story: the police fail to retrieve a letter containing evidence of the queen's perfidy. It appears that it was stolen openly in front of her. The thief, a Minister who relishes having the queen in his thrall, has hidden it. In despair when they cannot find it, the police go to Poe's famous fictional detective, Dupin and his colleague, who narrates the story, asking for help. The police maintain they have searched the perpetrator's apartment with no success. By appealing unknowingly (as Lacan explains it) to a mechanism similar to Freud's 'repetition compulsion', Poe's character, the enigmatic Dupin, locates the crumpled letter hidden in open sight in the Minister's front room.

Lacan approached Poe's story in his own way. He does not trawl through commentary or existing scholarly literature in the way Jung does in his approach to the Bologna enigma as we shall see. Any persuasive appeal an authority of the past may have does not move Lacan. It is not part of the discussion. Previous or contemporary commentators do not engage him either (except for Freud and he proposes that he is interpreting Freud as he was meant to be understood, so he is an authority on Freud in a re-reading). Like Descartes whom he refers to often in his writings, Lacan is creating a new way forward and won't be polluted by past and wrong ideas.

In fact, near the conclusion of the Poe story, Dupin uses a neat etymological display to reveal the Minister's personality which Lacan ignores. And, curiously, in light of Lacan's own Cartesian disposition to psychoanalysis, its rational leaning might have been applicable to his discussion and helpful for his conclusion. His goal, it appears, is to reveal, by any means, the psychoanalytic triad operating in Poe's story by finding Oedipal coordinates. However, ironically, Poe's Dupin's etymological excursion seems to disparage the kind of analysis Lacan engages in (we can only suppose that's why he missed it). Here is Poe setting out Dupin's exposition:

> With an art worthy of a better cause, for example, they [mathematicians] have insinuated the term 'analysis' into application to algebra. The French are the originators of this particular deception; but if a

> term is of any importance – if words derive any value from applicability – then 'analysis' conveys 'algebra' about as much as, in Latin, '*ambitus*' implies 'ambition', '*religio*' 'religion', or '*homines honesti*' a set of honorable men.
>
> (Poe 1845/1999: 468)

In other words, Dupin tells his friend, these derivative meanings are suspect, or, we might say, 'rhetorical'. He says that similarities in spellings do not necessarily make for significant associations. Hidden meanings are not out in the open with such obvious clues. (This displays Dupin's investigative method: the letter is out in the open and not concealed.)

But there are other issues with Lacan's partial analysis that engage with our theme of the problematic of representation and its impact on communication. He skirts other parts of Poe's text that don't fit his analysis too.

Barbara Johnson complains, for example, that Lacan focuses on the 'wrong' issue in thinking about Poe's recounting of police misinterpretation. It is true that the police looked everywhere possible for the hidden letter. But she points out that it is rather their nomenclature that has distracted them; they call their hunt a search for something 'hidden'. In fact, the letter is in plain sight. It is, therefore, in the very nature of how they search for meaning, for something 'hidden' that leads to their failure to find it. (Jung often recommended letting an image speak for itself without interpretations; and poets and painters often complain that their construction has significant impact without explanations.)

Johnson points out that it is the 'trauma of interpretation' rather than the 'compulsion to repeat' that Lacan focused on: a failure to focus on the meta-issues (Johnson 1977) of contexts, intentions and specific content. Lacan is not looking into the primary situation of the text as un-reality, as 'missing' object, in the very ways the police should have looked for the letter. Lacan, like they do, tries to find a transparent significance. (Unlike Dupin who focuses on the un-reality of the missing object, as Jung does when he looks at the Bologna text as we will explore below.)

Derrida complains there's something he circumvents too in his analysis. Lacan's *formal* analysis of the story means he mistakes the product. It is not first person narration as Lacan seems to read it. He leaves out mention of the narrator, which is a crucial literary and thematic device in Poe's story. He leaves this out because the triadic coordinates don't work when that extra fictional device, the narrator, is included. Too much distance . . .

Lacan throws the baby out with the bathwater – and actually he avoids even close examination of the fictional text itself. He abstracts a structured scenario that fits his theoretical idea of the 'imaginary'. Here, meaning and image are not identical – the analysed image points to a 'deeper' Oedipal construction. He leaves out discussion of the crucial narrator; he leaves out mention that this is one of three stories in which Poe featured Dupin (i.e. the context of this story). In fact, Derrida protests, Lacan reduces the story, and then he treats it as if it were 'real', i.e. as if it were not fiction, not 'nothing'.

Jung has already characterised such theorists as Lacan in his essay on the Bologna enigma to which text I will turn to next: 'there is revealed in them an extraordinary propensity to come out with the wildest fantasies and speculations – a psychic condition which we meet with today, in a correspondingly erudite milieu, only as an isolated pathological phenomenon' (ibid.: para 50).

It is that these scholars are not aware of the underlying nature of what they are exploring, i.e. that it is a 'nothing' they are examining, and missing the point, they are lead astray. And they do not let the text speak for itself. (Are their patients treated in this way?) I won't sidestep again here but Jung's comment on Joyce's *Ulysses* misses the forest for the trees too; he does not remember the meta-symbolic approach he takes in talking about the enigma of Bologna. More on that later.

The missing element in Lacan's examination seems to be his ignorance of the anomalies of psychic reaction. Lacan believes that the underpinnings of human product are rational, and so the elements must fit a causal and logical ordering. They don't speak for themselves partially because we don't accept their language and partially it's unconscious. Lacan does not believe his own theory that the unconscious has its own language – he won't let it 'speak' for itself after all.

In an earlier essay 'On the nature of the psyche', Jung argues that 'the soul was never able to get a word in as the object investigated' by psychologists, and he continues,

> The position of psychology is comparable with that of a psychic function which is inhibited by the conscious mind: only such components of it are admitted to exist as accord with the prevailing trend of consciousness. Whatever fails to accord is actually denied existence, in defiance of the fact that there are numerous phenomena or symptoms to prove the contrary.
>
> (Jung 1947: para 347)

Lacan is one such unaware psychologist, at least on the evidence of his seminar on the Purloined Letter. Jung's playful awareness of the ambiguities and paradoxes of all written or verbal 'text' makes his propositional approach authentic (and I deliberately bring up this phrase from his discussion of Abélard's 'propositional attitudes' – about hypothetical realities that are logically viable, at least).

By delving into what is familiar to humans, the artifice of 'nothing' or 'fiction', the foundation of the human psyche, we find results in a genuine engagement with human product.

Significant and transparent 'nothing' – it's all we know

We will see that Jung's exploration is about human modes of discovering meaning illustrated in the essays I want to investigate: first, 'The Enigma of Bologna' and then, written years later, his essays on 'Flying Saucers' and 'Synchronicity'. In the 'enigma' essay, Jung examines the text in its paradoxical totality, something significant and 'real' (in its transparently fictive way), based on its reception by commentators.

He makes again his point about judgement raised in *Psychological Types*:

> in such cases one always finds that the unconscious is under some kind of pressure and is charged with highly affective contents . . . . a differential diagnosis as between tomfoolery and creativity is difficult to make, and it happens again and against that the two are confused.
>
> (Jung CW14: para 52)

Paradoxical 'fictive' reality is all the reality we can expect of any text, or, indeed, of any human product. The contexts, the formal structures, the significance are the three elements comprising the paradox of human imaginative product. These elements are all taken on board as a totality in assessing human invention and understanding human communication.

Detailed analysis of the essay which appeared in *Mysterium coniunctiones* elucidates Jung's typical use of the trope of appearance/reality and his belief in paradox. A summary of its rhetorical organization will reveal other characteristic stylistic devices unique to Jung.

Briefly, here is the set-up to the Bologna enigma: Jung tells us that the

> epitaph is sheer nonsense, a joke, but one that for centuries brilliantly fulfilled its function as flypaper . . . it serves as a paradigm for that peculiar attitude of mind which made it possible for men of the Middle Ages to write hundreds of treatises about something that did not exist and was therefore unknowable.
>
> (Ibid.: para 52)

Jung adds to the number of treatises.

He cites the memorial poem in Latin alongside its German translation – here is a piece of the opening in the English translation as rendered by R. F. C. Hull:

> *Aelia Laelia Crispis,* neither man nor woman, nor mongrel, nor maid, nor boy, nor crone, nor chaste, nor whore, nor virtuous, but all.
>
> Carried away neither by hunger, not by sword, not by poison, but by all. – Neither in heaven, nor I nearth, nor in water, but everywhere is her resting place.

> *Lucius Agatho Priscius,* neither husband, not lover, nor kinsman, neither mourning, nor rejoicing, nor weeping, (raised up) neither mound, nor pyramid, nor tomb, but all.
> He knows and knows not (what) he raised up to whom.
> (This is a tomb that has no body in it.
> This is a body that has no tomb round it.
> But body and tomb are the same.)
>
> (Jung CW9: chapter 3)

Jung points out the riddles: old women referred to as young brides, coffins and cradles contrasted. Further, information is set out in the negative, i.e. x is not y, nor is it z. It is a poetical list of negations and contradictions.

The riddle opens up broad considerations of gender, alongside its overloaded nonsense, with recurring themes of fatality, loyalty and includes consideration of suppressed alchemical motifs of containment (which Jung is especially excited to excavate).

> the Enigma . . . has the same effect as the unintelligibility of chemical processes: the philosopher stared at the paradoxes of the Aelia inscription, just as he stared at the retort, until the archetypal structures of the collective unconscious began to illuminate the darkness.
>
> (Jung CW14: para 88)

Exordium: The *paradoxa* theme is engaged right from the start: a non-existent nonsensical inscription on a tomb is the surprising focus of a scholarly essay purporting to be scientific. Jung looks to establish a bond with the audience in preparation for his startling claims. He first softens the ground emotionally; let's share the anxiety that perhaps we are all wasting time considering this document. He wants us to recognise that he is not a crank, and so we can safely share his interest without losing self-respect. It is not the 'futile stalking horse but the projections it aroused' (para 52) that reveal something useful and meaningful for us, and this is the point of his attentions. So he exhorts us, after all, to engage with the message.

And not only does it have contemporary validity, he continues, for centuries 'it brilliantly fulfilled its function as a flypaper for every conceivable projection that buzzed in the human mind' (para 52); but it raises universal question of coherence: 'What is it that you do not understand and can only be expressed in unfathomable paradoxes?' (para 54).

Dispositio/Arrangement: And, now he sets out the common sense questions that are the usual criteria in assessing such a document, criteria used to set a document in context and in order to examine it accordingly. These enquiries are designed to draw us into agreement with his decision to pursue investigating the document by following a line of thought: Who wrote it? Why? And how was it discovered?

In each case, the answers are necessarily paradoxical, because it is not a document that exists. This anomaly is referred to throughout Jung's piece.

Jung follows the organisation of typical positivist, rational, scientific exploration: he sets out the questions; he sets out the evidence; he trawls through the commentators for further evidence and reaches a conclusion. But things are blocked right away. In each case, the question sets up contradictory response. We are brought to accept his preliminary conclusion: these are not the right questions; they are looking for irrelevant answers.

Does it matter who wrote it? Or when? Or why? It does not matter, he determines, after all, because even if it is a 'practical joke' perpetrated by an 'unknown humorist', the document has historical impact:

> [it] would become a *cause célèbre* . . . that . . . would lead his contemporaries and successors to question the nature of the psychic background – a question which, in the distant future, was to replace the certainties of revealed truth.
>
> (Ibid.: para 55)

We encounter paradox again. And, the 'victims [of the hoaxer's joke]', are 'as naïve and innocent as himself, [and] made their first, involuntary steps as psychologists.' To repeat and reframe the premise: 'this premonition of future discoveries in the psychic sphere expressed itself in the phantasmagoric speculations of philosophers who, until then, had appeared to be the arch-pedlars of sterile verbiage' (ibid.: para 53).

Philosophers wrote reams of commentary. We note that the alchemical language clearly fits Jung's theme, and those commentators who were most responsive to the riddle, Jung proposes, were alchemists. Their perceptions of what the text might be rescue the document, such as it is, from oblivion. Its worthiness is after all deemed to be its ability to inspire response.

Jung writes elaborately using almost an excess of adjectives, adverbs and detours to form his meaning. Copia/superfluity of images and meanings: aren't these multiple philological performances performed deliberately so that he is certain to touch on all perspectives not only to legitimise the text with contextual and linked proofs, but also to display his full engagement?

Perhaps it is about burying his reader with a wealth of persuasive evidence, 'proving' his propositions? Proof is by persuasive association not by logic. As he brings the commentators to 'discuss' the text among them, he adds his comments in too. In doing so, he dissects alchemical commentators of early times to discover his own themes. The style of his examination is not to link the recurring themes into a fable about how the ego interacts with dead material, but to link to the meanings unleashed by commentators' projections and receptivity.

The text opens those themes up for him as he lets it speak. It talks about wombs and containment and tombs – a fictional woman, or else a real, then (and now) dead bride, referred to as an infertile witch or as a phantasm – and the husband as a dismembered figure. Jung finds Jungian themes deep in the past, and implying that we share with him the notion that what's earlier in time is (1) authentic and (2) universal, except that this text is a hoax – nevertheless the commentaries and his too project universal, collective themes onto the reported provocation of an enigmatic text.

Maier's discussion is particularly important to Jung. He is an eminent ancient, alchemical scholar. 'These two persons, says Maier, *are* neither man nor woman, but they once *were*; similarly, the subject *was* in the beginning an hermaphrodite but no longer *is* so, . . . as a third thing it is new and unique' (Jung 1962: para 58).

He continues tracking Maier's argument, which involves all the combinations of images that a man and woman can be to each other, in age and in youth. The plenitude of images reveals his meaning: 'But "all" is the real explanation of the enigma: all these designations refer to qualities of the *one thing*, and these were thought of as existing, but they are not entities in themselves . . . ' (ibid.: para 58).

The negative cast of the riddle is critiqued. Maier dismisses the negativity as a salient feature, because it's all the same: everything is presented as 'not being', the opposite of what is. When it comes to the first positive statement of the inscription: 'This is the tomb', Jung quotes Maier's construal that it is a link to dismemberment: Maier thinks it has nothing to do with the tomb itself, but is a reference to the buried woman – a kind of metonymy: 'For she herself is the container, converting into herself the contained; and thus she is a tomb or wife, who was her own tomb without a body, and a body without a tomb' (ibid.: para 64).

Jung's revealed paradox leads him to dismemberment because of the way the woman absorbs her man into her own nature and thereby decomposes him; he becomes particles. Knowing we will find this idea startling, Jung tracks it in literature – the dismemberment of the king in his vessel, his tomb, is an ancient motif, perhaps starting with Osiris. The 'secret' of the union of opposites is revealed as a path to freedom. But with this surprising conclusion, Jung realises that he may lose us again.

Taking our part then, he asks himself, is the alchemical way the only way to interpret these riddles? It seems to reveal more about itself than about the text of the inscription. But here's another anomaly: Jung adds another 'nail in the coffin' to use his phrase. Not one of these commentators has actually seen the inscription. Not only is the commentary suspicious for its arcane discourse, but it is *entirely* fabricated.

An ancient scholar claims that he knew eyewitnesses who'd seen and copied the inscription out before the tomb was destroyed. Another scholar 'tries to be fair to the author of the epitaph' – here we are making allowances for a scholar who makes gestures of collegiality with a hoaxer. Testimony is acknowledged enthusiastically but finally it is unreliable and we are asked simply to rely on the authority of Jung's readings of commentary. In fact, to play it all out more effectively and to add gravitas to his material, he adds footnotes and Latin references to corroborate.

Of course, he implies, the 'truth' of the matter is in the construction of the 'facts' – whether they exist or not, which somewhat depends on your predisposition. Another obscure commentator is cited by Jung because he raises reference to an important emblematic figure, as Jung interprets it, for his psychology: 'In a metaphorical sense, as the feminine carrier of the anima projection, it is Jupiter's spouse and Agatho's beloved . . . . but psychologically they are anima projections, so far as masculine statements are concerned' (ibid.: para 70).

Other alchemists are cited – one brings the tree, the oak, into connection with the bath. It is the nuptial bath, says Jung. The crucial importance of the vessel and containment are highlighted. The importance of Tree is invoked; it is not that it refers to anything else, but that it participates in fables and myths that makes it significant. Or, rather, this participation reveals its importance – since it is a further reassurance of certainty if this is discovered material. Finally the tree is a metonymic figure for the death of gods – and the tree of life. He links us here to Christianity, to bring it home to us from the arcane and pagan attributions he has been accumulating. 'The grave-haunting numen is likewise a widespread idea that has lingered on into Christian legend. I have even met it in the dream of a 22-year-old theological student' (ibid.: para 75).

Jung recounts contemporaneous 'non-external historical events' like dreams to demonstrate the shared collective themes. Dreams are also the same kind of enigmatic 'nothing' that the inscription is. Jung tells us that even people not remotely linked to alchemy also seem to use such motifs in their dreams. This is an assumption by reversal: 'When did you start hitting your wife?' a lawyer asks. In order to answer that question, you implicate yourself. 'As the dreamer himself remarked, the dream had a numinous quality, and this is quite understandable in view of its meaning: it repeats the miracle of the phoenix, of transformation and rebirth' (ibid.: para 84).

Jung recounts a fable of the past, amplifying it to show us significance: finally he comes to the unconscious, the source of these images. Actions have psychic meaning:

> Cadmus loses his sister-anima because she has flown with the supreme deity into the realm of the supra-human and the subhuman, the unconscious. At the divine command he is not to regress to the incest situation and for this reason he is promised a wife. [His sister leads him to become the dragon-slayer, and he meets his wife, 'Harmonia' (the dragon's sister).] The dragon is obviously 'disharmony' as the armed men sprung from his teeth prove. . . . Cadmus holds fast to Harmonia while the opposites in projected form slaughter one another.

> This image is a representation of the way in which a split-off conflict behaves: it is its own battle-ground.
>
> (Ibid.: para 86)

From Vico, we can bring more to bear on this interpretation, but the paradox obtains too. In *The New Science* Cadmus has another function too; he is of course the ancient ruler who slays the serpent whose teeth he sows and who grow to be soldiers; but more important for Jung's amplifications here, he also carried the 'runes from Phoenicia and gave [to them the] order and values of those of the Hebrews'. Vico means that this is about Cadmus' fable of the spread of aristocratic power (he is transformed into a serpent) and he establishes that this poetic narrative is about the spread of language and its transformation, the empowerment of the 'vulgar' peoples, who revolt against the aristocratic blood authority of Cadmus.

> the fable of Cadmus contained several centuries of poetic history, and is a grand example of the inarticulateness with which the still infant world labored to express itself. . . . So easy it was for Cadmus to leave a written record of this history in the vulgar characters which he brought to the Greeks from Phoenicia . . . . that [it was evidence] the invention of letters by Cadmus . . . [brought] great benefit to the nations . . . [yet it] is concealed by Cadmus from the human race in Greece under the veil of this fable, which remained obscure . . . in order to keep hidden from the vulgar such a great invention of vulgar wisdom.
>
> (Vico 1976/1730–44: part 2, para 678–9)

Cadmus exercised aristocratic rule; writing undermined his authority although transported by him to a new land, handing power to people he ruled who turned on him – as evidence of the paradoxically creative and destructive performance, Cadmus founded Thebes, the site of wars for years to come centuries later. In the 'enigma of Bologna' the instability of language and its power links have other associations perhaps not exploited in full by Jung but which fit his theme. But while this is about transformation and paradoxical impact, it is not directly using alchemical language. The veil of obscurity the fable represents is directly relevant to my theme of the strangely revealing potential that the content of 'nothing' has.

Jung's next move is to build from this 'union of opposites' to the alchemists' realisation that by integrating the oppositions of 'good' and 'evil', which had been erroneously separated out by Christian dogma, they were in fact integrating the projections that these represented:

> it began to dawn on the adept that both opposites were of a psychic nature. They expressed themselves first of all in the duplicity of

> Mercurius, which, however, was cancelled out in the unity of the stone (the lapis) . . . . The *lapis* was recognised as an equivalent of the *homo totus* . . . an attempt to integrate opposites that were previously projected.
>
> (Ibid.: para 86)

He carries on demonstrating the close mix of psychic event and the alchemical fables that disclose them. His conclusion draws the enigma of Bologna into this contemplation of arcane and universal significance:

> the inscription itself seems to be a fantasy sprung from the same paradoxical *massa confusa* of the collective unconscious. . . . Any attempt to determine the nature of the unconscious state runs up against the same difficulties as atomic physics: the very act of observation alters the object observed.
>
> (Ibid.: para 88)

This excerpt is set out in full to show the various directions his thought takes him – the chaos of collective unconscious, inscriptions that are mysterious and ancient; the new physics is invoked. And he points out he has spotted in the matter, the 'collective unconscious': 'the collective unconscious through its archetypes provides the *a priori* condition for assignment of meaning' (ibid.: para 101).

Jung's analysis is a very different route through a text than Lacan's. His conclusion, after a thorough investigation of the associations and organisation of themes, and a discovery of the ubiquity of the collective unconscious among all the commentators, is the discovery of the tenets of analytical psychology. He arrives at those tenets from observable, empirical fact.

Further investigation of a text from later on in his career, brings up similar themes about 'made-up reality' and first using some ideas from Jameson and Ricoeur, and Vico's 'poetic key', I propose to investigate Jung's 'Flying Saucers' essay within this context.

How does 'fiction' make up real things, and what is its nature?

It is hard to account for Jung's essay 'Flying Saucers' until we begin to appreciate the rhetoric of paradox; but what sort of document is it? How did he come to work it up (there are other pieces of this period to examine which play with issues of realities: the Gnostic writings, his works of alchemical creation etc.)?

This essay purports to have sociological coordinates (there are statistics and references to other demographic data); direct reference to the external world was a secondary issue in the *Mysterium coniunctiones*. In a footnote there, however, he compares the essay to his earlier piece 'Wotan' which was a prophetic and historical warning of real and dangerous evil times to come. The 'Enigma' essay, 'Wotan' and the 'Flying Saucers' essay venture into a hybrid styles of text, lancing emotion and figural expression onto real history and society – emotional real event alongside 'fact'. When we read Vico's *New Science* especially and become accustomed to the nature of a mythopoetic world in which Vico finds the concrete 'realistic' laws of history, we realise we are in the same domain. Hybrid forms of writing are solutions for both philosopher and psychologist: Vico's poetic history, and Jung's swivelling on the appearance/ reality axis produce forms that strain their boundaries.

What are we being lead to expect from these writings? Focusing on genre to locate them as texts helps to predict expectations; how the writer is confined and what she knows commonly speaking about how it will play out. Cultural underpinnings and common storytelling form an underlay of prediction. Genre is a kind of radar to beam us through these hybrid texts. In modernist literary theory, the notion of a mix of genres that inform disturbing texts has come into its own and here it is useful. Later, discussion of the text *Answer to Job* plays with genre and emotion in similar ways with highly charged material.

'Flying Saucers' proposes that it is organised first of all in a comprehensive way: Jung discusses at great length in the opening sections UFOs as 'rumours' – by this he means rumour that haunt us in unconscious ways in the air around us (and this is about the collective unconscious). He sets up its ambient: out of the way in big spaces, lonely farmers report seeing UFOs; open skies are a feature and perhaps nearby government buildings. They are associated to visions, and some people report being carried off in these vehicles. Yet, scientists see UFOs too and they are as curious at their unlikely and irrational appearance as the farmers are. To investigate them, scientists bring their positivist, rationally designed tools to bear which measure in ways that fit into what reality they propose.

While these objects have been reported historically, Jung, in 1960, says that they are more insistent now. He means to alert us that their presence indicates something is happening. Since Jung is not a physical scientist or a religious commentator (because he might have associated these objects to gods mingling among us, as testimonies now and in the past refer to them), he does not. He will turn to analyse them as a 'psychological factor', he says.

They seem to be projections; there is a void in people's imaginations and psyches that used to be filled by Christianity (most recently) which is now undermined; where does that energy go now? The energy seeks to invest itself in something perceived to be flying in the sky. There is a radar, oscillating effect: we project anxiety in a collective way, and an object irrationally appearing in the sky throws energies back at us. The object attracts numinosity, established by viewers in reacting and projecting hopes and longing for meaning. Our psyches constitute this object but not as hallucinations of insanity, but as hallucinations of normal sight, normal perception.

The essay then moves on to demonstrate that these objects are universal – and so important as he says they are, they are features of the collective unconscious – and the first way, typically for Jung to prove this is to report on dreams from his patients in their numbers. He reverts to this immediately. Jung analyses several space travel or space object dreams closely to show us that there are typical elements that emerge from this psychic universality. He finds motifs of alienation, control, or phases of transformation in the dreamers' lives. And he points out associations to the cultural moment; he notes that the scientific status of the contemporary world is intruding into spirituality, not in a good, reassuring way.

Picking up his association also of dreams to works of art, especially modern painting, is typical of the organisation of his texts when he talks about this theme. Jung analyses pieces of art work and their demonstrations of themes crucial to his system – as they portray flying objects – cylindrical, or spheres moving through the skies, with platforms of light or of people. He interprets the paintings as aids in demonstrating that the themes emerging are associated to loss of meaning, or to quests. He chooses artists who are not well known, and he only refers to European products. Analysis of paintings is similar to analysis of dreams. They accrue collective significance, they are involuntary to one degree or another, reflecting the strengths and weaknesses of the time and peripherally of the artist.

To underscore his theme of the universality of these images appearing in human psyches in all time, he traces the flying object in history. This gives him space to explore scenes as they are described and depicted in ancient literature – he picks up the motif of the Holy Child as a star baby; shooting stars which no longer have otherworldly associations for us, did have meaning in medieval times and were reported accordingly. Jung presents an idea of the potentially radical differences of cultures, at the same time as also having similarities at the moment of an event (unlike Badiou's 'event' which is a serious rift or discrepancy with history).

This leads on to his dealing with the phenomena as a non-psychological feature to show the borders of the idea. He delves into how the collective unconscious operates in an external way to the human psyche, autonomously. He proposes that events of collective unconscious have independent agendas and timetables, and they are therefore not psychological problems. This short section summarises the motifs and brings them into global intellectual focus, i.e. he finds their quality of 'reasonableness'. His two epilogues describe lengthy books of visionaries who have travelled on space objects with aliens and return to tell us of spiritual lacks and fulfilments – along the lines of William James, and his own earlier discussions of the quest for meanings in his experiences with mediums; he is free here to talk with conviction about the other-worldly nature of these experiences and what they might mean for us, having established it earlier in the essay. Throughout, as he points out here again, he reminds us that scientists see traces on their objective and impersonal radar screens (he forgets to mention that these traces are interpreted by humans, of course, and therefore subject to irrationalities and subjective input).

And now back to locating its genre: the first call was to position the essay as if it were a kind of alternative history and humorous satire (except in the future which is always 'alternative' history too since the future is a projection of the past, and similarly based on familiar laws of history). Are they like those that Mark Twain might have written: like *A Connecticut Yankee in King Arthur's Court*, which tells the story of the dislocation of a contemporary American transported back to medieval England, or *The Prince and the Pauper* which played with class role reversal of look-alike boys in Elizabethan times. Twain's ironic assumption is that despite the distinctness of historical periods, time travel is possible, and time can be traversed as readers, and as physical motion, and men with technology of the future are gods, who can solve the real problems of the past (in *Connecticut Yankee)* – a kind of suppressed wish-fulfilment or Utopian vision.

The suggestive and playful stance in the opening pages of the 'Flying Saucers' essay suggests that; my lead comes not only from his preface to the English edition but to other introductory comments:

> it is difficult to form a correct estimate of the significance of contemporary events, and the danger that our judgment will remain caught in subjectivity is great. So I am fully aware of the risk I am taking in proposing to communicate my views concerning certain contemporary events. . . . I refer to those reports reaching us from all corners of the earth, rumours of round objects that flash through the troposphere and stratosphere and go by names of Flying Saucers.
>
> (Jung 1955: xi)

Another direction is suggested by Northrop Frye. Is it the kind of romance he discusses in 'Anatomy of Criticism'. The reader tucks up to a good story told by a wise old man around a warm fire in the evening, characteristics of the romantic genre, Frye says, which includes science fiction and fantasy, and which aims to 'maintain the integrity of an innocent world against the assault of experience' (Frye: 201). Since Jung's theme is about increasing numbers of flying saucers as a sign of the malaise of the times, and increasing alienations of the individual, the move into fantasy to withstand the assault of experience surely is a feature of this essay.

As further evidence that something of this escape is driving UFO appearance, Jung tells us stories of visionaries. He recounts the dreams of patients suggesting in his interpretations that these objects are protective, distorted displacements. He uses language that deliberately recalls a certain antique storytelling style, e.g. novels that begin, 'I found some documents in an old portmanteau that caused the strangest events in my life to occur.'

Or perhaps we could follow his other lead and think of this essay as a case study of quasi-sociological or scientific phenomena, in which he flips scientific data over to show its underside as emotive attachment to the dogma of causality? Might it be a kind of deconstruction of empiricism? Are facts evolved to explain unlikely interventions in reality? In other words, is it a critique of a certain type of empirical epistemology that mistakes plausibility for truth ('facticity')?

Associated to his discussions of wish-fulfilment and referrals to an 'as if' mode, often leads Jung in his writings to propound his notion of causality: synchronistic and meaningful associations that seem to occur independently undermining causality as a principle (see not only 'Archaic Man' which I will quote here, but also his discussion above of the 'Enigma of Bologna' in *Mysterium conjiuntiones* and various other texts, as in 'Synchronicity' with its long discussion of causality).

> it is a rational presupposition of ours that everything has a natural and perceptible cause. We are convinced of this. Causality, so understood, is one of our most sacred dogmas . . . unless, indeed, we follow the modern physicist in his scrutiny of the minute and secret world of the atom wherein, as it appears, curious things come to pass . . . we are not surrounded by a world that is obedient to rational laws.
>
> (Jung 1955: 'Archaic Man' 1931)

He concludes that we are resentful as a result. Jung's essay is *not* an ironic or satiric enquiry – its tone is similar to the 'Enigma' essay, for example. It is also *not* ironic displacement or a romantic fable constituted by wish-fulfilment, or a dream of Utopian formations. It is perhaps something along the lines, however, of an enquiry into a type of epistemology that might have the authority a positivist science has.

Jung grapples with the boundaries of a text that seeks the truth value of science, exploring how we account for events that seem to de-stabilise habitual external reality, including the result of statistical series of sequences. If we wish it hard enough, does something become 'real'? He says just that, however, in this essay in his conclusion:

> either psychic projections throwback a radar echo, or else the appearance of real objects affords an opportunity for mythic projections . . . even if UFOs are physically real, the corresponding psychic projections are not actually caused but are only occasioned by them . . . it is result of a profound psychic need . . . What happens to the energy that once kept the idea alive and dominant over the psyche?
>
> (Jung 1955: 148)

In this essay, however, it seems he is saying that energy displaces onto sightings of UFOs.

Jung is playing with dislocations of time and of appearance in a different way to Twain's alternate historical ironic stories: Twain indicates that we should take on these facts 'as if' they were real in order to contemplate his underlying themes of the dislocations of war and of class. He does not really push the boundaries of fable and reality as Jung intends to ask us to do here; as readers of Twain's speculative stories, we are transparently in suspension with him. There is underlying and ongoing commentary. As a form of fantasy, its attention to the detail of the dislocated time helps make the illusion 'more' real. (We all do this when we daydream: the fantasy has to be precise in all its detail: the girl or boy we've been ogling has to be wearing the exact sweater worn during the day to make the illusion persuasive.)

And so too for Jung in his descriptions of the cylindrical shapes, and smooth walls of a putative space craft which conform to the most advanced technology at the time (or what futuristic design presently indicates). In art and in dreams, and in visions – as well as in pictures NASA picks up on its radar – there is an uncanny lack of application about these UFOs. For the most part, and if we discount the people who suggest they've travelled on them, it is an alien object with no significance or purpose, except what is imputed to it by its viewers. And these assertions rather depend on the epistemologies and intentions of the enquirers.

This quandary is well defined in a novel by science fiction writer, Arthur C. Clarke. In his *Rendezvous with Rama* an alien object, 'Rama's' appearance is unaccountable for the world's scientists; but at long last, our protagonist starts to have an inkling what it's about. Rama makes no contact, and seems to have no purpose with the people of the earth, and so people react as they think it means them to. But, he suggests, what if, in its alienated way, it is simply appearing. In fact, in Clarke's story (among other things), Rama disappears after having altered the course of history in the places where it has touched down, and where it has been witnessed. Its intentions and presence are imputed to it by those who see it, and action is taken accordingly.

Jung explores here a psychic process that projects a metaphysical or transcendent space, a representation of a kind of longing or desire to be bamboozled, to be mystified, for pleasure or to exercise control which we long to do to make living in the world more bearable (he talks of this in *Answer to Job* too). He means for readers to reflect on what this might mean about the relation of longing to the independent reality of external objects. The nature of representation is caught up in this enquiry.

Certain questions arise: does the intensity of believing in the reality of UFOs – from farmers in a lonely field, to scientists at NASA – have anything to do with whether they are 'real'? Jung insists on this question, and on the cross-overs back and forth to fiction, psychological enquiry and independent 'real' science make this the hybrid text it is. Those elements of science fiction and Utopian reference and speculative scientific report hypothesise about an anomalous event. To expand on the nature of its hybrid qualities, we note it makes use of techniques of various modes of reporting to prod us to think about external event and its representation, along with its place in our lives and psyches. Knowing Jung's sensitivity to occult observation, he remarks on the lack of some of the usual elements of the occult, like a mediator. UFOs seem not to be mediated by a monitor of any sort (unlike séances, for example), it appears on its own.

In *Archaeologies of the Future,* Fredric Jameson explores science fiction writing, and points out that there is an excess of wish (superfluous wishing) that functions in the human psyche, but it seems required to maintain the innocence of experience. By creating a contrary alternative world, necessary boundaries are set. Jung's idea of energy seeking representation is close to this. But, while this notion may appear to be related to Lacan's *objet petit a*, the excess energy in Jung's conception re-dynamizes or revivifies an object that has manifested in relation to a collective urge or need. Lacan's notion makes the *objet a* a kind of fetish or vessel of incommensurate meaning standing outside normative experience. Just like his mathematical abstractions that he proposes stand for psychological significances, *objet a* is wholly an anomaly.

Paradoxes, otherwise excessive experiences or anomalies, are required in Jung's analytical psychology to shore up or balance reality as we perceive it. Speculative reality constitutes 'real' reality too. And it is the psychic component of this speculative experience which may appear to run counter to positivistic scientific, or so-called 'objective' data that Jung seeks to investigate in this essay.

In romance, or Utopian literature, super-natural events are 'told in quotation marks' as Jameson (2007: 202) points out. Listeners are not actually confronted; but our instruments of perception, eyes, nose and touch, etc. including our psyches are deeply implicated in sustaining the level of fantasy we need to live and to believe in what we see. We need anomalies. Caught in having to choose, Jameson says he would choose lies rather than corrosive truths.

6

HIGH PROFILE REPRESENTATIONS – METAPHOR AND METONYMY

Jung, Vico and Ricoeur, phenomenological anthropology

By turning 'fact' and 'truth' inside out, it becomes more important that the nature of metaphor and other figural devices, such as the tropes of metonymy, irony and synecdoche are investigated. Jung's use of amplification, paradox, fable, etc. fashions his rhetoric, and directly influences how analytical psychology works itself out in writings and, I'd propose, in practice (but that is another project I won't tackle here). Without his distinctive use of the tropes, and his choice of them, Jung's psychology could not happen.

Beginning with Vico, and following Ricoeur's book-length discussion of metaphor as well as referencing Perelman's explorations of the implications and functions of these strategies, I want to point out how Jung stretches the figural and comes to meet the logical and causal necessities in the scientific precepts of psychology in entirely adequate if contentious ways.

It is Vico who is credited with marking out the original derivations and functions of the figural devices of metaphor, metonymy, synecdoche and irony in chapters of book 2 on 'Poetic Logic', in *The New Science.*

> All the first tropes are corollaries of this poetic logic. The most luminous and therefore the most necessary and frequent is metaphor . . . every metaphor formed is a fable in brief.
>
> In such a logic, sprung from such a metaphysics, the first poets had to give names to things from the most particular and the most sensible ideas. Such ideas are the sources, respectively, of synecdoche and metonymy.
>
> Irony certainly could not have begun until the period of reflection because it is fashioned of falsehood by dint of a reflection which wears the mask of truth.
>
> From all this it follows that all the tropes (and they are all reducible to the four types above discussed), which have hitherto been

> considered ingenious inventions of writers, were necessary modes of expression of all the first poetic nations, and had originally their full native propriety.
>
> (Vico 1976/1730–44: part 2, para 400–11)

In other words, those writers who used them may not have known it, but they were using tropes of classical and universal, necessary derivation. In Aristotle's *Rhetoric* and *Poetics,* metaphor functions as genus to the species, including simile, metonymy, etc. which were all part of a general function of the transference of meaning by figural means. Although Aristotle highlighted the awesome capacity of metaphor, his favourite strategy, Vico presents these figural devices as means to new insights into human cognition, his 'poetic logic'. His most ambitious subsequent move was to correlate these devices to historical eras as all writers about Vico, and those influenced by him, have explored: see Vico, *New Science* books 2 and 3, and commentators, Verene, Berlin, White, Frye, Mooney, Pompa, Danesi, Shotter, Badoni, Joyce, Gross, etc. for a few instances.

There is a plethora of material about metaphor in rhetorical criticism since Aristotle first catalogued it. Ricouer's master work *The Rules of Metaphor* (1975) refers to ancient and contemporary discussions and I will use his work primarily, adding others to flesh out the discussion: Lakoff and Johnson, on metaphor's cognitive power; Perelman and Olbrechts-Tyteca on their status and persuasive faculties; Jean Fahnestock on their underlying presence and necessity in scientific writing; and James Kirby, spelling out the forms metaphor can take. Metaphor is central for Vico and 'poetic logic' and his commentary is included too.

Ricoeur investigates Aristotle's definition of metaphor. The Greek says metaphor seems to participate in two camps, the poetical and the functional (or 'rhetorical' as he terms it in his analysis). Ricoeur hypothesises that metaphor, as it is used in poetry, for example, is not generally felt first of all to be intent on persuasion (Ricoeur 1975: 12); but he goes on to re-position its functional place in argumentation, following Aristotle.

> With respect to structure, it can really consist in just one unique operation, the transfer of the meanings of words; but with respect to function, it follows the divergent destinies of oratory and tragedy. . . . This duality of function . . . represents a still more fundamental difference at the level of intention . . . [inasmuch as *Rhetoric* is a treatise on argumentation]. Aristotle defines it [rhetoric] as the art of inventing or finding proofs.
>
> (Ibid.: 12–13)

Poetry's intention (and metaphor participates in this) is to refer to mimesis; i.e. to tell the truth via fiction, fable, etc. Primarily, metaphor consists 'in giving the thing a name that belongs to something else' (*Poetics* 1457 b: 6–9).

After a discussion about Aristotle's focus on the semantic function of stand-alone nouns (which Ricoeur will later critique, insisting that predication is always implicated), Ricoeur explains a second characteristic: '*Metaphor is defined in terms of movement.* The *epiphora* ['movement' or energy – Aristotle's word] of a word is described as a sort of displacement, a movement "from . . . to . . . ". This notion of *epiphora* enlightens us and puzzles us.'

Ricoeur explains the dilemma. Aristotle not only designates metaphor as just one figure of speech among others, such as synecdoche and metonymy, he points out what many other critics also reckon, that for Aristotle the word *metaphor* applies to *every* transposition of terms . . . sometimes designating genus, and sometimes species (see Kirby 1997, Fahnestock 2000). Metaphor is both a broad designation and a specific device. The problems this creates will become clear as we explore other aspects.

A third characteristic is that metaphor 'is a transposition of a name'; it is defined here in terms of *deviation*, bringing along the negative connotation of that word; but it is *also* positive. It is a 'borrowing' too, Ricoeur says. It is always possible to find the source of this 'borrowing' and so there is nothing devious (as the negative sense of 'deviation' implies). These 'borrowings' include foreign words or neologisms. Often, as Ricoeur points out, this is represented by *substitutions* (ibid.: 16–19).

Fourth, *epiphora* also specifically moves the definition of metaphor to include *resemblance* by the dynamism of its powers of discernment. This includes analogy. Ricoeur analyses this facet of metaphor in relationship to the permutations of genus to species, similarities and dissimilarities, focusing on lexical distinctions. Perelman's treatment of analogy deepens this discussion, emphasising the relationships of types of resemblances (not of specific species to species as Ricouer's lexical resemblances entail). Analogy is important later in our discussion of Lacan's theories and so I expand on this aspect here, even if briefly.

Perelman and Olbrechts-Tyteca locate the device of analogy in Aristotle's idea of proportional metaphor in *Rhetoric* (Book 1) which Aristotle discusses at length. X is to Y as A is to B, and as X is to A, etc. This analogical formula hauls the discussion into the area of the functionality of metaphor in argumentation which both Perelman and Ricoeur maintain is perceived historically as a distinction of the strictly mimetic and poetical operation. Perelman, however, argues that metaphor as analogy, applied in its functional aspect, is the more appropriate way to consider metaphor in its dimension as a figural category.

Fifth: having established that metaphor has a functional purpose in argumentation and also that it has a poetic dimension, to please and to represent reality through fiction, Ricoeur takes a further step. (I pursue this, again, to anticipate my investigation of Lacan further on).

Ricoeur explains Jakobson's divisions as he sees it: '[Jakobson's] definition directly places the poetic function of language in opposition to the referential function through which the message is oriented towards the non-linguist contexts' (Ricoeur 1975: 222).

Reference is yet another problematic function of metaphor; 'problematic' since it refers to outside normal strictures and is too variable, too uncontrollable – wild.

Ricoeur extends this point further in proposing that it is by its referential capacity that metaphor instigates logical classifications in language. In this configuration, metaphor is a heuristic and it also generates taxonomies. To summarise, metaphor functions in referential and argumentative ways, using tropical 'turns' and creating alternate hierarchies. Metaphor is multi-faceted.

> The idea of an initial metaphorical impulse destroys oppositions between proper and figurative, ordinary and strange, order and transgression. It suggests the idea that order itself proceeds from the metaphorical constitution of semantic fields, which themselves give rise to genus and species.
>
> (Ibid.: 23)

The dilemma of metaphor's division into what seems to be opposite tendencies, function and trope, is reconciled in Ricoeur's observation. And, as Kirby also points out, after all, Aristotle's definition of metaphor hinges instead on a language of scientific taxonomy – he illustrates, citing Aristotle: 'Metaphor consists in giving the thing a name that belongs to something else: the transference being either from genus to species, or from species to genus, or from species to species, or on grounds of analogy' (*Poetics* 1457 b: 6–9).

Aristotle intertwines the dimensions of figural language. We have seen an example in Jung's theories when he recommended transfer from species to genus by transposing libido from a specific form of human sexual *energy* to a generic form, i.e. Jung's definition of libido moved it *from* species *to* genus. Libido comes to have a broad meaning in Jung's system that describes the *epiphora* of human personality, and transforms Freud's theory into one of the cornerstones of Jung's scheme. *Epiphora* here means the transforming energy of human personality, and the particular way it generates transformation.

Lakoff and Johnson set out the associative clusters that galvanize the cognitive powers of metaphor. They introduce a psychological element that is implicit in Aristotle's discussion (his *Rhetoric* has a long discussion of emotion which includes specific reference to metaphor in book 2). Linking of terms and concepts from one domain to another is a cognitive act. Fused elements form new meanings, related to (but not necessarily close to) the original necessity requiring their formation. Metaphoric transpositions are a common activity of language. Metaphor is not a specialist event, but a feature of everyday life. And, it is no longer recognised only in its poetical aspect. It is always functional either as generative action or as a mode of a perception.

Daniel Gross points out that in Vico's mythopoetic, original world, metaphor was generated pre-verbally; its primordial capacities were constitutive of human significance and of worlds. Comparing Vico's work to Lakoff and Johnson's research on metaphor, Gross says '[metaphor] renders the world interpretable by *instituting* linguistic convention . . . conceptual structure is meaningful "because it is embodied" – that is, it arises from, and is tied to, our pre-conceptual bodily experiences' (Gross 1996: 362).

Vico did not have the technical terms now developed to articulate his meanings, but it is apparent in how his argument is constructed what his insight is. Vico observed too that in languages the greater part of those expressions relating to inanimate things is formed by metaphor from the human body and its parts. This has been a truism since humankind spoke. In a passage just previous to the long extract above, Vico traces the way to meaning:

> thus, head for top or beginning; the brow and shoulders of a hill; the eyes of needles, and of potatoes; mouth for any opening . . . the blood of grapes for wine; the bowels of the earth . . . Heaven or the sea smiles, the wind whistles, the waves murmur; a body groans under a great weight.
>
> (Vico 1976: II: para 405)

And the list goes on.

It is a truism in psychology as well, that projections onto things we don't know with things we do, is a basic human strategy. Lakoff and Johnson agree with the thrust of Vico's argument, and maintain further, that metaphors are 'systematic clusters' that foster myths (Lakoff and Johnson 1980). Underlying these connections is not only wit of observation sparked off by sensation or thought, but also an approach to the ubiquity of analogy, and to the functionality of metaphor in communication. In all its phases, metaphor is a core strategy.

Expanding on his discussion of analogy, Perelman explores the power released in awakening a 'dormant metaphor' (Perelman 19: 409–10) of great interest to psychologists like Jung and Freud who refer back to events or people in the past to energise present analysis. The 'dormant metaphor' is a fixed analogy, firmly set in common parlance, a device awaiting enlivening, Perelman points out. We recall Jung's belief in the power of reviving symbols of the Catholic Church, for example, in a former believer, re-igniting passion in depressed patients, and his discussion on *fantasy* which we will develop later.

Jung's strategy in those cases implies a commitment to the constitutive nature of analogy or metaphor. Alongside 'free-flowing' metaphor (to use Ricoeur's descriptive phrase) or metonym (more prevalent in everyday speech) are those static metaphoric fusions that have become transformed into nominative forms due to their present and long-term embedding in the culture (Ricoeur 1977: 213–14).

These forms or phases are available for communicative exploitation. Contexts play a central role in metaphor and metonymy or synecdoche, and more crucially, in irony. Contexts and associations in the collective bring together different referents into one new form requiring 'communicative harmony' as Kovecses and Radden explore (1998) between listener or reader and speaker or writer. This is achieved by reference to common sense in deploying topical invention, which is characteristic of a discourse community.

Notable for his attentions to discourse, Lacan uses their differing approaches to figural language to distinguish Freud and Jung's differing attitudes. He is critical of Jung:

> The fact that the symbolic is located outside of man is the very notion of the unconscious. And Freud constantly proved that he stuck to it as if it were the very crux of his experience . . .
>
> This is witnessed by the point at which he made a clean break with Jung . . . when [he] published his *Study of the Transformations and Symbolisms of the Libido.* For the archetype makes the symbol into the blossoming of the soul, and that is that; the fact that the unconscious may be both individual and collective had little importance to the man who, explicitly in his *Moses and Monotheism,* and implicitly in his *Totem and Taboo,* admits that a forgotten drama comes down through the ages in the unconscious. But what we must say, following Aristotle's lead, is that it is not the soul that speaks by man who speaks with his soul, on the condition that we add that he receives the language he speaks and that, in order to bear it, he sinks more into it than his soul.
>
> (Lacan 2002: 392–3)

Lacan is sarcastic about what he calls Jung's eternal dedication to romanticism. He believes that language is a system of pre-existent signifiers which refer to other signifiers and only secondarily to signifiers of extrinsic reality. Humans use language as it is presented to them, generating an impermeable alienation because it is always at a deliberate remove from true meaning. The whole conscious and unconscious being is a separate entity from the ego within the same personality. It makes self-reflexivity a powerful player in the psychic life of each individual. Its reference is to a 'reality' that is always mediated by language, a kind of compulsory yet seeming self-chosen filter.

In his essay, 'The Instance of the Letter in the Unconscious' (Lacan 2002: 412–41), Lacan is equally sarcastic (cf. above, the soul 'blossoms' by itself). It is rather, he says, soul speaks through man, and there is at least a double step to signification. In Lacan's view, by my reading, Freud's 'Ego' sets off in search of significance but is then overshadowed by the 'Self' and itself becomes part of signification, absorbing without eliminating alienation. This is the constitutive potential moment of 'negation' that interests Lacan (Lacan 2002: 439) and Freud ('Negation', 1925).

Lacan's theoretical source is Roman Jakobson, referencing Saussure as structuralists mostly do. Jakobson suggests that one of metaphor's features is that it foregrounds figural language, and as poetry, evokes 'vertical' links to resemblances. Metaphor is on the cusp between signifiers and signification in his view. Its 'vertical' direction is polarised by 'metonymy' which participates in a chain of links, connections that are contiguous, 'horizontal'. Signifiers relate to signifiers and we find deeper meanings, leading to the unconscious, in our interpretation of this relationship. Both forms participate in repressions of the human personality, and reveal significance that is constitutionally always hidden. (In fact, significance for Lacan (and Freud) is always hidden in plain sight.)

This is important to Lacan for his development of ideas based on Jakobson's essay on *aphasia*. Jakobson notes that two disorders, inability to understand metaphor, i.e. everything has become literal and, secondly, the inability to connect elements of a unit to fulfil the 'reality' it suggests, are distinct and separate disorders. As is well known, Lacan takes this up, as others did too, as a way into Freud's idea of the unconscious. These are the operating coordinates of the language of the unconscious that Lacan postulates. Jakobson organises these human capacities in language as 'combination' and 'selection' which he calls the principal manoeuvres of language.

Lacan associates Freud's 'displacement' mechanism with metaphor, since it is a substitution for what the dreamer really means, motivated by repressed wish fulfilments. 'Condensation' is linked to metonymy; the dreamer highlights aspects of the signifier by its connection horizontally to another signifier. This provides Lacan with touchstones for a language of the unconscious in the observations of structural 'deviations'. Metaphor moves outside the domain of the signifier to make meaning while (to put it crudely) metonymy remains within a domain. (Needless to say extended metaphor appropriates the domain it 'invades', and sustains the shift throughout an argument until it may *become fixed* through repetitions.)

Lacan highlights Freud's *Totem and Taboo* because he says that in it Freud traces the history of an instinct that came to be embedded in humanity and in culture simultaneously. This 'articulation' becomes a 'given' foundation, an instinct. The structures of language are in place as givens *before* articulation. In Lacan's dismayed reaction (Lacan 2002: appendix 755–8) to Perelman's ideas about metaphor as analogy (see Perelman, *New Rhetoric*, 1972: 371–410), we explore further what I would propose is the erroneous and static nature of language that Lacan assigns it. This rationalist take on how language operates is widely divergent from Jung's orientation of course – not to speak of Vico's beliefs.

Perelman locates metaphor in an argumentative frame; its functional use is preeminent. Lacan disagrees with him: metaphor and metonymy are poetical devices, and emblematic of how the unconscious expresses itself. Analogy is too flexible in this analysis, Lacan complains. Coordinates 'only' reflect the contexts and the intentions of the speaker, and so do not represent the mode of language of the unconscious. And here's the problem for Lacan. Analogy is not essentially mathematically formulated, and Lacan wants it to be; rather it relies on framing. (It looks mathematical in Aristotle when he formulates syllogisms, for example, but, in fact most syllogisms are disguised enthymemes, dependent on inference and implication for meaning.) Lacan wants a metaphorical mode driven by stricter variables which do not function in the vague often uncontrolled ways of analogy. In any case, meaning is driven by specific unavailable coordinates.

Although Perelman did not respond to Lacan's objections (that I have found) Perelman and Olbrecht's discussion of analogy is close to Lakoff and Johnson's arguments about clusters of meaning (Perelman and Olbrechts-Tyteca 1969: 400 ff.). (And I'd say also similar to Jung's ideas.)

Perelman and Olbrechts-Tyteca explain that the coordinates of significance run along different threads, strings of associated meanings and images found in memory, both verbal and phonic. (I will not pursue discussion of the phonic chain of associations, although Kugler (2002) claims that phonic associations are very plausible and important proofs in Jung's word association experiments.)

Ricoeur protests that Lacan's (and Jakobson's) analyses remain too close to the surface, and they are not finally successful in claims they make about metaphor as the language of the unconscious. Further, he disagrees with Jakobson's focus on the primary status of the lexical aspect of metaphor (Ricoeur 1975: 198–202). He develops a theory of metaphor's dependence on predication. Other major thinkers of language like I. A. Richards also point to predication (sentences are a more meaningful way to explore language). But here I will point out that he means that predication implies a longer, deeper set of associations than Lacan allows. Predication tilts the meaning of a 'substitute' or 'deviation' word in its specific extensions.

Confining study of talk to semantic and to syntactical linguistics only surely limits Lacan's ideas. In effect, he leaves out the pragmatic perspective of language, its tone and the implications of feeling. Expert in the language of science which she maintains is fully committed to figural language, Fahnestock points out that this perspective does not 'focus on what utterance is supposed to accomplish for the speaker and how it functions in particular situations' (Fahnestock 2000: 171–2).

Metaphor and metonymy, for that matter, are used transparently as argument in Jung's work as a matter of course. They do not 'substitute' for something else. Using these tropes brings Jung closer to the source of meaning in his scheme. While Lacan's alienated ego interacts with significance at a distance, Jung's language user instantiates meaning.

Metaphors, metonymies, etc. are not so much mediators to deeper and other meanings as direct substantiation of significance in Jung's usage. They 'speak' for themselves. Images from dreams, and enacted in patterns of behaviour, are attended to as 'direct' talk. There are many examples, but I will use an instance demonstrating his method that appears in Jung's discussions in CW5: *Symbols of Transformation* written in 1956, based on his earlier volume of 1912. (The original version of this work finalised his break from Freud, as is well known, so differences between them were on Jung's mind as he wrote this – knowing it would trigger the break.)

Jung talks about theories of a libido that have broader scope than Freud's (or Lacan's) ideas. Here is another sample that relates to Jung's adeptness at figural interpretation, which he finds to be a dynamic activity.

In the essay, 'Two Kinds of Thinking' (in the volume, *Symbols of Transformation*), Jung interprets the activities and associative talk of Abbè Oegger which he takes from an Anatole Frances story. In the lead up to Oegger's 'case' Jung argues that libido is a space of 'neutral energy'. He pursues an image, then, as it elucidates and also enacts an axiom of his science (CW5: para 41–6). Here is the story and the trail:

A religious and dreamy fellow, Oegger had a vision following his meditation on the dilemma of free will in a creature necessary to the story of the crucifixion, Judas. Contemplating Judas's role changed Oegger's life, and he resolved to leave his monastery and to embark on the itinerant life of a preacher, spreading the message of God's mercy. Jung extrapolates from Oegger's life just how the argumentative mechanisms of fantasy operated, first as motivation to action, but also, then, secondly, as compensatory activity, susceptible to interpretation symbolically (or, you could say, 'topically').

First we read Jung's instruction: 'the conscious fantasy may be woven of mythological or any other material; it should not be taken literally, but must be interpreted according to its meaning' (Jung CW5 1956: para 44).

Fundamental to Oegger's decision to preach is a response to the dilemma of a legendary figure's guilt. Judas's betrayal is the ancient motif of the hero who is felled not by an enemy, but by a close associate.

> Though the myth is extremely old it is still a subject for repetition, as it expresses the simple fact that envy does not let mankind sleep in peace. This rule can be applied to the mythological tradition in general: it does not perpetuate accounts of ordinary everyday events in the past, but only of those which express the universal and ever-renewed thoughts of mankind.
>
> (Ibid.: para 42)

Not long afterwards Oegger's life as a preacher ran its course and he left the Church and became a follower of Swedenborg. And now for Jung's finale: Oegger's meaning is interpreted by Jung:

> Now we understand his Judas fantasy: *he* was the Judas who betrayed his Lord. Therefore he had first to insure himself of God's mercy in order to play the role of Judas undisturbed . . . his doubts and his hopes are only apparently concerned with the historical figure of Judas, but in reality revolve around his own personality, which was seeking a way to freedom through the solution of the Judas problem.
>
> (Ibid.: para 42–4)

Jung analyses the fable he reads of Oegger's life; he analyses dreams and other fantasies in similar ways. He discloses how the second way of thinking, fantasy-thinking, operates and how it is also present regularly in everyday life. 'Fantasy-thinking' refers to William James' analysis of less stressful, free association of thought, and also to Nietzsche's ideas. Earlier in this essay, he had quoted Nietzsche, and I will quote him here because it demonstrates clearly the stream of thought within a tradition that both Jung and earlier Vico followed:

> in sleep and in dreams we pass through the whole thought of earlier humanity . . . what I mean is this: as man now reasons in dreams, so humanity also reasoned for many thousands of years when awake . . . this atavistic element in man's nature still manifests itself in our dreams, for it is the foundation upon which the higher reason has developed and still develops in every individual. Dreams carry us back to remote conditions of human culture and give us a ready means of understanding them better.
>
> (Nietzsche, *Human, All too Human*, trans. Zimmern and Cohn, I, pp. 24–7, modified by Jung, in CW5 1956: para 27)

In his essay of 1912, written originally in English, and finally revised in 1948, 'General Aspects of Dream Psychology', Jung delves into the specific ways his kind of analysis of the unconscious in its dream manifestation differs from Freud's.

Freud's method is based on an assumption, Jung says in 'General Aspects of Dream Psychology', that images in a dream represent hidden meanings – and that, for example, long objects somehow always evolve 'monotonously' (to borrow Freud's word from another essay about sameness in interpretation) into meaning the phallus. Lacan's system repeats this fixedness: *desire* is always the *phallus.* So the relationship of image to meaning tends to be fixed. And, in Lacan's scheme, they are metonyms or metaphors inasmuch as the dreamer is compelled to deviant substitutions compelled by repressions in two ways: displacement or condensation. In his 1948 essay, Jung refers to this interpretive method of Freud's as 'causal'.

Jung sets out a more likely rhetorical approach. What is the purpose of the dream? How is it effective in accomplishing meaning? This he calls a method of analysis, toward 'finality'. He is interested in the functional aspects of meaning (which is all there is of meaning in any case . . .).

He establishes that dream images are what is left from the archaic *mode* of thinking, and he goes on to demonstrate that dreams are compensatory – a balancing of the conscious world and the unconscious world. The unconscious does not operate as if it were secretly conscious, after all, and its manifestations have their own mode of signification.

Symbols shift according to the purpose of the dream, and relate to the events and emotional life of the dreamer's conscious life during the time too. Analysing dreams is an exercise in topical thinking – links to common sense and to collective mores figure in. It is not the deductive and logical exercise of construing metaphors and symbols that Lacan and earlier Freud suggest.

> the images in a dream each have an intrinsic value of their own . . . significance lies precisely in the diversity of symbolical expressions in the dream, and not in their uniformity of meaning . . . the symbol in a dream has more the value of a parable: it does not conceal, it teaches.
>
> (Jung 1948: para 471)

The archaic mode of thinking suggests a notion of representation that William James explored especially in his *Varieties of Religious Experience*. Other issues James looks at in that volume and other essays of his on psychology make useful comparisons to Jung's rhetoric too, so I will bring his work in as a more sympathetic contrast with Jung than Lacan is, or than Freud is.

A simple definition of paraphrase is that it is saying the same thing in different words. But there are problems. By transposing one meaning into other words, there is undeniable and inevitable alteration. I want to propose that Jung engages in paraphrase as a form of amplification, and as *inventio* – location of the argument. Is this a different ploy than Lacan's deliberate finding of Oedipal coordinates in Poe's story 'The Purloined Letter'? I'd say it is. It is different in respect to how they arrive at what they intend to find. Jung arrives at his observations by amplification, engaging in *copia* and clusters of associations, paraphrase, etc.; Lacan arrives at his conclusion purportedly by logical or rational sequence, uncovering meanings using clues that are open for all to see, believing in sequences with causal necessity.

By enlarging or orienting meanings through paraphrase or amplification, Jung underscores his proposition that subjective associations are legitimate proofs. These rhetorical modes suit his psychology. In exploring the 'Enigma of Bologna' document, Jung exploits ambiguities and paradox. These are the universal forms of human sensibility and cognition.

Another question: is the source of ambiguity in the hoax or in its reception? Jung finds 'external' evidence in applying concepts of analytical psychology which serves to organise the evidence plausibly and adequately. (Think of the discussion of Abélard's propositional attitudes or Einstein's scientific stance of 'motivational realism' or formulation of hypotheses here.) Tactical awareness of uses of amplification and paraphrase are well deployed by Jung.

In *Psychology and Religion* (Jung CW11 1938/40), Jung insists that religious psychic experience reported by his patients are 'fact' since psychic event is as much 'fact' as physical evidence is. This conviction allows him to paraphrase their material which circumvents unreliable elements in the report. Jung's use of testimony as empirical evidence in paraphrastic form is categorically a species of 'interpersonal distortion' or otherwise its 'subjectivity'. Jung brings out the meaning his patient's testimony intends. James's use of what he calls *documents humains* in *Varieties of Religious Experience* clearly contrasts with Jung's style, since it is direct quotation – no distortions. But is it as legitimate as James thinks it is?

Testimony as 'fact' is subject to the same questions as material evidence is. Facts are 'probable' solutions to ambiguities rather than 'true' solutions. Definitions and narratives belong to their own time and place, and are deployed consciously or unconsciously. Human cognition operates on a level of probability engaged with rhetorical choice in exigent place and time. As John Schaeffer points out: 'The cognitivist view has become familiar . . . figures of speech are really conceptual structures, crucial both to cognition and culture' (Schaeffer and Eubanks 2004: 63).

I'd like to turn to Vico and to a Renaissance rhetorical writer, Erasmus, as well as to contemporary rhetorician, Perelman, to position Jung's point of view in a long tradition. Since his and James's Terry lectures touch on these themes, it is a propitious moment to bring in issues of facticity, certitude, paraphrase, invention and amplification and copiousness as rhetorical devices integrally involved in psychological theory and which have constitutive powers.

Inventio focuses the argument's source and location. Jung's use of the primary evidence of testimony is core in psychological theory. Jung relies on distinct and ancient awareness of language's function to interpret dreams which are primary evidence in his case for analytical psychology.

> I shall put some good work into my attempt to understand the dream. What I do is this. I adopt the method of the philologist, which is far from being free associations, and apply a logical principle which is called *amplification*. It is simply that of seeking the parallels . . . you try to put the formula you have established from the knowledge of other texts into the new text. . . . That is how we learned to read hieroglyphics and cuneiform inscriptions and that is how we can read dreams.
>
> (Jung 1968: 93)

He is talking not only about amplification here, but also paraphrase – and also another important manoeuvre for him, philological excavation.

Vico's definition of amplification, deriving from Cicero's and Quintilian's, focuses our understanding of Jung's strategies. 'Amplification is a certain type of a more elaborate affirmation which, by means of moving the spirits, wins credibility in what must be said . . . [it] arouses the spirit in addition [to an argument]' (Vico 1984/1711–41: 96).

In the handbook, Vico limits his definition of amplification to terms of forms of accumulation that go toward asserting credibility. The extended concept derives from persuasive force by exaggerated insistence. However, arousal, which Vico suggests is a major function of amplification, depends on personal and collective associations for greatest impact. Vico leads right up to Jungian formulations of amplification as finding hidden associations.

Examining Cicero and Quintilian's discussion of paraphrasing we will find that amplification is linked. In fact, one of the inventive exercises for the rhetorician was to contend with fellows in locating what is essential argument. Another related exercise is to vie in stating something one way or another appropriate to the argument; helping to develop the skill of deploying *copia*, an important strategy Erasmus devoted a popular volume to – responding to Cicero. Exercises about inspiring new associations in the use of material – by expansion – were also practiced in ancient schools.

These strategies mix with each other. Paraphrasing is related to books of commonplaces. Erasmus's *De Copia* was a bestseller used for pedagogic purposes and as a source book for practising rhetors. Erasmus emphasises paraphrastic use as a means of invention: 'Ideas are generated by linguistic variation rather than by logical inference'. In *De Copia* as Grendler discusses, Erasmus would set out examples of different ways to state the same thing. To paraphrase Erasmus, Grendler notes: 'Imitation did not mean exact reproductions; rather words could be added or subtracted, and a passage reworked in order to express the same or contrary view' (Grendler 1989).

Books of commonplaces – paraphrasing ideas for use in creating argumentation – also derived from medieval times, from *florilegia,* collections of sacred sayings used to construct sermons. These traditional paradigms of books inform the flavour of Jung's books with their compilations of medieval and alchemical etymologies and illustrations.

Vico advocated *copia* to his students referring to Cicero's *De Oratore*. Vico's emphasis on topics as strategy for invention is dependent on 'acute' consultation of compilations of common places. His definition of rhetoric in his handbook puts *copia* at the centre of the rhetor's domain: 'The orator is capable of speaking on all things whatsoever with a splendid style and a plethora of ideas (*ornate copioseque*)' (Vico 1984/1711–41: 9).

Vico continues in this section of the handbook to explore the rhetor's ability to remove constraints on 'particular' and 'universal questions' in presentation tactics, recommending that consideration of circumstance be undertaken, and using the 'best' appropriate language to bring it home be practised.

> This faculty of speaking with a splendid style and a plethora of ideas about whatever is proposed is acquired from nature, by art, and by exercise. For all things, it is nature which inclines us, art which directs us, and exercise which makes us proficient.
>
> (Ibid.: para 13)

Paraphrase is a form of commentary. It rephrases evidence, and generates argument. It is testimony that is transparently inflected by the rhetor's judgement of the material supplied. It is always and inevitably relational and intentional just as etymology is ideologically exercised.

Considerations of testimony participate in these themes. They explain why proof is about credibility and plausibility rather than 'truth'.

> For the Latins, *verum* [the true] and *factum* [what is made] are interchangeable, or to use the language of the Schools [the Scholastics], they are incontrovertible . . . The true is precisely what is made (Verum esse ipsum *factum*) . . . to know (*scire*) is to put together the elements of things. Hence the discursive thought (*cogitato*) is what is proper to the human mind, whereas intelligence *(intelligentia)* is proper to God's mind . . .
>
> (Vico 1968/1711: 45–6)

Vico circumscribes the realm of description and empirical observation. What is actually accessible to human science? For God, it is what is discerned and named that is created and made. Deduction is a basis for human truth. But *certainty* can only rest in discernment of God's truth. Human-deduced truth is a variable truth relying on humankind's limited perceptions. This is the core discovery of Vico's researches, answering Descartes' search for absolute truths, for one thing. But it is commentary on the results of human sciences too. There is another piece in *New Science* (Vico 1968) that applies here specifically:

> Human science was born of the vice of our mind, specifically from its extremely narrow compass, in that it is outside of everything and does not contain what it affects to know and because it does not contain them, it does not actualize the truths it aims at. The most certain sciences are those . . . that become similar to divine science through their creative activity . . . in these sciences that which is true and that which is made are convertible.
>
> (Ibid.: 52)

Logical deductions can pass for poof, deriving from the feeble, analytical approach of the mind and cannot compare thought to knowing deriving from discernment of significance. Empirical proof is *literally*, 'the true is the thing made [or done] for itself'.

Transparency is to do with certitude and probability, a kind of mystical proof but it is also rhetorical truth.

Contemporary rhetorician, Perelman, puts it in a similar way in his discussion of proof: 'A proposition is evident if it is evident at all before it is entertained . . . [it] depends on definitions being known beforehand' (Perelman 1963: 111). Self-evident propositions are arrived at by logic or by pre-convictions (prejudice?). They command a certainty that rests on absolute conviction, and this finally can only be arrived at by pre-logical knowing. As a pragmatist and an idealist, James contends too that what is self-evident is what we all agree on – it is what is plausible for us within the contexts of the community.

Jung takes us further than this: what we all agree about is deeply embedded if even unrealised by us in the collective unconscious, a collective complex which he refers to elsewhere as 'reality'. His instinctive and trained awareness certifies him to be our guide – to paraphrase and interpret dreams and visions, and, indeed irrational phenomena.

Perelman focuses on the anomalies of religious evidence, likening it to empirical truth. He articulates a position (ascribing it to Duns Scotus) which certainly sounds like a position Jung might take up:

> necessary and fundamental immediacy was ascribed . . . either to reliable witnesses or reliable authorities indispensable to make good the lack of immediate 'evidence', this same immediate 'evidence' being required in any testimony produced by intermediaries . . . to the testimony's truth . . . propositions guaranteed by faith, founded upon supernatural revelation, were comparable with the certainty conveyed by the propositions of science.
>
> (Perelman 1963: 110)

And,

> knowledge based on indubitable experience seems to provide knowledge with an absolute resting place while still maintaining mistrust in regard to our understanding . . . [these seekers are grouped in two categories]: mystics and empiricists . . . Empiricism if it is to lead to knowing, must transfer the structures of rationalism to the place of sensory experience.
>
> (Ibid.: 42)

Perelman and Olbrechts-Tyteca in their *The New Rhetoric* describe an underrated argument, the 'quasi-logical'. Propositions are rendered to effect adherence by combining snippets of logical ratiocination with emotive convictions. Already inclined to agree, the dressing confirms it: Jung constructs arguments along these lines in his religious discussions, knowing his audience is partially convinced already. The conviction of the visionary has its own power to persuade, appealing to a spiritual aspect in our selves.

James spells this out in an essay 'Types of philosophical thinking' which begins to make Jung's point about a universal dimension in the psyche: '[E]veryone's prone to claim that his conclusions are the logical ones, that they are necessities of universal reason, they being all the while, at bottom, accidents, more of less of personal vision' (James 1909: 10).

It suits Jung to talk in the Terry Lectures of mystical material in the form of dreams that he recounts to the audience; dream content has intention and a certain logic and structure and if it says it's talking about faith, so it is, he maintains. Evidence in his lectures is based on a sequence of dreams told him by a scientist who was undergoing a painful breakdown. We *assume* that Jung is quoting him verbatim. But what we learn later is what Jung does not mention: these dreams were told him by letter. Telling dreams aloud already places the dreamer at a distance from the personal internal experience. In the recounting it is shaped; writing down dreams places it at yet another remove. The dreamer/scientist in Jung's report has not, as far as we know, engaged in automatic writing. He expects his audience to agree that his paraphrasing of exemplary dreams and his rewording of his patients' experiences, are equally, on balance, plausible evidence.

James and Jung defend the factual basis of their evidence. But each considers fact as something very different. This appeal to the 'facticity' of the visions, or dreams, is a bid to present the material as scientific. Seeking this proof is an underlying 'complex', you might say, throughout their discussions, and it has a different flavour for each.

'Facticity' is a problematic explored in current rhetorical thought (Leff 2000); it has qualities of subjectivity and objectivity – it describes a quality of a piece of evidence. Ordinarily it is believed to be an extrinsic description applied by the perceiver. Does 'facticity' rest in the visionary or the dreamer, or in the observer – and how does this apply to psychic fact? Evidence takes interior form in psychology (and Jung would add that the new physics Einstein engaged in also included evidence to be taken on faith).

Jung is at pains to point out at the opening of his lecture that he is an empiricist, an observer and reporter of fact. In this case, evidential facts are religious phenomena as they present in the psyche. He insists that 'experience is not even possible without reflection, because "experience" is a process of assimilation without which there could be no understanding' (Jung CW11 1938/40: para 42).

Creeds are rigid 'congealed' structures of ideas and while these creeds do not interest him directly (as James had also claimed), the psyche's approach to ascribing meaning to creed does interest him.

Like the codified nature of dreams which Jung subscribed to, the factual constructions of religious psychic events, as told to him by his patients, have recognisable patterns deriving, he maintains, from collective 'complexes' embedded in the culture. The unconscious reveals a different aspect of embedded association when called upon to do so. In fact, 'the notion of the unconscious is an assumption for the sake of convenience'. This fact has rhetorical validity and that is sufficient. (He has used the dream of the man who thought he had cancer; Jung's treatment accommodated the patient's incorrect self-assessment, and he was healed.)

It is natural, as in the 'Flying Saucers' essay he pointed out, that we are suspicious of the fact of a UFO. But we re-position it as a 'visionary rumour' and it becomes manageable: the phrase associates to the concrete presence of an irrational and subjective fact. Jung finds the route to shift domain. 'The many thousands of individual testimonies just have an equally extensive causal basis. When an assertion of this kind of corroborated practically everywhere, we are driven to assume that a corresponding motive must be present everywhere' (Jung CW10: para 608).

This approach absorbs paraphrase into amplification. Not only do these devices work personally for him as keys to healing, but they appear as rhetorical strategies in history.

But what can we say about the errors? It is one thing to paraphrase as closely as you can to a verbatim reporting, understandable that you might shift emphases, or make associations that are misleading. It is another to make mistakes. Some dreamers reading Jung's reports of their interior night-lives complained they were not accurate.

Accuracy is another trope from ancient times, handled in certain classic ways, and excusable within certain parameters.

Erich Auerbach, literary theorist and author of *Mimesis* (1946) discusses forms of imitation in literature and contemplates links and associations that a word or phrase may have. His defence is characteristic of the humanist belief in heuristic argument designed to explore meaning rather than set up oppositions. Accuracy is a point of tension; but etymological research is controversial in just this way. Auerbach encourages tracing words to the most useful significance for the goals of an argument (1973).

Historians of rhetoric dismissed Vico's strategies because he got dates wrong, or picked the wrong Zeno for his discussion of mathematics. Avid readers of Jung wade through what amounts at times to lists of mythic figures, trails of definitions in Latin, Greek and English – all in aid of positioning and giving legitimacy to narratives seeking to be appropriate to primal depths. Metaphorical thinking is a kind of allegory of etymological thinking and research. Not only does the cognitive faculty of metaphor represent generative originary human product, it can be marked in history Vico claims. A word may come from Tuscany or from the Latin and etymological dictionaries not only pinpoint geographical locations but also attempt to note when a word appeared. The word's appearance occurred in contexts that remain part of that word. Its predicates and qualifiers shade meanings with great specificity.

Jung discusses how he positions dreams in light of discussion of facts, empirical evidence and interior material:

> as a matter of fact, the only form of existence of which we have immediate knowledge is psychic. We might well say, on the contrary, that physical existence is a mere inference, since we know of matter only in so far as we perceive psychic images mediated by the senses . . . . Although the mind cannot apprehend its own form of existence, owing to the lack of an Archimedean point outside, it nevertheless exists. Not only does the psyche exist, it is existence itself.
>
> (Ibid.: para 18)

However, contrary to his claims, there *is* an 'Archimedean point'. It is Jung's considered presentation of his patients' material, not only to his listeners and readers, but also back to his patient. The 'point outside' is Jung, and he proposes his 'commentary' or 'paraphrase', on their dreams or visions.

Vico pinned the laws of history on a type of creative vision of how time passed; he called it *fantasia*. Primordial significance abides in *fantasia*, and remains in the concrete institutions, civic organisations, etc. thereafter. Vico felt that a proliferation of words will eventually penetrate the soul of its reader or listener. The rhetor steers those meanings with *accutezza.*

7

AFFINITIES

Vico and Jung and the themes other scholars discover

> Vico and Jung have not one historical source in common. What they do have in common are all the classic texts of the Italians, Latins and Greeks which focus on aspects of the self that the Cartesian mentality excludes.
>
> (Verene 2002)

This section will provide a brief summary of commentators who make direct mention of specific correlation between Vico and Jung. While there may have been others writing about Vico who directly influenced Jung, like Wundt, commentators who claim similarities between Vico and Jung have more often mentioned they know this intuitively rather than having found evidence of direct influence.

Various theoretical issues repeatedly come up when commentators compare Vico and Jung. I will mention the most important issues and take each in turn to explore further. Commentators include philosophers, literary theorists, historians of science and psychologists/psychiatrists: philologist Ernst Robert Curtius, James Hillman, Donald Philip Verene and Marcel Danesi as well as analyst Silvio Arieti, among others, make explicit connections.

Here are the themes:

1 Jung's ideas of the archetypes and the collective unconscious have notable similarities to Vico's 'imaginative universals' and his ideas about *sensus communis*.
2 Vico and Jung both note the pre-eminence of imagination in cognition; related to this are their explorations of imagination's relation to myth-making and to narrative as matters of primal, cognitive 'necessity', and suggestions that the psychic mechanism of 'projection' is involved.
3 Jung and Vico frequently define and compare children and the mentally ill to what they call 'primitives'; both insist on the validity of 'archaic' insights. Vico read about the Indians of North America, while Jung visited the Pueblo Indians in the USA.

4 Etymology and philology are core methodologies for both. Vico felt that earlier languages lived on in vocabulary and metaphor, and was greatly dependent on *copia* and *amplificatio* as rhetorical ploys; and Jung explored using a technique of 'amplification' to discover 'buried' associations and meanings too.
5 They both have a Neo-Platonic orientation displayed in their rhetorical style and epistemology; both refer to the core and the source as the self-reflexive Self and refer to emanations out from the core.

Archetypes – imaginative universals

> whereas the personal unconscious consists of the most part of *complexes,* the content of the collective unconscious is made up essentially of *archetypes* . . . the 'archetype' . . . indicates the existence of definite forms in the psyche which seem to be present always and everywhere. Mythological research calls them 'motifs'; in the psychology of primitives they correspond to Lèvy-Bruhl's concept of '*réprésentations collectives*,' and in the field of comparative religion they have been defined by Hubert and Mauss as 'categories of the imagination'.
>
> (Jung CW9i 1957: para 89)

Ernst Robert Curtius refers succinctly to Vico/Jung similarities in his work on the history of poetic motifs in *European Literature and the Latin Middle Ages* (1953). His book traces poetic motifs from their earliest appearances and tracks them as they transform while also retaining their originary significance and, thereby, their power.

Curtius contrasts archetypes to the motifs/figures he traces in mythology. He finds Jung's claims that motifs have *primordial* universality utterly commendable. In his discussion of 'historical topics' Curtius shows the way to future research:

> these themes concern . . . relations of existence . . . they reflect the sequence of psychological periods . . . . To this class belong the 'aged boy' and the 'youthful old woman' [which] . . . have a twofold interest. First, as regards literary biology, we can observe in them the *genesis of new topoi* . . . . Secondly, these topoi are indications of a changed psychological state. . . . Thus our understanding of the psychology of the West is deepened, and we approach . . . the psychology C. G. Jung has explored.
>
> (Curtius 1953: 82)

Curtius characterises Vico's 'philologizing [of] history' as a technique of recounting events which are confirmed in narratives about where words come from, and narratives about what words and images 'mean' – how they evolve over the years and yet retain their beginnings. This has distinct resemblance to Jung's amplification technique – a technique, as I've suggested, deriving from Jung's immersion in rhetoric.

James Hillman, of course, who was one inspiration for this book, correlates Vico's work to Jung's in many places in his writings. He specifically considered Vico to be a 'precursor' of Jung: see his piece about Neo-Platonists which appeared in *Loose Ends* (1975): 'Plotinus, Ficino, and Vico as precursors of Archetypal Psychology'. He continued his discussion of Vico in *Re-visioning Psychology* (1976). He had also referred to Vico earlier in *The Myth of Analysis* (1972) and then, again, later, in *Healing Fiction* (1983).

> [Vico] presents typical aspects of the human mind as '*universale fantastici*' or universal images such as those found in myths. These are poetic characters, not mere inventions of a creative artist. . . . [It is] a mode of perceiving the world in the universals of God and Hero, each of whom is a type of a class concept and also a statement of metaphysical truth, a true account.
>
> (Hillman 1975: 158)

And more recently, Professor Donald Philip Verene focuses on Vico's 'universal imaginatives', as he translates the phrase, in *Vico's Science of the Imagination* (1981). Verene noted that few commentators on Vico had noticed how important the 'universal imaginatives' are to Vico's new science.

> Employed in the work of such thinkers as C. G. Jung and C. Kerenyi, . . . the concept of 'archetype' has played an important role as an instrument of analysing the structure of myths . . . the epistemological status and the internal logical structure of the archetype remains unexplored. . . . It is my view that in theory of myth, Vico's theory of imaginative universals suggests a view of the mythic concept that has significance not only for Cassirer's [work] . . . but [also] for the archetypal and thematic analysis of myth.
>
> (Verene 1981: 315 fn. 52)

Verene has more to say about Jung and Vico and synchronicity in work published in *Journal of Analytical Psychology* in 2002 which I will refer to below.

It is this axiom (among others) Verene refers to in Vico's *New Science:*

> imaginative class concepts or universals, to which, as to certain models or ideal portraits, to reduce all the particular species which resembled them . . . Egyptians reduced all their 'inventions' useful or necessary to the human race which are particular effects of civil wisdom, and because they could not abstract them to the intelligible genus 'civil

> sage', much less form the notion of civil wisdom in which these Egyptians were sages, they imaged it forth as Thrice-great Hermes.
>
> (Vico 1976/1730–44: para 205–9)

Abstractions were a secondary development after the poetic universals: history reflects human sequential development in this way.

Hillman also claims Vico's poetic characters are compatible with his own development of Jung's work: 'archetypal psychology'. He uses the fable of Apollo and Daphne, which Vico had also used as a demonstration. Hillman alters Vico's gloss on it in a revealing way that I think diverges from Vico (and Jung). For Hillman, Daphne's transformation is a story about escape from an importuning, all-powerful male lover – a power relationship with a personal meaning – but for Vico it is a story about *poetical* history, i.e. the truest 'true' history.

Apollo is a god, insisting on newly creating laws of family lineage in this fable. She represents a refusal to comply with family genealogy. The evasive human Daphne is eventually controlled by him, and branches of vegetation begin to sprout off her: those staffs/staves are the inception of genealogy of which Apollo is the god.

> Apollo begins this history pursuing Daphne, a vagabond maiden wandering through the forests (in the nefarious life); and she, by the aid she besought of the gods (whose auspices were necessary for solemn nuptials), on standing still changed into a laurel (a plant which is ever green in its certain and acknowledged offspring), in the same sense as the Latin use *stipites* for the stocks of families.
>
> (Ibid.: para 533)

However, Vico notes that the story was taken later to mean that Apollo was a libertine, and Daphne a woman pursued. But his own gloss is far more suitable to the level of 'imaginative universals' in their universal application to human history unlike Hillman's interpretation of what Vico intended with 'imaginative universals'. Hillman reduces Vico's meanings, in this case, and limits what he might usefully have taken on. He trivialises the fable as if it were a personal story. In fact, it seems to me that here, Hillman does not entirely come to terms with the cognitive, primordial aspect of Vico's universals.

Pre-eminence of imagination in cognition; its relation to mythmaking/narrative as primal, cognitive 'necessity'

Marcel Danesi also notes that Vico's *universali fantastici* (in his translation) are like Jung's archetypes and he emphasises the cognitive dimension:

> in modern Jungian psychoanalytic theory, the primordial percepts that the deepest layer of memory has stored away into genetic material have been labelled 'archetypes'. These are the mental models that have shaped genetic configuration of memory and have therefore come to form a 'collective unconscious' as the Jungians call it. The search for universal patterns of transformed perception in the deepest levels of the mind [as revealed in the narrative structure] of dreams is highly congruent with the Vichian model of primitive mentality.
>
> (Danesi 1993: 53)

For Danesi, primitive mentality is archaic or primordial mentality, undifferentiated consciousness. But while he refers correctly to Vico, it is not to Vico's 'imaginative universals' but rather to an evolved set of universals which Vico called the 'intellectual' universals. These are not the wholly originary 'imaginative universals' and I suggest that Danesi means rather this second level. These 'intellectual universals' are not the primal dimension; there is reflection or abstraction involved and that is not archaic. It is at the next level that poetical forms take on an aspect of reflection and are more accessible to conscious thought, and, perhaps to potential therapeutic manoeuvring. While moving into the therapeutic realm, Danesi and Hillman continue to cite Vico and to apply his insights to Jung, but without making Vico's distinctions.

> Vico's doctrine of poetical characters gives hints for an archetypal mode of therapy. The poetical character, a hero or a god, becomes the psychic structure by means of which we place events and see how well they conform with their universal types, or archetypes.
>
> (Hillman 1985: 159)

The personal dimension which generalises human types to individual and subjective entities is far from what Vico had in mind. Vico's 'imaginative universals' are concerned with how human mentality originates meaning at all. Vico had no sense of the personal as we think of it, no sense of an interior that could be delved into. But it is the key to human history and making meanings for humans.

Verene summarises Vico's great insight, talking about the conception of an originary mentality 'that ordered experience in terms of imaginative universals [which] is the "master key" of this new science' (Verene 1966: 66).

Marcel Danesi too stresses that Vico's primitive mind has an 'essential feature . . . the imagination'.

> It was therefore a mind that did its work on the basis of bodily experience, not analysis and deduction. Vico used the word 'poetic wisdom' to characterize the operation of the primordial mind, which can be defined, in essence, as the capacity to 'make sense' of perception.
>
> (Danesi 1993: 52)

But communicating with the 'primitive mind' across its blunt sensibility requires a certain mind set not all scholars have.

As a corollary but opposing notion to the achievement of adherence by identification, there is another similarity that arises here between Vico and Jung that is more important than it might seem initially. Both are capable of aiming at persuasion *not* through empathetic attachment, or allegiance, but by fostering alienation to engage audiences in their projects to convince.

Many theorists maintain that both Vico and Jung present their ideas with difficulty, engaging in obfuscation as a standard technique in their discourse. But, I would maintain that in this way, they actually express, and perform, startling insights.

Again, it is Erasmus (as Gowland also references in his work on Burton discussed earlier) in *De Copia* who pointed out that 'one should not write so that everyone can understand everything, but so that people should be compelled to investigate and learn something for themselves' (1999: Book 1).

As a challenger of Scholastic grammar (an attitude Vico would applaud), Erasmus recommended refreshing approaches to formulating ideas, rather than holding fast to arcane, overly conceitful vocabulary and 'rules'. Like Vico, he was reacting to Descartes' paradoxically 'conceitful' idea of 'clear and distinct' thought with its picayune solutions to philosophical conundrum. But Erasmus' refreshing approaches could take unusual forms.

In fact, as James R. Goetsch, Jr. cites from Frances Yates' book, *The Art of Memory* (1969: 132), one of Erasmus's secretaries was in touch with architects working on Camillo's theatre of memory, and commented on its utility as an aide-memoir in using grotesque or startling images wilfully associated to the object to be held in mind. The 'grotesque' or disquieting turn of phrase achieves similar attention.

Goetsch opens his book *Vico's Axioms* (1995) by referring to the viability of 'barbaric clarity' (meaning commonsensical or vernacular or 'vulgar' discourse as Vico would have it, as opposed to Cartesian casuistry), and comments,

> Vico's friends often seem less kind that his enemies. Not content with simply rejecting his claims, they praise the originality of his insights while denying the lucidity of his thought . . . the chief complaint of Vico's critics focuses on how he orders (or fails to order) his thought.
> (Goetsch 1995: xi)

Similarly one of the impulses of this book, inspired by Susan Rowland (2005), has been to explore the so-called difficulties of Jung's style and nevertheless show its effectiveness. As Vico notes in axiom II of *The New Science*, 'It is (a) property of the human mind that whenever men can form no idea of distant and unknown things, they judge them by what is familiar' (Vico 1948: para 122). This smugness, in effect, causes errors to arise; and so, Goetsch concludes:

'maybe Vico seems incoherent because we are' (1995: xii). Our mode of encountering unfamiliar things by distorting them reflects back on us, he says. Finding obfuscation is a mirror of our own distorted sensibilities. And so we cannot read something that is perfectly judicious.

While Rowland does not go quite as far in blaming the reader, she sees purpose in Jung's knotty stylistic choices. First of all, it was a necessity for him:

> Jung believed and *wrote as though he believed* that the thinking and discriminating mind – conventionally used to produce non-fictional argument – was situated within a sea of unconscious creativity.
>
> (Rowland 2005: 1)

For her, too, Jung's writing is a site of the deconstruction of scientific writing itself, and so he engages in digression and circumlocution to capture the nuance of what it is to investigate the psyche. She claims he needs to replicate the spontaneity of the unconscious thought as a component in his writing. Therefore, his writing enacts and performs its message.

On first encounter, the fact that Vico and Jung are difficult to read seems a superficial similarity; further, there are many unclear writers. I am proposing that it is in the similar nature of their styles in their bulky verbiage and hermetic associative organisation that a fellowship of thinking emerges between them. It is the privileging of imagination, the use of amplification, and reliance on virtues of *copia* that I have been arguing make the difficulties necessary. The reader senses something intricate yet engaging, and works hard to find significance. The reader transforms herself, you might say, in order to gain access to meaning. Engaging in this form of transformational thinking, ridding the personal of sensation, enables the reader to realise her individuality submerged in a universal type. You lose yourself when you struggle to find meaning on a difficult path.

In patriotically promoting Vico at Mussolini's (indirect) request, across European cultures, Grassi highlights the Neapolitan's idiosyncratic viewpoint. However, both Verene and Grassi point to the primal, sensual awareness of the particularity of individual self-awareness. This particularity is *identified* with an archetypal collective idea, an 'imaginative universal'. For Jung this is a heuristic for the individual in a way that it is not ever for Vico, who means it as a manifestation of the glue of a nation. Jung can accommodate the universal and the personal – and, as we have discussed – the impersonal too. Vico lacks language for the individual which he does not find relevant to any discussion. I'd like here to follow Grassi and Verene's lead in finding further direct affinities in Jung and Vico's work before bringing up 'projection'.

It is not only by ridding the personal of sensation that we come to realise the individuality submerged in a universal type. In fact, as any mystic tells you, or recommends, immersing oneself deeply in particularity is the way to know the self. Since the mind is active in forming itself, it can recognise itself best in these ideal portraits. The first men began to separate out emotion and sensation by these universal identifications: 'the human mind does not understand anything of which it has had no previous impression . . . from the senses. Now the mind uses the intellect when, from something it senses, it gathers something which does not fall under the senses' (Vico: 1948, 1730/1744: para 363).

Jung's archetypes are generated in the processing of human mentality at source too.

> Individuation means precisely the better and more complete fulfilment of the collective qualities of the human being, since adequate consideration of the peculiarity of the individual is more conducive to a better social performance . . . the idiosyncrasies of an individual are not to be understood as any strangeness in his substance or in his components, but rather a unique combination of already existent universal elements.
>
> (Jung CW7: para 257)

And in the introduction to his commentary on the 'Secret of the Golden Flower', Jung not only outlines a concept of how one culture must allow for the otherness of another culture, in line with Vichian historicism, but restates his idea of the cognitive value of the collective unconscious in similar terms to Vico's universal ideas: 'In purely psychological terms this means that mankind has common instincts of ideation and action. All conscious ideation and action have developed on the basis of these unconscious archetypal patterns and always remain dependent on them' (Jung CW13: para 12).

Another facet of cognition, which we recognise is similar to Jung's, is Vico's conception of projection. Projection is a core cognitive manoeuvre for Jung. Silvano Arieti (Tagliacazzo and Verene 1976: 81–94) asserts in his article on Freud that 'projection' had been anticipated before either Freud or Jung by Vico. Jung ascribes this 'mental mechanism' to archaic thinking, as Vico did.

Vico's axiom early on in *The New Science* spells this out: 'When men do not know the natural causes which produce things and cannot even give analogical explanation, they attribute to things their own nature. For instance, uneducated people say that the magnet loves iron (Vico 1948, 1730/44: para 180).

Arieti points out that Wilhelm Wundt wrote about Vico in his master work *Volkerpsycholgie* but he does not know if Jung or Freud noted these ideas from Vico, through Wundt, about 'projection' which was Wundt's theme. While projection is an essential manoeuvre of identification, there are pejorative aspects, and Vico knew them too.

Vico says projection undermines the ability of scholars to imagine the different mentality of either previous or other human cultures; they project their own values and cultural meanings when confronting something different. It is natural to find what we recognise and focus on that to explain a new principle or a fact, and we will alter it from our perspective (or Jung might say according to our type – extravert or introvert). Historians should resist this flaw in the best way they can. Through careful study and acknowledgement of differences they might succeed in their scholarly task.

Jung's projections are (most often) the perception of our 'shadow' attributes in another – we lay our own faults on to others because we cannot confront them in ourselves. Like Vico's scholars, we do this unconsciously. It is in bringing these unconscious projections into consciousness that we begin to achieve wholeness, in Jung's scheme.

> During the process of treatment the dialectical discussion leads logically to a meeting between the patient and his shadow, that dark half of the psyche which we invariably get rid of by means of projection: either by burdening our neighbours . . . with all the faults which we obviously have ourselves, or by casting our sins upon a divine mediator.
>
> (Jung CW12: para 36)

Although both Vico and Jung talk about a crucial awareness of particularity, the function of projection has different aspects for each. The difficulties of overcoming projection are recognised by both, but the ends are different. Vico's scholar may manage to shed his arrogance, but, Vico feels, it is finally impossible to get an insight into earlier mankind's sensibility. Jung's individuation-seeking analysand may succeed toward dissolving some projections, even if he or she does not reach perfect joining of consciousness and unconsciousness.

There are serious criticisms of Vico's belief that each era has its own style. Brian Vickers, for example, construes Vico's theory very differently from Verene. In Vickers' *In Defence of Rhetoric*, Vickers says that Vico's 'discovery' is not revelation; it is an 'invention', or an unstable argumentative position. These technical rhetorical terms designate different cognitive operations: 'discovery' is a revelation of what is there already. Vico retrieves ideas from memory by his imagination. As Vickers means it here, 'invention' is the location of an argument, a mental construction by analysis and deduction. While it may be that Vickers does not agree with Vico's cognitive stance, it is consistent with the epistemological underpinnings of *The New Science* (Vickers refers only to Freud); and Verene defends Vico's idea.

> certain social conditions and certain forms of thought necessarily go together and arise as co-determinative forces of history . . . Vico wishes to see a difference *in form* (my italics) in the production of these cultures and mentalities.
>
> (Verene 1981: 73)

Similarities in conception of 'the primitive'; comparisons to children and to mentally ill; validity of 'archaic' insights

Verene points out that Vico's comparison of primitives and children was a prevailing idea in Europe at the time. He cites as evidence the research in Frank Manuel's book, *The Eighteenth Century Confronts the Gods* (1959). Vico elaborated on the idea about the first men who behaved like children. For one thing they reacted just like children to fearsome occurrence.

Imagination is the first faculty of early humans and so it is the first faculty to emerge in children. Close to the earth, children, like the first humans, were '*auchthonic*' figures, whose sensual and concrete psyche registered the world like children did.

Vico's poetic discovery enabled him to propose with confidence the idea new in its time that humans first communicated in poetry. Children communicate in single words, and make metaphoric comparisons naturally. 'This principle is of the expressiveness of the poetic images that the world formed in its first childhood' (Vico 1948, 1730/44: para 212).

Erich Neumann explores this in his work on the origins of consciousness. Vico analysed history's phases by linking poetry to the first men, prose and abstractions to the heroes, and ironic criticism to 'modern man' and so clocked off history's laws. Jung concurred as others have, and developed a mythopoetic view of childhood psyche which Neumann explored using similar links to Vico's. This notion was explored in depth by historian Hayden White too in his work *Metahistory* (1974) and Northrop Frye in his *Anatomy of Criticism* (1957). Frye includes reference to Jung in his discussion.

Danesi contemplates these connections:

> The Vichian model of mental evolution holds an intriguing implication for modern developmental psychology that has seldom, if ever, been pointed out. It can be phrased in the form of a question: is it possible that the sequence of 'ages' that characterize the course of human history according to Vico are re-enacted in the mental and verbal development of the child in a chronologically compressed way? . . . Remarkably, a quick glance at the literature on child development suggests that this is a line of inquiry worth pursuing.
>
> (Danesi 1993: 65)

He highlights the overlap of ontology and phylogeny in Vico's concepts in terms that are not dissimilar to another Jungian who recognises Vico's similarities to Jung, Wolfgang Giegerich. He cites Vico's reference to original myth: 'defined as *vera narratio* or true speech' in his critical discussion of Hillman's archetypal psychology (Giegerich 1999: 171). Although he has not explored Vico explicitly, only mentioning the philosopher in several online seminars, in correspondence with me, and in a footnote, Giegerich contemplates the Darwinian law, 'ontogeny recapitulates phylogeny' as an important Vichian insight in his review of Erich Neumann's *The Origins and History of Consciousness* (1999). In Neumann's book, he traces the evolution of individual development within the collective developments of mythic history. Giegerich critiques Neumann's identification of the individual with the collective, proposing that their distinction is a more fruitful avenue to explore.

Grassi also points out that imaginative language is fundamental similarly to primitive and childhood communications, and that poetic language is the essential, archaic foundation to rationality as in Vico's scheme: 'importanza fondamentale del problema della metafora inteso in una dimensione "arcaica" cioè anteriore alla determinazione del linguaggio razionale' (Grassi 1990: 171) (the fundamental importance of the problem of metaphor meant (intended) in an archaic dimension which is prior to rational language [*my translation*]).

We have already encountered this concept of the similarity in cognition of children and primitives in Vico's discussion of 'imaginative class concepts':

> The first of these axioms shows the natural inclination of the vulgar to create them . . . the second shows that the first men, the children, as it were, of the human race, not being able to form intelligible class concepts of things, had a natural need to create poetic characters . . . In children memory is most vigorous, and imagination is therefore excessively vivid, for imagination is nothing but extended or compounded memory.
>
> (Vico, 1948, 1730/44: para 209–11)

And '[t]he nature of children is such that by the ideas and names of the men, women, and things they have known first, they afterward apprehend and name all the men, women, and things that bear any resemblance or relation to the first' (ibid.: para 206).

There are countless examples in Jung's own writings of his agreement with the view that children's and primitive's psyches are similar, but also, like Vico, they extend to the universal. And here is Jung expressing Vico's sentiments: 'The first attempts at mythmaking can be observed in children, whose games of make believe often contain historical echoes' (Jung CW5: para 29–32).

And although children are not capable of the mythmaking at the level of the adult psyche of early peoples, Jung continues, '[i]n the same way one can withhold the material content of primitive myths from a child but not take from him the need for mythology, and still less his ability to manufacture it for himself'. It is perhaps clearer to say, Jung recapitulates, continuing here, that 'archaic thinking is a peculiarity of children and primitives' (ibid.: para 32).

Verene points out that for Vico 'ancient primitives, contemporary savages, children, and peasants share a common form of mentality' (Verene 1981: 70) and he adds, they also share a common state of mind with 'mental defectives'. This is another concept that Vico shares with Jung, although they have different coordinates as philosopher and psychiatrist. 'Savages' are included here too – I make my own comparisons here.

Jung agreed with Vico in equating *contemporary* 'savages' with the primitive mind and with children, as well as mentally ill people. We see this clearly in Jung's memoirs when he recounts his travels and observations of the Pueblo Indians in the USA, and other groups in Africa. This was explored in discussion of the memoirs earlier.

But in *The New Science,* and elsewhere in his writings, Vico cites 'American Indians' (*sic*) as an example of a people for whom archaic thought existed presently – as they were 'contemporary savages':

> poetic wisdom, the first wisdom of the gentile world must have begun with a metaphysics not rational and abstract like that of learned men now, but felt and imagined as that of these first men must have been, who, without power of ratiocination, were all robust sense and vigorous imagination . . . [they felt things to be gods] . . . This is now confirmed by the American Indians, who call gods all the things that surpass their small understanding.
>
> (Vico 1948, 1730/44 : 375)

(Vico talks about American Indians, i.e. 'contemporary savages' elsewhere too in *The New Science,* see para 437, 470, 486, 517, 538, 542, 546, 562, 658, 841, 1033, 1095 – which demonstrates his excitement about these peoples who he'd only read about previously, in support of his theories.)

Vico commences to explore this theme with a discussion about how children use nouns as their earliest form of expression: Children, in fact, speak primarily in nouns, he says, 'leaving the verbs to be understood' (Vico 1948, 1730/44: para 453).

Vico compares this to a mentally defective man he observed: 'This good fellow who lived among us who, after a severe apoplectic stroke, utters nouns but has completely forgotten verbs' (ibid.: para 453). In homage to Vico's prescience, psychologists at Padua reiterate in psychological terms their contemporary research findings in tribute to Vico's observation in *New Science*:

> finalmente gli autori delle lingue si formarono i verbi come osserviamo i fanciulli spiegare nomi e particelle e tacere i verbi. Poiche' i nomi destano idee che lasciano ferme vestigi; le particelle, che significano modificazioni, fanno il medesimo; ma i verbi significano moti, i quali portano l'innanzi e il dopo, che sono misurati dall'indivisibile del presente, difficilissimo da intendersi dagli stessi filosofi. . . . Non regge orazione se non comincia da nome ch'espresso o taciuto la regga.
>
> (Those who created the languages have left the verbs last, in the same ways as children learn nouns and particles before verbs. For nouns elicit ideas that leave profound and lasting traces; the same holds for

> particles that carry modifications, whilst verbs, whose function is to denote movements, denoting what happens before and what afterwards, referring to the invisible present, which is very difficult to be understood even by philosophers . . . Every speech must necessarily start with nouns, either overtly expressed or subdued.)
>
> (Denes and Dalla Barba 1998: 31 – their translation)

Psychiatric insights such as these had impact on Vico's discussion of language and personality in ways very reminiscent of Jung's insights. In the opening section of Vico's *Autobiography* he notes a correlation between his melancholic personality and a fall he had on his head as a child. But he is an 'amateur' observer, he says, despite participating in an experimental scientific group whose principles were based on Francis Bacon's idea of deduction from example. He realises his approach is speculative.

Jung did not directly equate primitives' and children's cognitive faculties with the mentally defective that I can find. But he did recognise that somatic problems had impact symbolically and physically on mental processes. This awareness is at the centre of Jung's methodology as a therapist.

There are numerous instances, but I will use one depicted succinctly in Donald Kalshed's recent work. He describes Jung's treatment of a young woman who had developed a schizophrenic split after an incestuous encounter with her brother, and further sexual abuse from a 'friend'. She was a person frozen and physically ill when Jung met her.

Kalsched describes how Jung entered into the fable/dreamlife of this schizophrenic woman, enabling him to interact with her story of being imprisoned on the moon by taking the part of the demon vampire lover. This helped him to encourage the self-healing process which Kalsched identifies as Jung's therapeutic method (Kalshed 1996: 72–6). Kalsched insists that it was Freud's discovery that there were not lesions on the physical brain that lead to 'strangulated ideas' blocking behaviour; they were rather 'lesions of the psyche'. Jung was, perhaps, more interested in how *complexes* or psychic issues might effect somatic or cognitive processes in humans, and in this regard did not differentiate between children and adults, much less primitives.

Extending this idea, and imputing it to Vico, Hillman proposes that pathology has a role to play in health. He explores the notion that the gods are a disease. The struggle and suffering toward meaning and communication, i.e. overcoming the oppression of the *complex*, are themselves served up as a benefit. Healing is a settling in with pathology, as he explores in *Healing Fiction* and *The Myth of Analysis.*

Hillman uses mythological fable as consolatory therapeutic stories that the analysand works through analogically toward healing. Hillman starts from the end product, i.e. the cultural artefact, and reduces it to the 'universal'.

Hillman claims to discover this approach to myth in Vico's writings, and proposes that Vico is an early psychologist in this way. As a psychologist, Vico traced, in history, Hillman proposes, humanity's disturbing inclination to provoke transformation:

> Furthermore, is it most unusual to consider Vico a psychologist? . . . or is it more likely that psychology has never been truly psychological until Jung, who provided both a bridge to these unrecognised isolated sources and a means of drawing from them. It is through Jung that we can discover them [Plotino, Ficino and Jung, in this case] as psychologists.
>
> (Hillman 1975: 157)

Etymology and philology as primary methodological means

It is appropriate that a twentieth-century philologist such as Curtius would find similarities between Vico and Jung, and, indeed, similarities to his own method of working.

Tracing etymologies, and then exploring the 'layerings' of overlapping significance (as Danesi would call it) embedded in figures and texts, are typical Jungian methods of argumentation. These associations were sources of proof for his theories of the collective unconscious.

Vico used etymology to exploit revealed 'copious' primordial meanings. Meanings were linked in what might seem unlikely conjunctions. Vico's book, *On the Wisdom of the Ancient Italians,* speaks specifically of how meanings in the original words from Etruscan times permeate and illuminate contemporary Italy, and that these are valid demarcations of history, even if they are not always agreed by other historians.

He opens his work *On the Wisdom of the Ancient Italians* in this way:

> I noticed that [the origins of] many words were so learned as to seem derived from some inward learning rather than from the vernacular usage of the people . . . I conjectured that they had taken these expressions from some learned nation and used them unaware of their meaning . . . [after some discussion of Etruscan and Roman, and farther back, Ionian references] I take it as *certain* that the learned origins of Latin words came from these two peoples.
>
> (Vico 1988/1711: para 5)

He will not 'formulate a system by unearthing the causes of language . . . on the basis of philosophy . . . but I shall seek out the ancient wisdom of the Italians from the very origin of their words' (ibid.: 17). Finding self-evident proof in exploration of etymology is an exploitation of definition, and a further sample of his refutation of the logical dialectical organisation of epistemology as discussed earlier. Curtius and even more pointedly, a fellow literary theorist, investigated cultural output following the warranted authority bonded to topics that Vico recommended.

Critic and literary historicist Erich Auerbach based his philological work on Vico's principles. Like the aesthetician Wilhelm Dilthey, another philosopher greatly influenced by Vico, Auerbach believed that deep exploration by intuition and methodical contextual analysis of cultural product revealed the ethos of a culture.

In Vichian style, Auerbach's *Mimesis* and his *Literary Language and Its Public in Late Latin Antiquity* explore works that he explores as typical cultural artefacts of their period. In each essay, Auerbach focuses on a passage from a single work, and outlines the rhetorical strategies of the writer as he or she reflects the ethos of that culture. He acknowledges his debt to Vico in all his works. Relying on *expositio* ('narrative', really) for relevant organisation of sequence, circumvents dialectical necessities to find the reality of the culture.

In effect, etymology is *narrative* about a word, and Vico calls metaphors 'little fables'. As perceptions were separated out from the flux of external shapes and forces, early humans did not have sufficient words to distinguish a new entity (Vico derives this from Cicero's *De Oratore*). They drew on other words retrieved from memory by spotting similarities. Naturally it emerges that each culture spots different similarities. Using the topic of 'similitude' we can extrapolate what that culture made of its associations. Vico was also confident those early words were universally recognised in the *sensus communis* of that culture. Each had its own particular 'similarities' which became a kind of signature of that culture.

These new words, metaphors, derived from things we are *certain* of. They denoted a new entity. The story of their derivation is a fable of their being uncovered. The fables are *vera narrativa* revealed at source. The metaphoric term is identical to the referent. This discussion continues the earlier insight about the nature of the cognitive faculties Vico ascribes to human imagination. Auerbach relies on this insight to make his observations in his groundbreaking book.

Although Hillman and Giegerich disagree about it, both refer to Vico's notion of *vera narrativa* as living fable, a new discrete creation of reality. It is not just a similarity but a *new* 'particular'. This is not the job of a philosopher but the occupation of a poet, and the etymologist shares the poet's imagination in this respect as creating, i.e. *poesis.* 'Philology contemplates reason, whence comes knowledge of the true; philology observes that of which human choice is author, whence comes consciousness of the certain' (Vico 1948, 1730/44: para 138–40).

In Vico's system, the *true* is never finally achieved, and it is of problematic value once it is 'found' in any case. The *true* is the philosopher's aim; but philosophers came late on the scene in history. Vico excavates for meaning in words at their inception. There is no *truth* at that moment, in fact, *truth* is a reflective concept. Philosophers cannot help with the *truth* at inception. The nomination of a new entity generates *certainty* as we discussed earlier. The *certain* is a rhetorical concept in this instance, a belief that is not 'explained' but is known. The *certain* is what the rhetorician and the philologist seeks, and Dilthey and Auerbach find that, the best they can do, in their excavations in culture. I would claim that Jung seeks this too, and their aims are similar.

It is for this reason that clarity and rationality (words which Vico associates to his adversary Descartes) are not goals for Vico. In fact, in his disquisition on education (the 6th oration), he argues for imagination's priority also in education. Critical analysis too early in education destroys that first instinct for the *certain*, derived from common sense and memory, and the imagination in a young person. Vico's scheme demanded viability before it demanded causal and logical, dialectical, 'proof'. *Certainty* is derived from a sense of how and what words mean, from common sense, based on historical usage. It was dangerous for young minds to critique before they knew.

Donald R. Kelley confirms the importance of philology for Vico, quoting from Vico's *Il Diritto universale:* 'Philology is the study of speech . . . but since words represent the ideas of things, philology must first treat of the history of things' (Kelley in Tagliacozzo 1976: 214).

The significance of conceiving etymology as *narratio*/narrative about words, with beginnings in imaginative *choice* (found in the notion of discernment) is an important element to remember in analysing the case study of psychologists, and in interpreting dream narratives.

Jung interprets dreams as concrete 'containers' of feelings and significance, rather than narratives that point to repressed meanings. Here we see the similarities to these philologists, He treats dreams as an etymologist might.

> I have examined many such [important] dreams and often found in them a peculiarity which distinguishes them from other dreams. They contain symbolical images which we also come across in the mental history of mankind . . . in groups of images which occur not only at all times and in all places, but also in individual dreams, fantasies, visions and delusional ideas . . . their chief significance lies in their intrinsic meaning and not in any personal experience and its associations.
>
> (Jung CW8: para 554–5)

He asserts their universal significance, as Vico might. Vico's interpretation of narrative is closer to how dreams signify for Jung than the Freudian path to the unconscious. Jung's path takes him to the collective unconscious. Vico's narrative of words takes him into the common sense of the *gente* (the common people), which is an unconscious knowing.

Neoplatonic philosophy is expressed in specific style and epistemology and impacts on its corollary, the self-reflexive Self

In *The Realm of Rhetoric*, Perelman proposes that each philosophy has its appropriate style, a Vichian theme (Perelman 1982: 45).

Neo-Platonism would be inclined to use hierarchical poetics – i.e. etymological definitions revealing the derivation of words from earlier time; it would focus on 'discovery' and on *revelation* of meanings not on constructed argument. Again, it is a topical endeavour with warranties.

Neo-Platonic style dwells on 'decorum', an ancient rhetorical theme, as mentioned – in Aristotle's *Rhetoric*, Longinus' fragment, and as explored also by Augustine, one of Vico's important models. 'Decorum' refers to the appropriateness of presenting a theme in suitable style to its audience, its writer/speaker and its occasion.

As Longinus did, Augustine distinguished low, middle and high style in book 4 of *De Doctrina* (Augustine 1995, trans Green). Using the 'low style' in his own sermons, he sought to bring sublime concepts to the ordinary people of his congregations for educational purposes, hoping to stir them to rejoin the church. This was in contradiction to Aristotle's theorem in *Rhetorics* that the orator use 'high' style to talk about sublime matters. But in applying 'low' style to divine matters, Augustine sought to mimic Jesus' parables, and to bring the message home to his audience more effectively. This summary is taken from Auerbach's first chapter on Augustine in *Literary Language in Late Latin Antiquity* (Auerbach 1965).

Neo-Platonists look at allegory and analogy as heuristic devices to be shorn away in order to uncover, as through a veil, original, essential meaning, like parables. Attention to *dispositio* (arrangement) as it displays levels of significance, on the one hand, and etymological discussion (narratives of the history of words), and use of allegory to exemplify hidden meaning, etc., are approaches that a Neo-Platonic writer might take. Jung's alchemical writings and his Gnostic leanings are examples of this argumentative intention.

And Hillman would support this. After all the purpose of Hillman's essay on Plotino, Ficino and Vico is to establish common ground among Jungians and Neo-Platonists, and so find early authority and tradition. Plotino, whose *Enneads* is the classic compilation of Neo-Platonic ideas, is organised in layers, moving outward from the One, the source, to the specific individual soul, revealing steps along the way. Each level has certain capacities and levels of soul. The individual's soul and its steps away from the source focus the organisation of the material, and convey spiritual valence by its position.

The movement and placement of thoughts, as discrete concepts, are organised according to how important the material is assessed to be in relation to its hidden significance. The interpreter detects the symbolic level of the material or state of soul, and this enables an appropriate ordering of a hierarchy.

There are several aspects in which Neo-Platonic stylistic served good purpose and is useful for both Vico and Jung. They are the visual and conceptual attitudes, as well as a familiarity with discussing the soul.

Visual

Neo-Platonic ideas are congruent with abstracted (not directly realistically representational) images because they correlate to diagrams showing almost metaphysical, *spatial* hierarchy/placement. Plotino's work includes diagrams of spatial organisation that make hypostatical ideas or beings, and place them in rigid streams according to closeness to the One. Lesser beings and ideas are farther along the lines radiating from the One.

The graphics frontispiece to Vico's *The New Science* explores correspondences at the opening of the work which 'synopsise' his meanings, with rays of significance shooting up to the planets, the Sun, the zodiac and direct images of hidden meanings.

Jung's mandalas are emblematic of how potency accrues in the dazzle of the image as the eye travels into the central eye of the mandala. Mandalas are abstracted, not directly representational, but emblematic representation.

Conceptual category, 'precursor', suffuses Neo-Platonism

This idea assumes that the source closest to the origin is the most authentic. To find the precursor is an important proof of authenticity. 'Precursors' are invented if necessary. Vico and Jung and Neo-Platonic philosophers Hillman cites use such a rhetorical tactic. We have already noted the anomalies of Vico's and Jung's etymological efforts. It was customary to cite Egyptians or Persians such as Hermes Trimegisthus, as both Jung and Vico frequently do, to give weight to an argument. The *topos* of 'accuracy' has its own history as explored. In the same way Homer, as investigated by Vico, is a 'real' emblematic universal figure – the blind poet who spanned centuries.

Pre-eminence of and familiarity with the Soul

Jung would agree, Hillman proposes, with Plotino's agenda: 'This first inquiry obliges us to consider at the outset the nature of the Soul' (Hillman cites Plotino, book 1, para 2.2 here of *Enneads*).

But later in this essay, Hillman differentiates Plotino's 'mode of symbolic perception' from Jung's 'psychologizing' of mythology. 'By connecting the images of myth and the Neo-Platonic mode of symbolic perception with psychiatry, he [Jung] could link Gods with diseases (CW13: para 54) and so was able to devise an archetypal basis for the therapy of our psychic suffering' (Hillman 1975: 154). 'To these defects of mind and tongue are joined the most pernicious of all, those of soul, created to be open and sharing but overpowered through sin by an overweening self-love' (ibid.: 155).

For Vico mention of the soul is the closest he comes to a sense of a personal individuality. Because Vico, Jung and the Neo-Platonists operate comfortably with metaphor, they are psychologists, according to Hillman. His archetypal psychology exploits this idea. Their methods are metaphoric, so he establishes these precursors as his authorities. Neo-Platonists uncover hidden meanings to reveal Soul. Jung in his alchemical work, and Vico with his deep exploration of poetical history, fulfil this criterion which makes them Neo-Platonist authorities for Hillman.

Disposed to Neo-Kantianism, Verene approaches the Neo-Platonic theme from another point of view. Verene finds Jung's theories viable specifically in relationship to Vico. Verene's article, published in the *Journal of Analytical Psychology*, focuses on Jung's work on synchronicity, highlighting Joyce's exploitation of Vico's *The New Science* in creating the *corsi e ricorsi* of *Finnegans Wake.*

To summarise his piece: Verene first commends Jung for his work on coincidence. Verene cites Jung's anti-Cartesian orientation, similar to Vico's in questioning logical causality as the first explanation. He cites Jung's work on the *I Ching.* Vico's argument similarly rests on the anomalies of proof, he says.

Synchronicity signifies more than simple coincidence, Verene explains; he sets out three ways that Jung means synchronicity, but, finally Verene concludes, it is for Jung a means to the discovery of the Self which he commends.

In order to achieve self-discovery, we recognise that we find ourselves in our own place and time over against cyclical historical event. When we interpret the *I Ching*, we find or discern our own meanings in the rubric. Vico's famous *corsi* and *ricorsi* is a recognition of the cyclical principles of event. Events recur and link to earlier events with a significance that we can discover in the discovery of the Self. This is the self-reflexivity of the Neo-Platonic attitude. 'Jung notes that the wisdom of the *I Ching* is the same as self-knowledge. The self apprehends its own nature in the nature of things through the interpretation of the hexagrams' (Verene 2002: 466).

Verene recalls Jung's view of the 'primitive' mind: '[F]or the primitive mind [says Jung] synchronicity is a self-evident fact; consequently at this stage there is no such thing as chance' (Jung 1952 para 941 – Verene's citation). Verene draws out the implication of this viewpoint, using Vichian rhetorical language:

> Nothing occurs by chance or accident. What in logic is a fallacy of false cause, in the sense of *post hoc ergo propter hoc,* becomes in the mythical world, a principle to establish cause . . . because a particular species of bird appears repeatedly at the beginning of spring it is seen as the bringer of spring.
>
> (Ibid.: 464)

Verene points out meaning is discovered in Vico's *schema* by the 'prudent' man with a discerning 'acute' mind; human beings discover significance by having 'a good eye' for what the repetition refers to. With 'discernment' comes a recognition of self-knowledge – we remember where we fit into the cycle of repetition in the world.

> The *I Ching*'s hexagrams correspond to Vico's mental dictionary, which like Jung's archetypes of the collective unconscious, contains all the basic symbols of the world's mythologies and the languages of the nations as they develop their conscious memories from them. Vico has no specific means to tap these meanings other than meditation and narration on the patterns of repetition perceivable in the 'great city' of the human race.
>
> . . . Joyce's work {*Ulysses*} is a book of wisdom in that it contains all that there is in human experience. Whoever and whatever we look for in it we find.
>
> (Ibid.: 469)

Verene concludes that

> the philosophy of self-knowledge can turn to Jung as a way to see the non-Cartesian side of the self, a great deal of which depends upon the self's ability to confront in practice and in thought the presence of coincidence in human experience.
>
> (Ibid.: 475

The self-reflexivity of the Neo-Platonic soul is finally explored in Jung's idea of individuation.

8

WORD ASSOCIATION TESTS AND DELIBERATIVE LOGIC

Forensic Jung

> the evidence of the senses is also an operation of the mind in which conviction creates the evidence
>
> (Proust, *The Captive*, 1999: 141)

Proust's idea of the role of memory is distinctive; the senses are gateways into memory (interior) and into reality (exterior). The resulting connection brings empirical evidence together with memory to make significance. In *Swann's Way*, the madeleine dipped in tea triggers specific memories of his childhood and this process and event shapes the novel, closely interweaving interior perception with real exterior event.

At nearly the same time Proust was writing this work, in Switzerland, Jung was initiating word association experiments but after the first excitement, he realised he had disappointing results. He was struggling to bring human sensory material to bear as evidence in a scientific context. The results frustrated him, and, years later, in 1927, Jung proclaimed, "whosoever wishes to know about the human mind will learn nothing, or almost nothing, from experimental psychology . . . ' (Jung CW2: 1904/1973). Yet he had made his name internationally with the association experiments despite setbacks.

This work was the basis of an important stream in Jung's career that began before his encounter with Freud's psychoanalysis. To explore development of what he hoped would be reliable tools to evaluate anomalous data, I propose to apply the heuristic of deliberative rhetoric as a mode of enquiry. However, the failures of the logical, positivist and causal rationale of this experimental method set Jung not only to be receptive to Freud, but also to turn to other speculative modes of enquiry.

Jung's work on the word association experiments had followed on from hospital director Bleuler's and colleague Riklin's work at the clinic, following ideas set out by earlier psychologists, Kraeplin and Wundt. The association tests were an attempt to find an objective way to assess mental patients' internal worlds. With this knowledge, the doctor could communicate with the patient on her own ground, and treat her. Despite his own disappointments, as Ellenberger tells us (1970: 667), the association tests were used as a diagnostic tool for years afterwards.

Jung presented his paper, 'Association experiments on normal subjects' (CW2: 1905), and had hopes that the tests could be used in criminal cases. But despite what appeared often to be valuable results later contrasting results from 'abnormal' subjects, he concluded that this technique was not useful in detecting specific criminal behaviour.

Many psychologists, including William Stern, were critical; and Freud too had a negative response. Freud published a paper in 1907 (translated 1924) in which he thought results were interesting but not reliable.

Months after Jung published the results Freud mentioned the experiments during a lecture to law students. He was interested to note how these new experiments used objective scientific probes into the criminal mind. He referred to both Jung's and Stern's work. He also reminded them of his own earlier work in the 'Psychopathology of everyday life' (1901) that had laid down similar groundwork. He had proposed then that certain deep-seated neuroses in the individual seemed to interfere in their daily living. He compliments Jung for discovering the principles of these results again, and for developing a new concept of influence from his own 'ideational content' i.e. the 'complex': 'Examples like those given by Jung (1906) are well calculated to make us doubt the occurrence of chance or of what is alleged to be arbitrary in mental events' (Freud 1901: 104).

While extolling the possibilities that key words might stimulate revelation of 'secret' meaning, Freud also comments results are unreliable. Perhaps by recording all the results over a number of years, he says, it may prove to be significant. In this early essay, Freud does not seem to recognise the distinctions Jung made about the complex. In fact, it emerges years later that Freud's comprehension of the 'complex' as a kind of repressed cluster of sexual associations, was not a broad enough definition for the results of Jung's work. But the experiments did establish that feeling-toned complexes or tensions are constellated around related associated links.

In 1914, after their break, Freud dismissed the importance of the 'complex' not by logically refuting the concept, but by reducing and distorting its meaning.

> No other term . . . has been so misapplied to the detriment of the construction of clearer concepts. Analysts began to speak among themselves of a 'return of a complex' where they meant a 'return of the repressed', or fell into the habit of saying 'I have a complex against him,' where the only correct expression would be have a 'resistance against him'.
>
> (Freud SE14 1957: 29)

Arguing by misdirection (as Jung might have seen it) and hearsay, Freud misconstrues Jung's deep-seated emotional clusters for shallow neuroses. Considering the distinctions along modes of rhetorical heuristic, we might say that the way 'complexes' as underlying figural transformations (like metaphor) manifest reflects precisely what they are. Mechanical methods in the early work indicated their presence but it is only a significant discovery when psychologists learn what they are.

Discovery of scientific method that is *not* logically and causally based (i.e. *logos*-based) but a method more suited to psychological empirical data that accommodates subjectivity, irrationalities, images of significance and emotion was the important endeavour of Jung's working life. Exploring his work rhetorically reveals the underlying drives of the scientific discourse.

Juridical or forensic rhetoric

To propose deliberative or forensic applications of Jung's word association technique, Vico's discussion of the tenets of ancient juridical rhetoric is useful. In fact, it is the inventional primacy that he applies to juridical rhetoric that reorients his adherence to causality as a driving force in seeking the 'true' or the 'certain'.

Aristotle's *Rhetoric* sets out forensic rhetoric as the first of three parts. Forensics specifically deals with issues of 'truth', i.e. establishment of *fact*, taken as empirical phenomena. Gathering material from Vico's lectures on the occasion of scholarly year openings, and the handbook of rhetoric taken from his lectures at university, Vico establishes an adversarial approach.

The first task is to establish the *nature* of the 'truth' we seek in each case. The rhetor's professional goal is necessarily intertwined with her personal motivation, i.e. getting her salary in pursuit of her job, and successfully representing her client to gain esteem, etc. The 'truth' she seeks influences the discovery of fact. Adversarial lawyers appreciate the dimensions of this 'responsive' kind of fact and this conception better enables a rhetorician to achieve her aims. (See Shotter 1993: chapter 3 for analogous discussion in the social world.)

Syllogistic, dialectical investigation, *logos*-based, relies on the notion of 'incontrovertible truth'. Like scientific work this approach to legal investigation privileges *logos* processes in seeking to confirm and persuade; it seeks to persuade by 'objective' means, and deals in rational necessity rather than emotional or moral certitude. Context, circumstance and intention, however, are accommodated in complicated ways.

In the context of forensics, Aristotle's *Rhetoric* describes argument using logical strategies as 'artificial' proof; these are proofs derived from constructed self-evident corroboration. However, testimony supplied by witnesses counted as 'natural' proof. A witness may well make biased errors in recollection, so this 'natural' proof can be arbitrary and unreliable. Rhetorical ('artificial') 'truths' are more powerful but since they are sometimes reliant on arbitrary testimony, they must be treated carefully.

Deliberations about truth are at the core of forensic argument. In fact, it is the underlying preoccupation of the court. In Jung's parlance, it is a 'constellation', a complex: an underlying preoccupation or 'truth-complex'. We can say that seeking truth is the fundamental *topos* or *schema* driving juridical rhetoric. But this is always contingent on what the nature of 'truth' is. The participants in the courtroom process must agree on that. (Just as agreement must be reached about the nature and appropriateness of scientific data in a series of procedures.)

I'd suggest that in applying analysis of the truth 'complex' to Jung's word association work, a new idea about the 'truth' of human personality emerged. These ideas devolved into Jung's major innovative work on 'complexes' and discoveries about human personality and 'type' theory, *Psychological Types* (CW 6 1921).

> The predominance of one or the other point of view depends less upon the objective behaviour of things than upon the psychological attitude of the investigator or thinker. Empathy leads to the mechanistic view, abstraction to the energic [*sic*] view . . . both . . . make the mistake of assuming that the subjective concept is identical with the behaviour of the thing itself; that, for example, causality, as we experience it, is also to be found objectively in the behaviour of things.
>
> (Jung CW8 1928: para 5)

His propositional theory of types supersedes the inchoate results of gathering what purported to be 'objective' data in the word association tests.

Methods of proof

Stasis theory

Stasis theory, a rhetorical mechanism used to judge event in a methodical way, provides coordinates to seek certainty. It was developed by Isocrates and Cicero and used by legally minded rhetoricians (Ijsseling 1976).

In order to define 'reality', the forensic rhetorician concentrates on evidence as it applies to the operating *topos* of the courtroom, accusation and defence. Based on the reality (from her perspective), the rhetor selects the evidence. Those facts of evidence are organised rhetorically to assess truth. The conclusion is *plausible* and repeatable reality, i.e. *verifiable* in the way mathematic results are readily demonstrable.

There are three questions of *stasis theory* Vico sets out from sources: *an sit* – was the deed a crime? (Vico calls this *conjectural*); *quid sit* – what crime was it? (Vico calls this *definitional*); and *quae sint eius proprietates* – was the deed just?

(Vico calls this *qualitative*). There is another question too, Vico reminds us: is this court qualified to judge the case? Every law student, and student of logic, knew this formula and used it to focus their enquiries (Vico 1984/1711–41: 57–9).

Where the rhetor sources the truth corresponds to how she sifts through evidence. Is it the bloody knife that is germane, or the broken dishes on the dinner table? Tracing to source is germane in Jung's experimental and scientific work as well.

It is nearly impossible to ascertain opinion about fact from a stance outside the community because sources of meaning are particular to culture and time. Vico's conjectural question raises this issue: a fatal act of aggression might be a murder or it might be self-defence. In Jung's experiments, the conjectural mechanism operates similarly for individual reaction. Where the source of action is, i.e. its motivation, defines the reaction. The issue of motivation is a leitmotif in Jung's *complex* theory. It is a ruling precept that strongly visceral and anxious reactions that 'perseverate' several words on in the sequence of response indicate the presence of a 'hidden truth'. Participation in courtroom proceedings reinforces the idea that tracing action back to motivation reveals the significance of the action.

Reverting to the *topos* accusation vs. defence, we admit that consistent arguments on each side often derive from various, even contradictory, sources. People commit acts either 'voluntarily' or 'involuntarily'. Doing something 'involuntarily' is either an act committed by chance, being in the wrong place at the wrong time, or else by flaw in human nature (such as mental illness), or under control by someone or something else. Accordingly, the defence will use the argument of 'diminished will'.

Courts use psychologists' opinions about mental derangement in exploring the guilt or innocence of the perpetrator. To trace motivations effectively depends on effective interrogation. Indeed, in Jung's association tests, once he gathered that clusters of association and emotion were operating 'underground', he believed he was finding what seemed to be autonomous sub-personalities, or 'complexes'. He had to develop inventive and consistent ways of tracking these sub-personalities or entities. But, in the end, despite exploiting techniques of objective data compilation, he could get no closer than noting that something was there. As is true for argumentation based on inventional means as a starting point, without proposing the answer, knowing where you were going, you cannot ask the right questions.

Jung felt that he knew the guilt or otherwise of the person on the stand, and so he could make judgements. And, in his investigations in the criminal field, he assumed that there was a connection between mental illness and criminal behaviour. But we sense ambivalence about the aim of assessments in court, and it led him into equivocations in both his private work and in the courts. Such equivocation rendered the scientific results unstable, if not unusable.

> every habitual criminal is morally defective, and is thus ill in a scientific sense. The law, however, as it stands at present, claims all individuals who recognise the punishable nature of their action and who are not acting under an irresistible compulsion.
>
> (Jung CW1: 469)

Applying stasis theory in the courtroom, and in Jung's experiments

Vico proposed various strategies the defendant might use to protect her client. The advocate searches through arguments for evidence to support her argument but she also seeks to anticipate the accuser's response. The high stakes in the case, winning or losing, shape the exchange between adversaries. Vico itemises inventional approaches to counter a series of questions.

The principal places of argument at the *conjectural* level are several: what was the motive? (e.g. impulse – an outburst of anger or hate – or calculated – deliberately done for gain?); was there possibility? (e.g. the occasion to commit crime without detection); and the opportunity to better oneself once the crime is achieved?; or, were there what Vico calls 'signs' – words or deeds that preceded the act – threats, plans or instruments [weapons] secreted away. Vico suggests (based on Cicero's advice) that the defender prepare herself to reject any such imputations of motive, or possibility, and to digress from or invent undeniable signs.

To withstand the *definitional* accusation, be prepared with 'variant definitions; confirm one related definition by proposing a weaker one'.

The *qualitative* dilemma encompasses several issues. Has the person/patient committed this action 'voluntarily': is it a calculated act? 'Is it a repeat of earlier performance of a harmful act? Did harm to someone else bring pleasure, so that desire is engaged?'

I will use some cases Jung was involved with to continue analysis:

DEMONSTRATION NO. 1: NURSE'S THEFT CASE (JUNG 1909: 439–65)

Stasis theory suggests finding a sequence of biased perspectives that will come to function as guidelines in looking at a set of facts. The questions lead the arguer into a choice of either conflicting or supporting proposals. This ploy is especially relevant to one case Jung participated in.

In this case, Jung called on his idea of types to help. There was a history to this notion, which he relates to his readers in *Psychological Types.* William James was thinking along these lines too. In an early lecture, 'The One and the Many', James (1907: lecture 4) points out that links among particulars can certainly be arranged in many different ways. He focuses on the vicissitudes of temperament and applications to argument choice. Analysis of a set of facts depends on a person's 'type' James says.

If you are inclined to see unity everywhere, all facts will have similarities to every other fact, and you *will* find a unity, a one-ness in all. If you view the world in material particulars, you will be noting differences among things, and the world will fragment into myriad, discrete items. Finally, James concludes, these two viewpoints are inextricably intertwined, and in their negotiation with each other, a sequence of facts that is 'truth' is constructed.

The magistrate or the rhetor recognises the tension about 'truth' that is created by a constellating preoccupation of guilt among all the participants. Eventually this tension will accrue to a sequence of events that reveal a plausible truth.

There are many variables. The courtroom is the 'rhetorical space' (to be discussed later) and I will maintain that so is Jung's consulting room, and the space of his experiments. The common, pressing awareness extends 'the space' out into the community, and similarly extends this (uneasy) truth complex. The results are inevitably compromised. The variables were apparent to Jung.

He acknowledged William Stern's critiques about the calculated choice of words Jung made in the association test. Stern and his partner, Clara Stern, had experimented on the nature of children's lies and had made deductions about the effect of an extrinsic 'symbol' on human reactions (Stern 1907/1999). Freud made similar deductions he reported on in 'Two lies told by children' (1924/1913): he noted hesitancies related to the purpose of the lie in children's testimonies. He applied them to adults.

It is true, Jung says, answering Stern, that the tone of voice and very presence of the interrogator (and in the courtroom, with the shared obsession with the crime itself – whether you are the guilty party or not) influences the interrogation and the responses.

Jung is certain however that he can distinguish the culprit from the innocent party intuitively from knowledge he has learned about typical responses in his clinical experience: 'Experience has shown that a defendant who is sure of his innocence will concentrate more on the general fact of the injustice of being suspected than on any particular detail of the evidence, which is for him irrelevant" (Jung CW2 1937: para 612).

The assumption that he can tell a person's guilt (which is their secret) by intuition and by noting other evidential hints he thinks are 'telling' is a deeply held conviction. Jung claims he does this by assessing reactions that are not even conscious to the speaker. The culprit, the innocent or the informed will reveal their roles to him in the scenario of culpability. The fact that 'stimulus-words touch upon emotionally charged complexes . . . is the foundation of what is called the *diagnosis of evidence*, i.e. the art of detecting, by means of an association experiment, the real culprit among a number of people suspected of a crime' (Jung CW2 1904–7: para 452).

The theft narrative I focus on here demonstrates a few elements of forensic interrogation as they correlate to Jung's theories.

Six nurses were suspected of the theft of money from a locked cupboard. Two shared the room, and both knew where the key was. There was time during every day when the room was empty. The 'charge nurse' helped her friend, the victim, to search high and low for the missing money with no result. Then they raised the alarm about the theft, and Jung was called in to help find out who the crook was.

He quickly established that only three of the six had 'possibility' – designating at once his targets as well as broaching the *conjectural* argument: was this a crime at all? His view and the court's was that it was a fact that the money has been stolen. But there is little discussion. Perhaps the money had been borrowed. Maybe it was never there. But, according to the story, it's gone missing after it had been locked up. The key is easily obtainable. Only three people knew that the money was missing, where it was kept, and had opportunity – he asks these three designates to submit to the association test.

He has assessed them though even before he listens and considers their responses. In fact, he must in order to question them. He strongly suspects the charge nurse who had ostensibly helped look for the money. In fact, so convinced is Jung of her guilt that he sets out to incriminate her with his questions.

The significant words Jung chooses – 'red' (like the colour of the door), 'key', which the guilty nurse had to find, use, and hide away again, etc. – will feel like aggravated entrapment to the guilty charge nurse; it arouses the suspicions of the third nurse, an innocent party, when she realises that she is a suspect too – her associations become more considered, and lengthy as the data reveals. But it is not directly for the reason to hand. He has proved that there is an alliance between the impulse to find 'pure' truth and a credible and persuasive truth that serves the purpose of the seeker.

In this case, he does not set words that target what a motive might be (something associated to poverty, for example), if there is motive, or whether there was a crime. He takes it for granted it is thievery or else the result of some defect in her personality which made this an act of diminished responsibility. To look at Vico's criteria in this context: Jung never asks *definitional* queries about this event. Nor does he enquire into their relationship, to find out if there were resentments or history between the nurses that would mitigate the guilt. In other words, he does not search out *qualitative* arguments. Based on his opinion about her apparently dismissive attitude, and the ease she'd have had in accomplishing the theft, he prepares his words to entrap her. And then, he is 'proved right' because the pressure of submitting to the association test itself induces her to confess her guilt. Did he find the right woman?

We might say he did not follow precepts of juridical proof seeking – but temperamentally he seems not to have been able to. His questions were skewed, and savvy nurses knew how to manipulate his tools of enquiry. These point up all the human variables that make such enquiry unsuccessful.

As with Freud's guilty child who seems to acknowledge a specific wrongdoing by displacing guilt from the real event to another, the fixation of guilt on the wrong nurse is not contemplated when Jung deliberately chooses his words to test them. Rhetorical variables of the courtroom surpass objective questioning to arrive at agreed-upon credible truth.

DEMONSTRATION NO. 2: THE ELDERLY GENTLEMAN SUSPECTS THEFT

In another case, it was fear of the test itself that threatened the subject, who confessed all. Jung interrogated a young man after an older gentleman asked Jung to apply the association testing. He suspected the younger man, a student living in his house, of stealing from him. Jung prepared his word lists accordingly, having got the details from the elderly man. Soon the terrified younger fellow is confessing all to Jung, confirming Jung's and the old man's suspicions.

The culprit's personal testimony confirms his guilt; Jung does not realise that he is engaged in entrapment. Does he realise that the very form of the inquisition, the inexplicable (for the young man) ritual of words thrown out, responses timed, and noted, aimed at discovering secrets, carries menace? In fact, hysterical subjects might well confess to anything to relieve the pressure. Again the subject's visceral experience undermines the stated intention to get at the truth.

Jung proceeds just as if he were an adversarial rhetorician. He has already determined who and what his target is, i.e. where the truth – the guilt – is hidden, and he goes about uncovering it. In the first case, it is the charge nurse's psyche. He loads the stimulus-words to obtain her admission of guilt. In pursuit of this goal, he has unwittingly revealed to all three nurses he examines that he already knows who the guilty party is. Doubtless this influenced his result. Clearly the same happened to the student in demonstration number 2.

DEMONSTRATION NO. 3: A MURDERER IN THE CONSULTING ROOM

In private consultation, Jung relieved a woman of her obsessive behaviour by releasing her guilty secret. It emerged, under his questioning, that she'd allowed her baby to drink contaminated water which killed the child, and she'd always hidden her guilt. It is not just that it was an error; she had not wanted the child and knew exactly what was happening. As in the instance of the young student above, or in the revelation of a nurse's theft, Jung reveals all to us in his report with a flourish, they are acts of bravura for him. I believe they are presented this way to mitigate his responsibility.

Did the mother in this instance overstate her case, taking on the generalised guilt and grief about the child's death as her own personal responsibility, so it became her guilt? Freud had pointed out to his law students in the lecture cited above that transference of guilt is a common mechanism. Would a policeman investigating the supposedly contaminated water, and the timing of events, and the compunction determine guilt and agree with Jung? The revelation remained in his private study, except as he used it as further published proof of the viability of his experimental method.

But his concluding remarks do not yet get to the most important discovery: that these people were certain types, with certain dispositions and worldviews that determined their choices. They were simultaneously reacting to 'complexes' he'd aroused either in their personal lives or in ways to deep-seated convictions in the community or in archetypal situations. Or his method had inculcated certain dispositions or choices (the integrity of the volleys of questions and answers). The inadequacies as I think he perceives them will move Jung to other solutions.

In the discussions at the opening of the word association volume, CW2, an innovative codification of the relationship between the psyche and words is proposed. I will explore the ramifications now.

The 'truth' complex in forensic rhetoric: definitions, sources, techniques

Elocutio *(including figural devices) vs.* logos *as argument*

'Peithos', the Greek nymph of persuasion, was part of Aphrodite's entourage; she epitomised allure, connections and soft talking. She did not engage in any attempt to go beyond the gods to a place where she might find *absolute* truth: after all, she was already on the upper plane: a goddess was her best friend. In Peithos's mythic guise, persuasion has no broad conceptual aspiration.

However, throughout its history, rhetoric often did aspire to broader scope. Rhetoric was originally subsumed to philosophy and influential philosophers/rhetoricians in France and England, like Pierre Ramus (1515–72) wanted to transcend the stylistic moorings of communication. (Plato had disparaged rhetoric – which included poetry – and turned to Pythagoras, a 'magical' mathematician, to resolve his issues.) Ramus attacked Aristotle, and wanted a closer union with dialectical logic. Aesthetic forms tied meanings down into distorting contexts, he felt. Their concern was to purify philosophy.

As a result, rhetoric degenerated in Renaissance times when, broadly speaking, 'ornamentation' was set outside any necessary connection to argument – often in long compilations of aesthetic formulas. By the time of the early Enlightenment period in Europe, rhetoric was a pejorative word. It meant empty talk, superfluous and excessive.

Before its degeneration rhetoric had been essential study as part of philosophy. Vico (and other theoreticians) reunited 'ornamental' or *elocutio* to philosophy in innovative ways, and raised the stakes for rhetorical philosophy again. For one thing, the need to speak for yourself *effectively* in the courtroom

– using forensic rhetorical tools to present the plausible truth of your case – could mean your life or death. Presenting a case plausibly meant skilful manoeuvring of the facts to display their truth. Theoretical underpinnings had to be systematically and persuasively thought out. Truth had to be particularised and significant, and presented with allure to engage adherence. Truth purified of context was a meaning without voice. *Logos* alone would not succeed.

Struever comments that Vico disengaged rhetorical forms from superfluous aestheticisation (*sic*), where Ramus and others had consigned rhetoric, bringing it back to impersonal objectified levels of indubitable necessity. Casuistry and dialectical rationalisations did not carry sufficient conviction.

Argument is shaped to achieve intent: the intention in juridical cases is to discover the 'real' truth of what happened. 'Real' is based, however, on figural argument, beautiful and arousing, persuading susceptible listeners or readers with the allure of Peithos. Vico placed juridical rhetoric at the centre of his system, and recommended *elocutio* as primary argumentation for its powers in establishing adherence. It may seem that imagination is far from the persuasive power of *logos* but 'poetic logic' had great influence, and served functional purpose – and was not only to be deployed for hedonistic purposes.

Sensus communis and sensory argumentation – sources

(a) Customs and perceptions change from place to place. Descartes disparages *ethos* as a source of argument overturning Cicero, Quintilian and other ancient rhetoricians' convictions. Precepts deriving from the 'common sense' cannot stand independently as axioms of necessary truth, Descartes thought.

Guidelines of the community are often set down as 'common places'. 'Common place' aphorisms are part of the storehouse of arguments and ideas that a speaker might use as touchstones for a like-minded audience.

Jung subscribed to common sense support for his insights in the long history of language, for example:

> It must have been a considerable psychic achievement in the beginning of language and conscious thought to separate contrasts in speech and concept . . . we are verbally very practiced in these closely connected concepts, which are very often supported by quotations and rhymes.
>
> (Jung CW2: 18)

His arguments often rest on common-sense propositions. Arguments from common sense are traditional aspects of juridical argumentation too especially in front of a jury. As Jean Fahnestock points out, however, this might seem unusual to contemporary rhetors who feel that the particular cases will throw up their own arguments in their own specific contexts (Fahnestock 1988). *Inventio* for Jung, however, began in primal topics, universal and commonsensical; and then he exploited the parameters to shock and transform given beliefs. The entirely self-evident abstractions of mathematics may be logical bases for 'certain' truths but these certainties exist outside worldy influence. Scientific language rested in objectified abstractions, and Jung's struggles with conclusions of word association tests had to do with orientation to a neutral abstracted view of *logos* rather than a *logos* based on *topical* and plausible truths. Rational and logical conclusions devoid of human contexts were irrelevant.

In his considerations of Descartes' philosophies which he tried to counter in his time, Vico argues that too much ratiocination leaves rhetors without experience of deploying the useful tools of *elocutio* (or 'eloquence'), founded by instigating arguments based on common sense or *topics*.

> I may add that common sense, besides being the criterion of practical judgement, is also the guiding standard of eloquence. It frequently occurs, in fact, that orators in a law court have greater difficulty with a case, which is based on truth, but does not seem so, than with a case that is false but plausible.
>
> (Vico 1990/1709: 13)

Descartes' focus on dialectical logic made students unfit to practice in courtrooms, or in the world. William James's pragmatist colleague, Peirce, attacked Cartesianism with a ferocity that was shared by James, and that echoes Vico's complaints:

> But what are the conditions, Peirce asks, for Descartes to begin his 'solitary' questionings? Where does he stand when he reflects his consciousness within itself? Why suppose that consciousness is a self-standing domain sealed off within itself? Consciousness fades off on every side through fuzzy fringes.
>
> (cited in Wilshire 1997)

Assessment of action depended on common sense and also on bodily 'topics', and furthermore, the rational was not isolated from worldly or physical constraints either. Vico discusses another ramification when he discusses 'personification' – a persuasive, figural device that makes the argument. An orator might use 'grotesque' and/or sentimental means to make the point. Create a tableau, for example, of a deeply sentimental 'pattern' (calling on typical configurations of sentiment): a female thief might appear alongside her wailing children whose husband has been killed, to get her off a maritorious murder charge (Vico 1984/1711–14: 187). Personifications of gods can be used to browbeat an audience into fearful submission. Compilations of maxims and commonplaces in handbooks provide numerous tableaux – used to clinch an argument alluding to formulae of sentiment and allegiance to accepted opinion about females, etc. in the community.

Vico recommended utilising the imaginative and generative capacities of rhetoric since, used cleverly, it penetrated to human pre-verbal responsiveness. Jung's use of fable, fairy tale and myth throughout his work recognises the effectiveness of primal forms in penetrating the psyche. We recognise those forms; they appeal deeply to us.

In Vico's handbook on rhetoric, 'sensory topics' generate words and afford the rhetor access to affect or 'moving eloquence'. Could Vico have measured how effective these types of topics were, he'd have tried to measure them but not in the ways Jung attempted to in his association tests. Measuring times of reactions, or guidelines to achieving adherence to conviction, was not the point. Aristotle's book 2 in *Rhetoric* set out psychological means to reach an audience. To catechise those formulae and their deployment, as Vico proposed, seems natural to Jung's chosen domain once he recognised it.

> It is noteworthy that in all languages the greater part of the expressions relating to inanimate things are formed by metaphor from the human body and its parts and from the human sense and passions. . . . Heaven or the sea smiles; the wind whistles; the waves murmur; a body groans under a great weight.
>
> (Vico 1948, 1730/44: para 405)

Experiential, sensory memory in a word or phrase alongside its presentation and context linger on in that word. Jung investigated distractions that disturbed the results he'd expected.

Freud has pointed out in his lecture cited earlier, that a game played by children at parties consisted of calling a word out at random, and someone adds a second word, and a compound word is formed. This game is part of childhood for many people. In fact, the German language is made up of compound words made up of added-on single words (Freud 1907: 103 in 'Psycho-analysis and the establishment of the facts in legal proceedings'). While I see no evidence that Jung read that paper before analysing results, the game may well have been in the German part of Switzerland where most of his subjects came from.

So Jung's questions elicited certain childhood exchanges in his tests that were extraneous in some respects, but absolutely on target in other (more important?) aspects. But the fact is that associations were brought on board uncontrollably negating the results – or did they? Were the criteria simply being judged in irrelevant ways?

He realised too that the words could have the visceral impact of a command: one word shouted out felt imperious. He noted that this oriented their response accordingly; further at times, the word is sensed as a verb, and response is as if to action.

Other forensic techniques: Presentation/fluency; Notatio – word choice and arrangement; Narratio – fable; Logos techniques – elenchus; Invention – the difficulties of categories and enthymeme

Presentation/fluency

Recalling Vico's opening paean to fluency, it is a common experience that when a speaker *sounds* spontaneous, we are disposed to trust her sincerity. Rhetoricians strive to reconstruct spontaneity by using fluency to gain adherence. The speed of an answer indicates lack of premeditation; it indicates authenticity or truth. In his experiments, Jung relied on response time to measure consistency and authenticity of meaning. But knowing the variables of human communication, he knew to be suspicious. When he subjected former or suspected culprits to lists of words, for example, he knew his subject's responses would no doubt have an element of calculation. It proved to be impossible to outmanoeuvre them.

Stern explored this suspicion in his work with his wife on children's lying. A fellow lecturer at Clark University where Jung made his first American trip, he had constructive points in his talk, such as: 'Spontaneous testimony is not as susceptible to error as is testimony in response to questioning' (Stern 1905: 28). But the difficulty, he continues, is that 'freely given reports' lack specificity, and make it difficult to test the accuracy of the testimony. He is also alert to the suggestibility of the questioning itself.

Jung's deductions about the rate of response lead him to see there must be deeper meanings buried in the psyche, but he was also suspicious from several similar points of view: 'the purely intra-psychic association cannot become the object of another's consciousness without being transformed into familiar symbolism of language' (Jung CW2 1904–7: para 21).

We cannot assume that we will comprehend the material. All that we can know is that the material may point to a consistency of theme. And this is similar to how we understand fluency. The most we can say about fluidity of expression is that it indicates at least a desire to be seen to be sincere; its actual referents need checking. The speaker or writer's external circumstances, motivations and intentions need investigation. Guilt and innocence are rhetorical decisions and, in his way, Jung both exploited and was subject to that anomaly.

Notatio; and arrangement

The word association experiments marked psychic truths indirectly. Jung is at great pains to make this point clear. Experimental techniques were designed to get at the individual's distinctive and negotiable truths, contained in the unconscious. Although Vico is not referring here to psychic experience, he can start our discussion:

> *'It has ever been and ever will be permitted to issue words stamped with mint mark every day'* [Horace's *Ars poetica*] . . . And indeed words are the marks of things. Hence *notatio* is a locus in topics that provides an argument for the power of the word itself. Words are like money by which man transacts the commerce of the spirit.
>
> (Vico's commentary on Horace *Ars Poetica* verses 46–72, cited in Crifò's notes, Vico 1984/1711–41: 227)

Words mark meanings, but in unexpected ways: 'it is a false assumption that psychic phenomenon corresponds to stimulus-words'. The nurse in the theft case study did not react to 'key' by imitating in action or in the response a releasing action with her hand (or at least Jung does not tell us she made this gesture). She reacts to the tension in the word for her and takes extra time to respond. She is perhaps recalling what it felt like when she took the hidden key. '[T]he stimulus word [is] merely the stimulus in the strict sense of the word and in the reaction merely a symptom of psychological processes the nature of which we cannot judge' (Jung CW2 1907–11: para 20, p. 10).

Jung describes his technique – here taken from the text of his lecture at Clark University: 'The Association Method' (1909) (reprinted in CW2): 'The words are carefully chosen and partially arranged in such a manner as to strike easily almost all complexes of practical occurrence . . .' (ibid.: para 942); 'the stimulus words are therefore merely a part of reality acting up on us; indeed, a person who shows disturbances to the stimulus words, is in a certain sense really but imperfectly adapted to reality' (ibid.: para 944).

Words have independent power in their semantic sense and also in their affective impact, i.e. how they are presented to us, in what order (arrangement), or in the tone.

Jung tries to accommodate this inherent power. He puts a potentially loaded word to his subject, and then follows it with two irrelevant words, knowing that the effect of a strong reaction will 'perseverate'. In other words, energies/distractions from the semantic meaning of a word will also leak over into reaction-responses immediately after the strong word is declared. He can 'sensitise the effect of a perseverating emotion' (ibid.: para 946, p. 55–6).

The prolongation of a disturbance, well on into reaction to the words following in sequence, reveals an underlying complex.

Then, he anticipates another objection to his method: 'with a suspected culprit as a test person, critical stimulus words are words which have a direct bearing upon the crime' – the entrapped participant is implicated already, since they are being questioned, and the context cannot be free of foregone conclusions about guilt even if the specifics are not clear.

The style of presentation is part of the argument itself. The responses are 'beyond the control of the will', he says. The *antimetabole* he uses to express the foreboding a criminal subject may have, works in its way to flaunt this power beyond semantics:

> If you submit you're done for and if you do not submit you are done for too, because one knows why you are unwilling to do so . . . if you put it to a criminal that he can refuse, but that is fatal because one knows why he refuses. If he gives in he hangs himself.
>
> (Ibid.: para 944)

The 'arrangement' of this statement makes the point too. 'If' you do one thing, something happens, and then 'if' another, usually something altogether different should happen – or that is what we are expecting to conclude from the sequence of these words.

But he undermines our expectations. Jung is pointing the finger at us all. He gives us pause to think – slows us down to ponder the implications – it could be us too; we are implicated alongside this person, a criminal, by what our words may reveal about us. Their words reveal who they are and their guilt. Jung uses the visceral impact of words and their organisation to target pre-linguistic communication.

Techniques of arrangement also include methods of emphasis that convey their own significance. Jung uses repetition, including *ploche* – i.e. repetition of a word or phrase for emphasis – to create an underlying sense that we are all implicated and he knows why:

> 'Can *you* do something with these words?' I said: 'little enough, but I can tell *you* something. Quite recently *you* have had worries about money, *you* have too little of it. *You* are afraid of dying of heart disease. *You* must have studied in France, where *you* had a love affair, and it is coming back to *your* mind, as often, when one has thoughts of dying, old sweet memories come back from the womb of time'. He said: 'How do *you* know?'
>
> (Ibid.: 57)

'You' is used again and again. It is finger-pointing, and the bringing-it-home-to-roost sense of revealing, unveiling, that Jung uses in the very presentation of his point, in his fable. This emphasis has effect on his listeners too.

Words are not only potent due to their arrangement, there is an element of fable and of embedded magical potency in words that Jung exploits. He had misgivings about it, however, not only because it was manipulative but because it seemed unscientific.

While it is the case, as writers such as Alan Goss in *The Rhetoric of Science* (1997) and Jeanne Fahnestock in *Figural Rhetoric in Science* (1999) demonstrate, there is much semantic and figural configuration in scientific writing, which is not only decorative but which is instrumental.

For example, as before, the expression 'if one thing' or 'if another' implies choice in a grammatical proposition. The response must be to choose, or to contradict the set-up of the proposition entirely. Buried metaphors of hierarchy or energy can drive an argument. These modes are not often acknowledged (or recognised) in scientific work. As Vico had proposed, *elocutio* has instrumental use; Jung confronts this directly in the association tests.

In lecture 2 at the Tavistock, Jung reveals his concern that his material will not be acknowledged as scientific. The tension leaks into his vocabulary and style. Despite his intention to be 'objective', his defensiveness emerges. But, perhaps irritating, although he capitalises on it, he complains that because of the disclosures that his association tests found, he has been called a 'sorcerer', or a magician.

When people challenge him about the validity of his tests, 'I ask them to bring some material of a person *they* know and *I* do not know and I show them how to read the story of that individual' (ibid.: 56). He deliberately suggests witchcraft or shamanism, asking for a piece of the target subject's own person: it could be a strand of hair or cloth. He reads secret emotions and reveals hidden truths in the material like a medicine man. He explores *narratio* in this respect to his own ends (which we will investigate further in discussion of his memoirs). He seems here to create fable opportunistically, exploiting embedded residues of enchantment.

He frames his stories to exploit fabulist elements. As he gives us the interpretation of an elderly man's words, he suddenly stops: 'Then things became rather startling to me' (ibid.: 57). He uncovers a secret hidden in the words: the old professor had an affair when he was a young lawyer in Paris. The truth had suddenly overcome him and now Jung moves into the passive voice as the English translation of the German indicates. He is the passive recipient of truth, overcome from outside. The grammatical form makes his point: incontrovertible fact has overtaken him, like a secret charm.

The showman's bravura extends to a flare for irony. Jung habitually uses reversal – uncovering the truth contradictory to what appears on the surface. It is the hidden truth, and buried in the psyche. And it's a fable that has its own autonomy and speaks in its own way.

Jung also brings common sense into his analyses. In recounting his story as a young man to Jung, an elderly man, a judge, he uses a French word that Jung construes as relating to the falling value of the currency. Jung works out instinctively and with the speed and accuracy of a courtroom prosecutor, that there had not been such a currency failure in Zurich, so it must have been in a foreign place. It is the residue of energies left over from an unrequited love. This is sheer but informed guess work.

Jung, the magician, uses grounded, real and shared sense of the world in making discoveries . . . adding credibility to his magical interpretations. He knows this style of assessment is problematic but common-sense deductions are designed to appeal to 'normal' common authority. He also dips his tone conspiratorially in the prose at times – as if he is talking conspiratorially to a familiar who shares values with him. Given the extreme value of storytelling to Jung, focusing on narration in its rhetorical sense here functions as a preamble to later material in this book on his memoirs, and a discussion of *Answer to Job*.

Narratio

Fables are used as scientific evidence and proof in Jung's work. Case studies are the standard, evidential form of psychological reporting. They are proffered as 'real' and the implication is that it is 'true' experience. True and neutral experience is what scientists accept, and what people of reason accept, as ample evidence for interpretation of facts. They are what make meaning of fact. By using fable, Jung uses reassuring phenomena, material that purports to be 'natural' unproblematic testimony. But he also indicates that ironically surface stories may mean something else, and he is a magician who can see below the surface.

In demonstration no. 3 above, Jung relishes the revelation of the 'truth'. Using the backdrop of the melodramatic *schema* of the innocent mother suffering the loss of her child, he drops the unexpected on us; he reveals he's uncovered that she'd murdered her child. He relies on our sense of inevitability by using the *topos* of reversal to underscore the surprise – her guilt is brought to light. 'You begin with relatively harmless words and you are likely to get an honest reply' (ibid.: 58).

Jung's underlying message is that it is by these means that his technique of questioning is so effective. Words have an independent power that he taps and they are set in contexts. Vico discerns this distinction:

> *Nota* is that from which an argument is obtained from the power of the word itself. The Greeks called this 'etymology,' that is, a word from a word, a true speech. But we, avoiding the novelty of a word not well suited, called this locus *notatio* because words are characters of things. And thus, Aristotle spoke of 'symbol' when we Latins mean *nota*.
>
> (Vico 1984/1711–41: 117)

From etymological sources too, we sense the meaning embedded in a word from its history – and its juxtaposition to other words revitalises its prelinguistic power. When we attempt to speak with these words, and arrange them to obtain maximum experiential (or visceral) power, we are targeting the 'universal audience' – the collectivity shared by the unconscious of all human beings.

Logos technique – elenchus

A familiar technique in adversarial legal rhetoric is the series of questions. Jung's word association experiments are also founded on this ancient *topos* of searching for knowledge. There is a compelling force field: questions require answers.

In his fable of meeting with an elderly man, discussed briefly above, Jung tells us how the gentleman unwittingly revealed he'd had an affair after Jung had resorted to questioning. It is assumed that Protagoras invented this technique of interrogation, although it is often called 'Socratic'. But there is a confusion here that is pertinent to understand Jung's use of question-and-answer technique.

Billing comments it is originally credited to Protagoras because of his perspectival approach to rhetoric. His skill was to anticipate his interlocutor's response in arguing both sides effectively. But Plato's Socratic dialogue is different than Protagoras's. Socrates was interested in making a specific point, often about ignorance or paradox. Protagoras performed endless perspective shifts. Socrates made his point, and stopped. Fahnestock (1998) also points out that when we attend to the audience's experience of *elenchus*, it is felt as methodical moves to refute a point, not to seek an answer. The popular online site *Silvia Rhetoricus* (http://silvia rhetoricus/rhetoric.byu.edu [accessed February 2012]) defines *elenchus* as 'syllogistic refutation – use of questions and answers to show untenability of opponent's position'.

Deriving from dialectical probing, as Socrates performs it, it is plain and directed enquiry which gives readers (or listeners) a sense of 'honing in' on the truth, while it goes about its ritual query and response. It both imitates pursuit, and functions as pursuit in getting at the truth. This could be the truth of a complex, of a criminal act, or of a 'true' diagnosis. By its drive, questions and answers move, we feel, inexorably, to get at a concealed truth. As the interrogation is pursued, we are lured along to intimated hidden truths. This drive operated in the word association test.

This same judge, the elderly man who'd challenged him about the association test, became a professor of criminology in a later 1935 version of Jung's tale. It adds to the irony, of course. We are meant to feel that even someone long-versed in assessing criminals' stories has been caught out by Jung.

Invention – the difficulties of categories and enthymeme

In order to conform to how results are presented in a scientific community, the word association tests had to be set out in a series of objective categories which organised data toward scientific conclusions. The search for these categories, and his failures in systematising them, is the over-riding 'story' of the word association tests.

Despite the difficulties, Jung arrived at the innovative 'complex' theory (you could say the 'failures' were a prompt). He arrived at the 'complex' theory, I'd suggest, by altering taxonomies in new ways – he redefined things.

> as long as we still know so little about the connection between psychic events, we must refrain from formulating the principles for a classification of external phenomena from inner psychic data. . . . The examination of associations is an indirect one and is susceptible to numerous sources of error caused by the great complexity of the process.
>
> (Jung CW2: para 11 and 13)

As every scientist does, in his word association test Jung went about organising his data and trying to draw conclusions. There are various means of organising data. They can be organised to suit your conclusions. Or the experimenter can identify what is similar in each fact that might help to determine a category and organise from there. But in the case of the results based on subjective personality, the similarities are hard to gauge, and the conclusions are unknown. Scientists engaged in this kind of research face these questions. In Jung's case he tries to re-categorise objective data into subjective groupings. And thereby the attempt to bring objective judgements to bear on subjective data is defeated.

In Jung's Tavistock lectures in 1935, he defends his experimental method, including how the data is organised, founded on scientifically accepted common assumptions and styles of argument about the substance of his data.

He attempts to find a self-evident rule that differentiates 'external' and 'internal' associations to organise his data. But the definition of the rule is the difficulty. Using the *topos* 'either . . . or' he hopes to list the qualities of each, but it doesn't work for long. Each individual has her own sense of inner and outer. He determines that what he comes to call the 'complex' drives the definition; and it is comprised of themes and associations particular to that individual. The method Jung and colleagues arrive at rests in correlating motivations by intuition. In fact, the cluster of feeling-toned associations became primary in his theories. He concludes that the problem has been that 'we are not classifying the associations but their symptoms' (Jung CW2: para 22) and while this may have important implications, it is not conducive to 'objective' scientific tabulation or to significant conclusions in themselves.

> [we try to] refrain from formulating the principles for a classification of external phenomenon for inner psychic data . . . the purely intra-psychic association cannot become the object of another's consciousness without being transformed into familiar symbolism of language.
>
> (Jung CW2: p. 11 'Association test of normal subjects')

His initial categorisations had fallen apart. 'Normal' people populate the first division. He tries, by elimination, to discover what pathology is. He assesses a subject as 'normal' and then applies their responses to the 'normal' column in his data. By accumulation of data, he hopes to arrive at a formula that will show its opposite, pathology. But he can never settle on this.

Jung and his colleagues try to find meanings by categorising in terms of gender, but they have mixed results. Nothing meaningful emerges. Then they focus on educational levels, assuming that this test may be more realistic among people who have verbal facility. Then, further, Jung isolated linguistic divisions: the 'predicate' type is a fruitful category, more than 'educated' or 'uneducated' man. Jung's data suggests the 'educated' and 'uneducated' women share this 'predicate' disposition while 'educated' men do not.

So while education and gender are not useful categories – there is too much overlap – something about *predication* is meaningful. He thought it revealed intellectual capacity related to abstraction. (But they had the added complication of the Swiss-Deutscher dialect, which most of his population spoke. Predication is implicated in a different linguistic scheme in that dialect. This skewed the categorisations.)

In the process, he and colleagues intuit that there are other organisational elements of communication they might use, and they search for it. They look deeper into personality, and new categories subdivide earlier groupings and refine them.

They decide to tabulate patterns of sensory reaction. As we learn from Vico's sensory topics (Vico 1948,1730/44: para 495–7), the senses generate language at source. This direction proves fruitful. It is not only that sensory responses are recognisable 'objective' phenomena but they are a cognitive bridge in creation of meaning. In the case of Jung's experimentation, there are certain sensory themes he defined which we have mentioned: hearing a one-word sound as a command; the rhythmic instinct of breathing, of the beating heart, etc. embedded in instinct and in cognition; acoustic reactions to words that associate them with fear, etc. In trying to assess and then tabulate how a word was experienced, outside its semantic presence, Jung was tackling its pre-linguistic dimension.

But even as they defined data by sensual association in greater particularity, the outlines of the categories blurred. The number of categories proliferated. Jung's focus on basic visceral pre-linguistic processes kept leading to other categories.

Final frustrations and inadequacies

In a long extract from the Word Association Test volume (CW2: p. 19), Jung struggles to assess responses using a mixture of intuition and calculation.

> Thus we see here a relationship analogous to that between 'coordination by external relationship' and 'coordination by internal

> relationship'. In concept *pencil/length: length* is essentially contained in the concept or is co-existent, while in *father/worry* the concept *worry* adds something new and therefore causes a shifting of concept. We should readily accept the grouping of judgement-reactions into analytic and synthetic if there were not a considerable practical difficulty: we have no way of knowing in the individual case whether the analytic predicate is an essential part of the concept or not.
>
> (Jung CW2: p. 11)

Billig characterises this frustration in *Arguing and Thinking* (1987): 'there is an inevitable intertwining of category (the impulse to generalise from characteristics) and particular (the individuation of collective data), which [keeps] demonstrates they are compensatory' (Billing 1987: 19). They keep slipping out of category.

If the rhetor, or as in this case, the experimenter, recognises the balancing nature of these impulses, she can remain open to other 'constellations' of tensions. In these essays in the first volumes of his collected works, Jung is drawing on the organisation of social categories, applying individual criteria (as a lawyer must do in the courtroom), and revealing new *topical* (or paradigmatic, or, otherwise 'archetypal') criteria. They don't remain distinct; they rely on each other to make boundaries and definition, balancing each other rather than remaining separate.

Jung increasingly focused on trying to categorise *how* people reacted rather than *what* they say. He compares the similarities in one family, and discovers that they have a leaning toward predicate responses. Another woman's associations are consistently visual, another acoustic – the words sound like each other, so the connection is 'external' – a distraction may cause unusual reactions, or slow them up – but there are no apparent external circumstances (like the ticking of a metronome, for example). It appears there is something internal that is distracting the subject's focus. Jung focuses himself on *attention*, which, he says, is of 'cardinal importance'.

And then there is the other great difficulty. He questions the significance of the criteria he has developed to assess the data.

Why does it matter that uneducated women react more to internal associations because they lack verbal facility? What is significant about educated women's strong reaction to external language-play? Other matters take on significance when he interprets them in a new way, however. He notes family resemblances in communication among a mother and two daughters. Not only are their associations similar, but their construction of talk is similar. There is a familial link that is crucial and that is at the bottom of their similar associations and communication patterns.

Something outside the direct data is impacting on this group of subjects. The missing premise is the family 'complex' perhaps in this instance (to put it crudely). It is a form of proof that is used in developing arguments in the first stage of the rhetorical process: *inventio* and the *enthymeme*; and here the rhetorical syllogism is relevant.

> shifts in attention only occur when the inner image to be expressed does not command the intensity of attention necessary to set going the appropriate speech mechanism. Deviations into by-ways only occur when what has to be enunciated is not intense enough i.e. it does not reach a sufficient degree of consciousness.
>
> (Jung CW2: para 470)

Jung starts thinking about the underlying impulses of rhetoric. He recognises that *how* he looks at his data impacts *what comprises* the data. Vico articulates the nature of this search in chapter 11 of *The Art of Rhetoric:*

> Invention is the devising of suitable arguments intended for persuasion. Moreover, an argument, derived from a source, is the reason which, when applied, confirms and explains the matter under consideration. This source from which the reason is derived is therefore called the 'locus'. The locus is the dwelling place where the argument resides.
>
> (Vico 1984/1711–41: 25)

Jung bridges his data among associations, and he finds common assumptions and understandings. The link in this family inflects his data, and the existence of such independently operating motivation, the 'complex', is his rhetorical discovery.

Jung's attempt to exploit logical, forensic means of expressing his new psychology was not adequate to his purpose, so he set about redefining 'objectivity' and its proofs. This period in his career generated his ideas about the 'complex' and included his recognition that subjective, figural rhetoric must be an acceptable and scientific style of expressing fact.

9

PATHÉ AND JUNG'S PASSIONATE AGONY OVER *ANSWER TO JOB*

Pathé is increasingly given attention as rhetorical strategy. *Pathé* is the technical equivalent of emotion and passion. Rhetorical uses of passion and emotion have powerful and immediate impact on motivation to act, and part of how we are in the world depends on human emotion. But as we know instinctively, passion needs to be carefully gauged in communication and in motivating action owing to its inherent irrationality and often personal/biased intent.

We experience strong emotion as having primordial, autonomous meaning as in Jung's system; we are passive in front of such powerful feeling; it is visited upon us. But (especially) when we witness it in others, we attribute arbitrary significance to it. A rhetor must take into account in what ways such emotion is reliable or unreliable. However, when emotion is used by design, it is not only the force of its presence that is assessed by the audience – its strength or weakness – but who it is that displays the emotion. These contribute to its being more or less persuasive. Sincerity and reputation undergo close scrutiny but within the parameters of intent of the emotion as it is perceived.

Another crucial question about persuasiveness: does the rhetor herself need to experience the emotion to convey it more effectively? Must you be angry to incite others to anger? This is an important issue in considering Jung's book on Job and we will address this farther on.

It is evident on a straightforward reading of Aristotle's *Rhetoric* that in his considerations, emotion or passion has visceral and unthinking force and must be deployed within carefully judged contexts to be persuasive. Similar to Jung's *Psychological Types* (chapter 8) in approach: they both catechize scenarios, in Jung's case showing types of psychological organisation, ways of processing. In Aristotle's book 6, he enumerates forms of anger – in revenge, private and public – shame, fear, indignation, etc. These scenarios form a comprehensive look at human emotion on universal rather than personal levels. (This choice of presentation is unlike most of Vico's scenarios serving as illustrations; his 'stories' are set out to show specific impact in deliberative or juridical rhetoric.) The permutations of intent and variety are a rolling-out of character interrelations without psychological/personal discussion. Implied by both these methods – Jung's and Aristotle's – is emphatically that all humans without number and in all diversity are included. (Reference to male gender nevertheless also implies females.)

Considerations of the strategy of 'emotional invention' would include these elements and suggests an overriding design of being, a mood of communication, i.e. its modal propositioning. (Conditional? Emphatic? Or assertive? Or fearful?) These represent a few instances of cognitive and ontological postures in this understanding of Aristotle's *Rhetoric* (see Agosta 2010).

'Emotional invention' would clearly be a recommendable start in arguing a point about human rights, for example. If you are a corrupt advocate showing great anger, your intent in hoping to gain freedom for a specific corporate boss might be suspect on various accounts. In discussing the nature of the psyche and its relation to a God figure that he posits is a given of human longing and projection, Jung might well engage in anger as a passional/inventional approach. Indeed, as we are exploring, Aristotle sets out numerous circumstances and variables about using passion or emotion in persuasive circumstances. To reiterate, 'emotional invention' is focused on seeing emotion in its own right as a 'propositional attitude', representing modes of cognition, suggesting action.

Heidegger's discussion of Aristotle's book 2 in *Rhetoric,* edited and published in English recently (2009) specifically celebrates the classical Greek's work on passions, claiming its participation in an ontological dimension, as Vico claimed for passional rhetoric in pedagogic and juridical domains.

In discussing Heidegger's claim, Scult (1999) suggests that: 'the rhetorical situations in which we find ourselves are defined by an emotional urgency that calls for a response'. In many ways, this is a paradigm of the rhetorical situation Bitzer set out in an essay I will apply again to Jung's *Memoirs, Dreams, Reflections* below. Exigency is created, contexts assessed in all their varieties, and an argument deployed.

Emotional rhetoric is how we cope in a world we are 'thrown into' at birth (referencing Heidegger's concept of 'throwness') when we find we call on the pre-ordained interpretations of a rhetorical pre-set of discourse with and among our fellows. Emotion brings concreteness to bear on rhetorical being-in-the-world. 'We are able to make our way in the world, day by day, minute by minute, because our world is already "there" for us, pre-packaged in the meaningfulness of everyday speech' (Scult 1999: 148). For Heidegger, Scult points out, 'everyday speech' is rhetoric.

Vico engages in similar ideas. He takes on the 'moving force' of rhetoric as Gross explains: its affective power induces change, to keep up with shifts in mood within the community. (Although he does not say so, Gross here seems to be referencing Heidegger's sense of our being 'thrown into' again, but more: a temporal world constantly moving forward; to match it or cope with it, we find ourselves meeting it with rhetorical capacity as a moving force, capturing this forward drive).

Gross cites a case Vico uses to show the particular (in this case, the personal) oscillating with the contexts of civic 'impersonal' law. Vico uses a metaphor to indict illegitimate children – they are 'monstrosities' who should be thrown into the river according to the Twelve Tablets of Roman law. He does not mean this in the personalised way we might think. But it is also not an analogy. He proposes to shift the underlying identity of these beings.

> In Vico's scheme, an illegitimate child would not become an official threat just because some were convinced of its monstrosity. Fear of this sort might still have disastrous consequences for a child, but those consequences need not be categorical; other illegitimate children would not necessarily have to die. However, when passion became institution . . . written into law as a way to protect patrilineal inheritance, illegitimate children were *moved in their very identity* [my emphasis]. What we have then is persuasion of a sort tangential to individuals and intentions . . . Vico applies rhetorical analysis to a historical moment in which a particular kind of rhetorical activity becomes institution – in this case a moment in which social passion is articulated in law.
>
> (Gross 2005: 13)

Historical rhetoric provides unique access to the history of emotion, in this case fear of a child's threat transforming the child into a monstrosity. I am contending here that Jung brings this form of definitional shift in the ontology of the human in his discussion of Job.

A kind of belief in transformation set on by anger, in the case of Jung's book on Job, moves a culture on to recognition of a new kind of God, implying definitionally, a mutable essence, based in the psyche of the human collectivity.

Affect/feeling and emotion are closely related in Aristotle's work, where such analytical considerations began. In Jung's work, he distinguishes feeling from emotion. Roughly speaking, feeling is closely aligned to taste, or judgement and attitude, while emotion is more instinctual, more an irruptive reaction and drive. There is some value in maintaining this distinction, and I will sometimes bring it up. In my view they are more on a continuum for Jung rather than strictly operating within different domains.

Jung displays emotion in much of his writing, as strategies of engagement or as sheer expressive ornamentation or as gestures of bravura, but I am proposing to focus on anger in the form of indignation for this investigation of Jung's book on Job because of its relevance. It was a book begun in anger and indignation, engaged with anger as a primal and universal force, and which was met with great anger.

In his book, Jung seeks to assuage his own anger and by empathetic means of techniques of identification, to assuage his readers' anger. Jung assumes that the audience, the readers, share Job's indignation at the pain Yahweh settles on him in the Biblical book. It is this singular injustice that undermines belief in Yahweh and Job seeks to grasp Yahweh's reasons. The pain Job experiences presents his friends with a dilemma; they witness his physical and moral pain but seek to justify Yahweh's reasons and purposes too; they do not sympathise much, then – a different reaction to Jung's audience in feeling compassion for human suffering. We might propose that only when they can feel pain on his terms will they join with him in a new community of recognising human being-in-the-world in a new way. A new agreement about ontology, how it is to be human, will come to be resolved in agreement about what Yahweh is. Jung seeks to persuade us, in what I am not alone in perceiving is a sermon, what this shift in recognising the nature of what the Lord means for humanity.

The sermon is the discursive form most appropriate to what underlies the intention of Jung's book. But he manoeuvres the sermon form, as I will explain about Negri's book, into a radical homiletics: Jung changes the ground plan. Sermons draw on common ground among rhetor and audience. Articulating the nature of that community is the primary job of the homily; re-gaining adherence to a set of precepts is necessary when there is a problem. Discussion about the Book of Job takes on the task of re-integrating a sense of the good God; and in this way Jung finds psychological means to achieve that. He is proselytising: re-setting ground as well as then seeking to regain adherence as if it were primarily simply recognition of what that ground is, despite our instinctive emotional reactions.

Persuading his readers is a parallel to Job's rhetorical dilemma. Pain is not something Yahweh experiences therefore using that physical and moral compunction advocated for use on judges in a courtroom won't be effective.

And, the other dilemma is that the judge is being judged. Jung's attempts to elicit shared pain are feasible between him and his audience, but the grounds of sharing the pain are not agreed. He expects his audience in the first instance to share the instinctive reaction of Job's friends: there must be something Job has done wrong. (There is something wrong with Jung's blasphemous analysis of an evil God.) Yahweh is who he is, and pain is a stage on the way to redemption after all. Jung's moral pain at the injustice of the Lord's visiting pain and destruction on humankind as on his patients is an appeal to recognising a different Lord than the Old Testament Lord who is the one Job seeks to persuade. The Lord forfeits his rightness and goodness in acts of these kinds which stand outside a relationship among compassionate humans, and what a Christian audience expects. The result is loss of faith, and Jung's effort is to persuade his readers that maintaining faith can be achieved if the nature of Yahweh (and related to that, an understanding of how we accommodate our longing and sureness about there being a Lord at all) is re-defined.

Yahweh in the Old Testament, Jung is proposing, is a Lord we accept knowing the Messiah is to come. Yahweh must be seen to be brought to awareness of what is to come. Yahweh is, after all, omniscient – and this dilemma is important in Jung's discussion. We know what Yahweh must be brought to recognise he also knows – there is a Messiah coming.

Antonio Negri proposes that pain is not a 'price to pay' for being human, 'but the destiny of man [*sic*] on the path to salvation' (Negri 2009: 95). What history provides humankind with – and in the Book of Job, Yahweh comes to remember that he 'knows' this – is a 'mediator, a messiah, a redeemer as element which would solve a drama otherwise excessive and insoluble' (ibid.: 96). Jung proposes that this perception of Yahweh and, indeed, his making his presence directly felt in a vision, i.e. his coming into Job's world, subjects Yahweh to human criteria. His immanence in Job's world brings Job into participation in divinity – and this is Jung's purpose in his sermon. The source of divinity is part of the makeup of humankind: the divine and humankind are intermingled in the world. The Christ figure is the incarnation of the divine, and participates in the world. Jung is showing us a link to the ontological presence of the divinity, not by moral means or by rational means but by means of analysis of the commonality of our outrage, our indignation and anger at evil visited unnecessarily in the world.

Historical theme of 'emotional invention' or emotional rhetoric

The chronological movement of perceiving emotion as irrational (and therefore useless in making judgements or engaging in persuasion) to its respected use as a method of persuasion engages themes that are pertinent to my investigation of Jung's writings. Before I enumerate the specific strategies he used in *Job* I want to set out a brief diversion on how emotion came to be so highly regarded in rhetoric (apart from the recognition by philosophers which I have been partially engaged in so far).

Aristotle's proposition about emotion is that it is a form of cognition with equal power to reason. According to Fortenbaugh, this was innovative. Pre-Aristotle, Fortenbaugh suggests, emotion was

> viewed as an affliction divorced from cognition . . . considered in opposition to reason and hostile to thoughtful judgment. It was Aristotle's contribution to offer a very different view of emotion, so that emotional appeal would no longer be viewed as an extra-rational enchantment. Once Aristotle focuses on the cognitive side of emotional responses and made clear that an emotion can be altered by argument, because beliefs can be altered in this way, it was possible to adopt a positive attitude towards emotional appeal.
>
> (Fortenbaugh 1975: 18)

While recognising emotion's power in persuasion, its unreliability is acknowledged. If a rhetor is too passionate, she cannot control communication. And, further, if passion is not aroused most adeptly in an audience, it swerves in unplanned directions. These are issues Jung is aware of in his essay as we will note.

In *Rhetoric* and *Poetics,* Aristotle concentrates for the most part on passion in relation to the audience; it is a force to be stimulated with intent ('emotional invention'). (Passions among the players onstage in the tragedy are more or less a reflection of this awareness.) Expiation of emotion, the *catharsis,* is the sign of a tragedy, and a means to transformation. Although commentators are not necessarily happy to merge Aristotle's analyses from both books, his comments in *Poetics* indicates the effectiveness of artistic (and political or juridical) fashioning within shared contexts, in this case, on stage.

> A tragedy . . . is the imitation of an action that is serious and also, as having magnitude, complete in itself; in language with pleasurable accessories, each kind brought in separately in the parts of the work; in a dramatic, not in a narrative form; with incidents arousing pity and fear, wherewith to accomplish its catharsis of such emotions.
>
> (Aristotle, *Poetics* 6.1)

Catharsis is the critical aim of representations in theatre among audiences. However, emotion in tragedy is a public expression associated to ruling families. Lower classes do not enact emotion on stage, nor did they appeal to emotion in the courtroom since their position was not an important element in public life. In Aristotle's discussion (and later in Cicero's) there is not the personal or psychological dimension that we expect. Emotion was not a democratic faculty. It is this 'impersonal' element we will find in Vico's story of his life that we will try to compare to the mythical fable of his life Jung creates – the relationship 'universal' and 'impersonal' figure in a discussion of emotion. You can say there is a hierarchy of emotion – rage was for kings, sentimental quibbles for the chorus or females in a play lower down the scale (Gill 1984).

Daniel M. Gross explains the background, talking about anger and arrives at a similar approach to Aristotle's work as Fortenbaugh does. In Aristotle's scheme, anger is a 'social passion provoked by perceived, unjustified slights, and it presupposes a public stage, where social status is always insecure' (Gross 2006: 15–16). He goes on to say that 'anger is constituted not in the biology nor even in the dignity that all humans are supposed to share equally, but rather in relationships of inequity' (ibid.: 16). Aristotle uses the *Iliad* to prove his point: a king is overcome by rage because he's suffered a 'concrete insult' despite belonging to a class of people entitled to be 'treated with respect by those inferior' (ibid.: 16; citing Aristotle, *Rhetoric* 1378b).

Aristotle is not referring entirely to the personal anger among characters who are familiar to us, i.e. figures who are psychologically informed; we expect feelings that are bursts of emotion, permeating a drama or narrative. Conrad expresses this in a brief aside in *Nostromo* when the idealistic mine owner discusses politics with his wife: 'they discussed it because the sentiment of love can enter into any subject and live ardently in remote phrases of talk' (Conrad 2007/1904: 47). But anger, as Gross puts it, is a 'psychosocial' event for Aristotle. In its instrumental use, Aristotle describes *pathé* as 'productive of an emotion in the audience' (Gill 1984: 155). What is emerging is recognition that all humans share emotion's cognitive function. This is how Aristotle justifies using passional tactics on an audience; it might well be effective in changing beliefs as acts of persuasion. Manipulating emotion at a universal level in such a way that it has impact on the personal level is a dramatist's skill, and is analogous to the aims of Jung's work in responding to primal anger in discussion of an archetypal work about the injustice of evil. But before I turn to Jung, I want to insert another element that impacted on Vico.

The idea of emotion as impulse contained in our biological nature began partly with his predecessor, Descartes, in *Les Passions* (1629). Vico attended to Descartes' work closely, changing from an ardent supporter to a critic, as discussed earlier. Undoubtedly there is a bodily element contributing to the passions, providing a way to measure strengths of conviction. Indeed Jung relied on this in his word association tests.

Descartes specifically locates passion in the pineal gland, and historically, this is where we might pinpoint contemporary ideas of 'psychophysiology' beginning, Gross claims (ibid.: 18). There is a related past set of ideas in Aristotle's character types who display emotional characteristics based on biological fluids or 'humours', i.e. physiology. The melancholic figure has an imbalance of bile that pushes him to act in demoralised, angry ways (see Aristotle, *Problems X)*. It is a similar, if still not completely formulated, idea of 'psychophysiology' which Gross finds in Descartes. Vico refers to this saturnine figure in his *Autobiography* as we will see, and Jung draws on its universal associations too in *Memories, Dreams, Reflections* (chapter 20) which we will explore further below.

Whether in sermons, taking Augustine's passionate sermons to the Donati as exemplary models in this field, or in the courtroom, the rhetor seeks to arouse physical reaction by means of passion, to motivate an audience to action. As Vico considers it, in the mid-eighteenth century, picking up from Cicero and Aristotle, *pathé* is a rhetorical, deliberative tactic – in other words, there is a future element, a moving forward element to action implicated. Vico sorts through types of effective passion (leaning on Aristotle's phrasing and divisions):

> the first and source of all the emotions is love by which we pursue the good; its first-born son is hate by which we avoid the evil. . . . The best of orators will be he who knows which men are ordinarily lead either to this or that emotion of arousal or calmness, towards whom, and for what reasons they are thus lead.

> . . . manners and emotions must be commingled with the issues themselves and, as blood throughout the body. They are thus diffused throughout the entire oration.
>
> (Vico 1984, 1711/41: 45)

Aristotle also talked about stylistics: '"emotional" style is typified by the presence of compound words and many epithets, and unusual words' (see Aristotle in *Rhetoric* 1408b); this is opposed to 'an "ethical style" which is related to external features of "character" – age, sex, nationality or degree of education . . . features that can be conspicuously brought out in vocabulary of phrasing', but have no emotion attached to them (Gill 1984: 155).

While an orator or writer does not want to appear uncontrollably possessed by emotion which serves to undermine audience confidence, the experience of such passion, as Longinus discusses it in *On the sublime,* can have numinous qualities. The rhetor most readily conveys the sheer intensity of passion to an audience while in its grip (ibid.: 161, 164). Longinus conceives of *pathos* as originating in the writer, empowering the writing. Writer, orator and audience are all 'taken out of themselves' by the emotional power of the sublime (the 'poetic frenzy' of Plato). Poets are inspired creators, transported out of themselves and capable of communicating this power.

My investigation in this section concerns how Jung particularly uses passion of anger in *Answer to Job.* Does anger drive his argument, does it only and also serve as distraction to offset controversy, and does it offer persuasive support in the realm of the mystical or religious, normally conceived of as irrational?

Jung and passion as transformative techne (bringing in association to poesis and fashioning)

Answer to Job originated in Jung's anger reflecting his patients' distresses, he tells us, and the traditional response to the problematic of evil it raises. Its conclusions and arguments aroused controversy for Jung but, after all, he had shaped it as an 'intervention' (an inducement to transformation) rather than commentary (as Negri calls his own discussion of the Book of Job in *The Labor of Job* (2009)), which aims at change with equally powerful polemical force. Many other writers, from Biblical commentators to Marx and Ernst Bloch saw radical possibilities in the text of the Book of Job too in ways related to Jung's approach. Jung's position situates him in a particular tradition of exegesis; in this case, what Boer calls 'radical homiletics'. My investigation includes consideration of his book as a sermon of sorts.

Jung attempted to design his argument to deflect from angry reception. He feared it would cloud reception of his radical point about what God and evil are. He focused on the Biblical theme of incommensurability of bodily pain, in humankind, to evil, here as divine power and judgement, and thereby its impact on what belief is. God visits physical pain on Job for no reason. Either Yahweh is not a benevolent God, or conceptions of God are wrong, or else this injustice is not commensurate with what a relationship between God and human can be or ever is. Further, Yahweh's own strategic coming-into presence to talk directly to Job is remarkable for reasons that Jung makes much of in his own way.

But despite a cautious approach, Jung drew anger and pain from Jewish and Christian theologians, and lost at least one close friend.

Mogenson proposes that Jung's insights replicated the trauma of our lives with God; did Jung replace or draw on himself this trauma? And he then suffered the consequences of such action: 'Jung . . . [the psychologist] must write without inhibition with the afflicted psyche's voice if he is "to give expression to the shattered emotion which the unvarnished spectacle of divine savagery and ruthlessness produces in us"' (Mogenson 2005: 11).

The rhetorical importance of emotion was of course very clear to Jung: prior to his work on the *Job* volume, in *Aion* (1951), Jung explored the significance of the intensity of conflicts of emotion situated within the individual psyche:

> The feeling-value is a very important criterion which psychology cannot do without, because it determines in large measure the role which the content will play in the psychic economy. That is to say, the affective value gives the measure of the intensity of an idea, and the intensity in its turn expresses that idea's energic tension, its effective potential.
>
> (Jung CW9ii 1951: para 53)

Nussbaum establishes a link from affective feeling-tone to a rhetorical perspective as well that expands on the philosophical implications of Jung's ideas which implicates the ontological dimension I am attempting to establish: 'Judgment, or some intentional activity very like judgment, is necessary for emotion; and emotions can be individuated only with reference to their characteristic cognitive/intentional content' (Nussbaum 2001: 261).

The oscillation between the personal and the universal dimensions have additional level in Jung's writings when he extends it to living in the world. Hillman explains how Jung makes this extension: 'the affect system is a predicting device which anticipates the future in terms of the past; it is a way of knowing, a way of adapting and a way of being in the world' (Hillman 1960: 188–90, citing Jung).

Perceiving emotion as a cognitive instrument, a 'propositional attitude', Hillman establishes it as a kind of 'reasoning' for Jung. Our emotional life, Hillman points out, is personal to us in a way intellectual life cannot be, 'in that it alone contains the motives from which our conduct springs' (ibid.: 191). But here the impersonal coordinates of rhetoric, the pre-ordained set of communications we live in accommodate both the universal and the personal and Jung instinctively brings this insight to bear in extending past Hillman's restrictions, as Nussbaum suggests about the breadth of affectivity.

Buber not only critiqued Jung's bathetic style of presentation, but complained he'd brought 'psychologisms' to bear on theologians' ground illegitimately. While I think Jung's approach has broader implications than Hillman thought it did, Dourley points out that Jung had perhaps a failure of confidence in the broader scope of emotional argument too:

> Given the irritable tone of Jung's reply there can be little doubt, in the face of Buber's evenness of writing and self-assurance, who won the debate in terms of literary style and suavity. Nor does the exchange leave much doubt that Jung, on his part, was deeply emotionally engaged in the issues at stake Buber had touched a tender spot, especially in one who denied a metaphysical implication in such conceptions as the archetypes and the nature of their influence on consciousness as the basis of humanity's religious instinct and so of the religions.
>
> (Dourley 1994: 125–45)

But although Jung did not offer a calm and reasoned response, as Buber did (although Buber wrote sarcastic and angry letters about Jung's work to friends), Jung felt unfairly undermined by Buber's reference to a piece of Gnostic writing Jung had published privately. It was personal. In letters and published response, he protests too much, defensively it appears, in disowning that earlier work (i.e. *VII Sermones ad Mortuum*).

Intellectual discussion in dispassionate ways is deemed the appropriate and effective mood: Buber's measured public responses were presented as self-evident conclusions. All rational people must invariably agree, even in this religious matter. Defensive, passionate response is deemed to be biased, and not at all self-evident.

But in the religious field where this dispute takes place we often expect heat and personal invective. Theology has its constraints as a discipline but Jung believes it is those constraints which are skewing religious practice and beliefs of real people. It is a matter of the psyche; and he claims his arguments stop short of 'psychologisms', i.e. the illegitimate attribution of personality traits to religious behaviour. For Buber theology claims to have extrinsic, even objective foundation to his theories of God-as-discrete-Other. The rhetoric of religious discussion is founded on accepting mystical notions as absolutes of reality, not subject to dispositions of belief or individual certitudes.

And, despite Jung's disclaimers, it appears Jung challenges the discipline's borders. He anticipated the affront theologians would feel and tried with middling success to waylay it, but without great conviction (and then took it hard when they disputed with him). His 'universal audience' was composed of the ordinary believer, people who lived by religion in their immediate lives with all the passion and subjectivity implied. Theologians could take it or leave it.

Bishop contends in his work on *Job*, that Jung's arguments propose parallels between individual and collective belief motifs founded in universal rhetoric: '*Answer to Job* is . . . so to speak, a phylogenetic version of the ontogenetic *Individuationasprozess*; a "diachronic" version throughout historical times – across many centuries and aeons – of the "synchronic" process traced with regard to the individual in Jung's other papers' (Bishop 1999: 160).

As Dourley has described elsewhere about other discussion of Jung's, the conjunction of the immanent and the transcendent – out into real external space – creates (in this case) 'real' universal anger symbolised in angry Yahweh contending and shaped by individual psychic anger that extends outward by virtue of its rhetoric, its establishment of emotional propositional contingency. The pressure to establish exigency impacts on the immanent contingency of the pressure of emotion. In establishing the exigency, affective power induces change, and shifts the collectivity. It is transformative.

In the case of *Answer to Job* emotion provides the bridge to create and to convey Jung's controversial, conceptual points about God and about God's relationship to evil.

> But, although our whole world of religious ideas consists of anthropomorphic images that could never stand up to rational criticism we should never forget that they are based on numinous archetypes, i.e. on an emotional foundation which is unassailable by reason.
>
> (Jung CW11 1958/1952: 556)

Surges of emotion or feeling are gradients for determining the psychic and transcendent truths; emotion is legitimate scientific and intellectual argument and thereby a cornerstone of Jung's work. Objective logical or dialectical argument is counterproductive in the field:

> feeling is challenged quite as much as my intellect. I cannot, therefore, write in a coolly objective manner, but must allow my emotional subjectivity to speak if I want to describe what I feel . . . I also speak in the name of many who have had similar experiences.
>
> (Ibid.: xviii)

In the Book of Job, Job's anger at Yahweh reflects an interplay between personal and communal that is a *topos* of the Old Testament. In Genesis 10:21–33, Abraham called the Lord to a reckoning about Sodom and Gomorrah: Abraham negotiates with the Lord who intends to destroy the city, he beats him down in numbers to be destroyed (quasi-logical since it looks objective and mathematical!) and, finally:

> Abraham spoke up: 'See how I am presuming to speak to my Lord, though I am but dust and ashes! What if there is one less than five innocent people? Will you destroy the whole city because of those four?' 'I will not destroy it,' he answered, 'if I find even one there.'
>
> (Genesis 10:21–33)

Job objects to the Lord's injustice and expresses profound disappointment. Who will be his advocate to represent Job to the Lord in this case when Yahweh is not judicious? Jung's offensive responses to these anomalies drive the emotional level of the argument.

Jung's emotive justifications: identifiable rhetorical devices

There are five passional devices we might trace which Jung applies in writing his book: sincerity; defensive justification of the emotive foundation of rational psychological discourse and argumentation; use of distinct vocabulary; the physicality of passion; and the tangibility of passion. These are intertwined with other discursive strategies like reversals, ironies of conceptions, etc. But I think this essay is predominately galvanized by passion.

First of all, as a persuasive ploy, a display of sincerity is disarming, a form of indirect persuasion: *insinuato*, an appeal to sympathy. If used too often or too noticeably, it puts an audience on guard. If the rhetor is not skilful, the message is: 'this argument is so shaky, I must appeal to you on other grounds to obtain adherence'. These other grounds are personal when emotion is appealed to. But, used well, as Perelman and Olbrechts-Tyteca point out,

> [a] choice of arguments that are 'irrelevant' to the discussion, but that closely affect the feelings of the speaker, will in the same way as the tone of his voice, serve as an indication of sincerity . . . the perfectly suited argument is not always the best.
>
> (1969: 456)

In other words, if an argument is all too pat, it feels like a rationalisation. A little break in the voice can indicate a sincerity that might overcome this sense of contrivance. What is more sincere than an outburst of passion? Referencing Aristotle's applications, Perelman and Olbrechts-Tyteca enumerate the ways a rhetor might make a display of emotion more persuasive: 'hesitation, hyperbaton or inversion in which an order brought about by emotion is substituted for natural order of the phrase. . . . The absence of conjunction and mixing of figures' are the most relevant expressive applications (ibid.: 456). They go on to point out that an ironic confession, pretended passion, is, after all, also a normal mechanism of persuasion, which 'as [if] by strengthening them they make the desires more likely to be fulfilled' (ibid.: 61).

In the midst of his discussion, Jung writes seemingly in a great rush, listing examples, mixing up grammatical form, etc. to convey his points. He goes on in the final sections, piling up more phrases and sentences that amount to lists pouring out of him as he relieves himself to get to the final conclusion.

And, secondly, to pick up a point Nussbaum makes, intertwined judgement and emotion actually determine the direction and methods of arguments. Emotion drives his enquiry into the psychological ramifications of injustice. He insists it is a scientific and not a theological enquiry. In fact, emotional and subjective enquiry would seem appropriate to his scientific/psychological theorising. Many commentators have claimed those scientific argumentations as well as any arguments claiming to be objective or empirical including fact-based scientific contention are founded on emotive propositions.

Alan Gross contends that assertions of value which are constitutive of emotion paradoxically make up what scientific claims are.

> [T]he general freedom of scientific prose from emotional appeal must be understood not as neutrality but as a deliberate abstinence: the assertion of a value. The objectivity of scientific prose is a carefully crafted rhetorical invention, a non-rational appeal to the authority of reason; scientific reports are the product of verbal choices designed to capitalize on the attractiveness of an enterprise that embodies a convenient myth, a myth in which, apparently, reason has subjugated the passions. But the disciplined denial of emotion in science is only a tribute to our passionate investment in its methods and goals.
>
> (Gross 1990: 15)

This leads to the third technique Jung instinctively uses which reveals passion; it is what Perelman and Olbrechts-Tyteca refer to as 'persuasive' vocabulary, when a designation of what appears to be a 'value judgment' is transmuted in the telling into a 'judgment of fact' (Perelman and Olbrechts-Tyteca 1964: 446). Definitions/vocabulary reflects intention. They cite an example of definitional shift in a discussion of Cicero that Vico undertakes in *Instituzioni oratorie*: Vico sets up an opposition between types of law. He defines a domain: 'There you have not written law, but natural law' (ibid.: 448, citing Vico in *Art of Rhetoric*: 150). Cicero's 'written law' is crafted by definitional shift into becoming its opposite, i.e. 'natural' law, laws that emerge from the ways of nature. Vico redefines 'written law': that it is 'natural' law is made to be the result of artifice.

To justify a definition, 'appeal is sometimes made to scientific or popular etymology' (ibid.: 448) in order to highlight its category status. Here is a brief example from the opening section of Jung's essay in which he leans hard on a definition to lay the groundwork for his position: 'The possibility of this development lies, one must suppose, in man's "godlikeness", which one should certainly not look for in human morphology. Yahweh himself had guarded against this error by expressly forbidding the making of images' (Jung 1964: 449).

'Godlikeness' is under semantic stress here. Its definition is transmuted from something 'objective' and alien to human ken into human potential. The sarcasm helps make the transition to new meaning. It highlights an alternative: i.e. that there is a god-like quality that is part of human makeup despite Yahweh's conjectures and prohibitions. Definitional ambivalence indicates and exploits core passions. And of course Jung often called on scientific words, redefining them, to borrow their prestige from the public sphere.

Generally underlying Jung's arguments and judgements of Yahweh in *Answer to Job* is the anger at hypocrisy, and anger at Yahweh's renunciation of obligations. (Auerbach in *Mimesis* sees a transformation of style from the expository, axiomatic narrative of myths in Homer's *Iliad*, to personal, intimate relations with a God we track emotionally in the Old Testament – meanings become symbolic exchanges, rather than concrete, specific and timeless interchange. Yahweh engages in direct exchange with humans in the Book of Job, unlike the distant communications with Jove or Apollo in Homer's stories.) The underlying category of genre, you might say, has shifted from impersonal to personal already in the move from consideration of Homer's works to the Bible – and as we will note later in Jung's discussions, this is a moving forward in time that is pertinent to definitional categories.

And, next, in Jung's psychological schema, judgement is visceral, and expressed in the feeling function. As in Vico's system cognition evolves from sensory categories: 'the human mind is naturally inclined by the senses to see itself externally in the body and the etymology is universal; words are carried over from bodies and passions' (Vico 1948. 1730/44: para 78).

The body is the site of emotion, and the crucial location for effective argument. From the time of Aristotle the physical element was a sign of communicative success as a criterion of engagement, however unreliable it proved to be in the long term.

Related to this is the last point: it is essential to be tangible. Hillman points out that concrete terms rather than abstract ones make best long-term impact. When abstractions are used, they are laden with personal associations outside the control of the rhetor. 'Patriotism' evokes your own home, your family, etc. Since it does not mean anything specific, its blandness makes no impact, unless a rhetor indicates the symbolic tangibles of the community, for example a country's flag, or mascot. To demonstrate how a symbol evolves, Hillman cites Jung's example of what a knife means to an individual who has attached a fearful memory to it. 'The image of the knife thus becomes a symbol', and forever after its power to arouse fear will make the heart beat faster, the blood run cold, etc. 'Emotion is an adaptive function, and a way of being in the world', Hillman continues (1960: 173) and this emotional extra acts rhetorically to induce reaction.

Jung and his patients make suppositions based on emotional judgements about a reality that instantiates the 'facticity' of that reality. The anger is a reaction to the abuse of a power that is supposed to be benevolent. As Bishop discusses, there is a projection of cultural ethic onto a being created subjectively (projected) into a purportedly extrinsic world. The anger is about a transformation in cultural mores and in personal expectation. Extended 'objective' reality, as Gross goes on to argue, is a 'complex', a cluster of emotional attachments to a passional notion of meaning (Gross 1990).

Jung's book on Job opens by inviting us to sympathise with personal anger which amounts to a plea to sustain Jung's definitions, his perspective as he tracks the cultural evolution of a God who is outmoded and who is lethal. He looks to the future from the perspective of the outmoded Old Testament, past Christ, to the Holy Spirit.

Emotional reaction is traditionally part of religious, Biblical material. Jung uses passion to move from one mode of investigation to another: from taking a text literally to its being an inducement to transform by absorbing his radical interpretation.

Jung's conclusion is that the symbol of the Self is a kind of Christ whose image welds together the symbolic and the irrational to make a numinous, transforming image. Bishop explains that the Christ symbol, as set out by Jung, is a combination of all the elements of sympathy, personalisation and transformation that constitute the demarcation (or 'incarnation', a God becoming man). Jung redefines what humanity is in this essay. To extend this point, I propose that Jung uses passion in *Answer to Job* to bring about transformation in his readers by bringing new meaning to Job's dilemma, and to demonstrate the place of passion in propelling history forward. Jung exploits the passion that the Christ image attracts to do this. But Jung's appeal is not unreasonable.

Jung's argument in *Answer to Job*

The argument of *Answer to Job* is a movement through Jungian psychic principle and its impact on cultural/theological support systems. Job functions individually but also as a mythic figure, representing the individual, but a collective symbol at the same time.

The book opens with a discussion of *privatum bonum* and its vicissitudes – how it was arrived at and its inadequacies. Jung mounts his discussion from a disarming position of transparent subjectivity. The expression of anger is used as a forced resignation of responsibility, an excuse in anticipation for causing serious offence. This posture seeks adherence to the sincere Jung, whose re-reading of the Bible we are asked to attend to with our hearts open.

Anger is the driving force. Yahweh's anger, incited by Job's complaints, alters the relationship not only between the Lord and Job, but the Lord and humanity as placed in theological/cultural history. As Bishop traces in his book, a new form of God will emerge, omniscient but contained by the constraints of time, and the judgements of human consciousness. Jung raises this issue early on. The emergence of this collective God (already pre-figured, so Godhood is a 'discovery' rather than an evolution) is aligned to processes of individuation in Bishop's reading.

After the opening *insinuato* of the preface, and in the opening paragraphs of part 1, Jung discusses the elements of evil in Yahweh, and the relationship the Lord has with Job. The problem is the nature of this Lord/God who demands reverence but who accepts Satan's evil challenge to test a good man. These matters cause distress but this reaction is mainly due to standard, limited theological comprehension of what God is.

To investigate this dilemma, and to set it in context, Jung looks at the foundational backdrop to the Book of Job; he calls upon the Greek books of Wisdom, and the presence of Sophia, the feminine principle, who is more powerful in her essence than the brutal force Yahweh wields. Jung is not referring to the aesthetics of the Book of Job; instead he refers to the embedded ethos of those early books. Despite Christianity's excision of those elements that conflict with the notion of the perfection of the Lord, the 'wisdom' remains.

Pre-fall, there was a feminine principle in play in the mythopoetic world of that time. But then, in the Bible, the story/fable focuses on Adam, Cain and Abel, and the tale of the serpent's corruption of Eve. The argument is that man is perfection and woman, completion. Egyptian times disclosed a Lord with no Eros, and no connectedness to humankind. The perfection of the Christ figure is prefigured; he is a creature who exists in eternity, along side with the incarnation to come. A pre-existing pattern (an archetype?) is disclosed to be in place if anything is to happen at all. The enshrined energies and potential will manifest in time.

Earlier acts of creation are reviewed then in Jung's argument: what happened to Satan/Lucifer; future apocalyptic events that are reinstated and the time to come after Christ; his death over against incarnation as a new yet predetermined God is contemplated; and the presence of the mercurial Paraclete on earth in his place. Yahweh's unconscious is not as wily as Satan's, we are told, and human consciousness of salvation, meant to free man from the fear of God is rather a one-sided conception of salvation. As Christianity defined salvation, it is not adequate to counter the anxiety of a God who accommodates evil. The theological argument of *summum bonum* is seen to be inadequate in Jung's discussion. Salvation is not a release from the fear of God and yet it was promised to be such a release. Rather, 'salvation' is an insight into the processes of the Lord's interactions with the fluctuations of the human psyche. This affords a resolution, Jung tells us.

Yahweh proves to be evil for Job, ineluctably foisting ills and disaster on this good man. The easement of pain Jung points to is a process of the recognition of Yahweh's unconscious longing for human capacities of judgement and conscience. The human recognition of Yahweh's intent embodies potentiality for change. The psyche's image of the Lord is revealed to be of a limited creature. The anguish of suppressed anger brings about seismic change, but it is a focus on all aspects of the Lord that is the result.

The Lord is to be both feared *and* loved, we learn from Jung's discussion, and Ezekiel's vision (the fourth friend) is invoked to look forward to a vision of a higher man to come. Mogenson puts that in Jung's account, 'the wrath of God and the kindness of God are complexly interwoven' (Mogenson 2005: 28).

A disturbance in the unconscious is located, and the ascendancy of the Virgin Mary, the feminine principle, is confirmed, raised into place on earth by the Catholic church, as it is in heaven, to form a quaternity raised up from the trinity. It is an acceptance of the 'unity of antinomies' that Jung arrives at, and its expression is in paradox. Jung proposes an integration of evil into the God concept; the Christ figure is to be superseded by the Paraclete. Anger is potentially resolved in ironic resignation to paradox.

Extremities of passion

After the irresolution of uncontrolled passion, the other extremity of passional argument is polemic. Its meaning (taken from the OED) refers to 'controversial argument or discussion', from the Greek *polemikos* 'warlike, belligerent', from *polemos* 'war'.

Jung's passional appeal draws his audience into agreement with his contentious message of a more whole God, primarily by identification. Thus, he draws his audience of general humanity into the psychic circle of what God paradoxically is, a 'union of antinomies'. Passion moves the world, and it moves Yahweh onto a new god, Christ and then on to the Paraclete. His primary, targeted audience is not the professional theologians or other psychologists, in fact, but his patients, general humanity.

> I hope to act as a voice for many who feel the same way as I do. . . . Even if we know by hearsay about the suffering and discord in the Deity, they are so unconscious and hence so ineffectual morally, that they arouse no human sympathy or understanding. Instead, they give rise to an equally ill considered outburst of affect, and a smoldering resentment that may be compared to a slowly healing wound. And just as there is a secret tie between the wound and the weapon, so the affect corresponds to the violence of the deed that caused it.
>
> (Jung CW11 1971: 526)

When the Lord is brought to talk to Job to answer the dilemmas of human existence, we are presented with an insight into a mystical vision that inculcates absolute certainty and truth. It resolves itself for Job in commitment to a Lord he perceives back in his rightful posture, vindicating Job's human activity in consorting faithfully with the god-figure he'd believed.

10

ETHOS, THE RHETORIC OF *MEMORIES, DREAMS, REFLECTIONS* AND PERJURIES OF SELF-PRESENTATIONS

With two-part preamble

My seeking links between Vico and Jung continues in Joyce's fictional enquiries begun in *Finnegans Wake.* By the time he came to write it, Joyce had accomplished a thorough reading of both Jung and Vico. Both figures make appearances in his novel as eponymous qualifiers; Joyce devised adjectives, adverbs and verbs using their names. Joyce clearly picked up Vico's ideas of *poesis* and the *corsi recorsi* which he refers to, and which he uses as guideline to structure the fictional text.

Following demonstration of striking similarities among Joyce, Vico and Jung's works of self-presentation, I will focus more closely on Jung's *Memories, Dreams, Reflections.* I propose to demonstrate its use of *ethos* as a means of persuasion using the classic breakdown of a rhetorical space proffered by Bitzer: its exigency, constraints and audience, to flesh out another aspect of Jung's *techné.* In his way, Jung's use of 'enactment' is distinct in following the tradition of fictional 'true' memoir. His presentation of the events of his life, as he deems them to be, is not only a performative and instrumental element seeking change in his readers (which Susan Rowland explores in her essay on *MDR* in *Jung as Writer* (2005), but it also enacts its precepts of individuation. I am claiming it achieves in its setting forth the kind of mythopoetic fable Jung aims to create with his memoir.

Part 1 Setting up the background for comparisons

Historians of law and philosophy know Vico in direct line with their disciplines, but students of literature may well first find Vico when reading Joyce's work. As I mention earlier, it is just this route I took in coming to read Vico's colossal work *The New Science* and discovered the idea of the correlation of historical moment to rhetorical style, heroic and imaginative figures, axioms of re-cyclical nature of history, etc.

Comparing the openings of Joyce's novel *Portrait of the Artist as a Young Man* (hereinafter *Portrait*) and Vico's earlier book, his autobiography (hereinafter *Vita*), 'the story of himself', as he calls it, is a useful place for me to start an examination of Jung's *Memoirs, Dreams, Reflections* (hereinafter *MDR*).

Jung and Joyce seemed to feel they'd failed each other. Joyce refers to Jung in his novel in pejorative ways, but he also enlisted help with his schizophrenic daughter. Jung could not help her. And Jung dismissed Joyce's *Ulysses*, saying it read the same way going forward as going backward, which drew Joyce's contempt.

But Jung understood very well the alienation he thought Joyce was depicting, and found the writer's volume displayed demoralisation and associated decadent impulse. The urge to reconcile fragmented parts of reality is shared by both, and drives their prose. They share the discursive poetic elements that often occur in autobiography and memoir too and, such is the nature of memoir that we are not surprised fictional values apply.

Joyce absorbed Vico's ideas into his fiction as stylistic 'law' along with a poetic sense of history. Narrative impulse in all three of these writers is guided by topical logic and association which are appropriate to their intentions. The guidelines provided by rhetorical investigation bring Vico, Joyce and Jung together. The psychologist's system and theories are manifest in an inclination to expression that is close to imaginative sources. Vico's recommendations of poetic logic and Joyce's related perception of how the world works inform our look at Jungian psychology in many ways, consciously and unconsciously.

Representations of childhood

MDR is a problematic memoir for many reasons. It is a memoir that does not include names or dates, and far from being a wholly personal document, it is collaborative. This last trait is not unusual in Jung's approach. Jung is sensitive to anticipated reaction. He often attempts to forestall certain reactions; in this case I suspect, he forestalls his family objections by incorporating a kind of 'censor' in the form of a collaborator. Aniela Jaffé's full participation is set out for all to see on the title page of *MDR*.

Following the first three chapters about childhood, *MDR* is non-sequential, customised rather to its writers' thematic points rather than to the ordinary chronological progression of memoir. Also, when we check it over against what we know are the facts in Jung's public and private life, we realise that a great deal has been left out.

The reasons I am proposing that this is so is that as with other notable and equivocal autobiographies, such as Augustine's *Confessions* (which instigated the genre in many ways and which swerved into polemics) and Vico's *Vita*, *MDR* is focused on *enacting* its agenda of individuation – inspiring recognition of individuation process in its readers (as a way to transformation) and showing it.

'Enactment' in the case of Joyce suits his theme of the appreciation of evolving consciousness of the artist from birth. Jung's attentions to using enactment are deeper, and are without demurral (or transparency) derived from fictional precepts. The *ethos* of *MDR* is reflected in its shape and intent. And while it is not unusual in respect of autobiography or memoir that it includes fictional elements, it is not what we expect when we read contemporary narratives of a historical person. We expect an accounting of ups and downs – praise and blame, real life contextualizing, the bulwark of *ethotic* prose. We expect accounting from this public figure, after all, participant in controversial world events. In only small ways do we get it.

I propose first to explore the fictional values of Joyce's representation of childhood alongside Jung's memoir to build the case; and to demonstrate that a deep-seated commitment to 'enactment' as rhetorical device to persuade is operating in both.

James Joyce's depiction of childhood

In the opening chapter of Joyce's *Portrait of the Artist as a Young Man,* Joyce replicates the language of children. His creative notion of a fictional biography of an artist demanded that the opening *exemplify* or 'show forth' the interior of the early days of the artist. It begins with the nonsense talk of children but it is decipherable:

> Once upon a time and a very good time it was there was a moocow coming down along the road and this moocow that was coming down along the road met a nicens little boy named baby tuckoo.
>
> His father told him that story: his father looked at him through a glass: he had a hairy face.
>
> He was baby tuckoo. The moocow came down the road where Betty Byrne lived: she sold lemon platt.
>
> O, the wild rose blossoms
> On the little green place.
>
> He sang that song. That was his song.
>
> O, the green wothe botheth.
>
> When you wet the bed first it is warm then it gets cold. His mother put on the oilsheet. That had the queer smell.
>
> His mother had a nicer smell than his father. She played on the piano the sailor's hornpipe for him to dance. He danced:
>
> Tralala lala. . . . . .
>
> Uncle Charles and Dante clapped. They were older than his father and mother but uncle Charles was older than Dante.

(This is a long selection for better comparison to *MDR*.)

In this opening sequence of *Portrait,* what we read is set out as if it were a fairy tale; the baby experiences smells, sees light and feels warm and cold damp (from his own excretions); he hears songs and rhythmic clapping, among other sensual experiences. He breathes a simple 'tune' in strophes.

And, in the sequence immediately following this one, in *Portrait,* the child learns about right and wrong: he is told to apologise for his behaviour. In miniature, his sensibility opens up, recognises its borders over against the external sensibilities of his uncle, friend and mother; this is incipient identity and abstraction about personality, morality, the child's own. The child is beginning to separate out from his associations immersed in the world around him. The philosophical gloss on this that Vico might make we explore later on, because he has similar themes.

In *MDR* we find a similar sense of how the psyche of a young child unfolds through its senses, and moves toward 'individuation' in Jung's terms, or particularisation, as Jung intends to demonstrate. The abstraction evolving from unconsciousness into rational consciousness via a move from poetry to prose and philosophy is a phase Vico expertly analyses in terms of phylogeny. But it is present in Jung's sequence about an individual here. The poetics of the recounting enacts how the child's psyche performs.

Jung's childhood representations in MDR

MDR's opening chapter is a comparable sequence of sensual, pre-logical and pre-linguistic association, even if it is not a representation that re-enacts a child's idiom. (Joyce presents his work as fiction, after all; but as I will explore below, there is a strong fabulist element in Jung's purported set of real-life memoirs.)

> It was a fine, warm summer day, the sky blue, and golden sunlight darting through green leaves. The hood of the pram has been left up. I have just awakened to the glorious beauty of the day, and have a sense of indescribable well-being. I see the sun glittering through the leaves and blossoms of the bushes. Everything is wholly wonderful, colourful, and splendid.
>
> (Jung 1961: 6)

In the sequence following this one, Jung describes the smell and taste of drinking warm milk; he moves on to the sight of the lake beckoning him away from home to other children's places. Jung describes by chronological, internal association, the awakening of the senses in his self as a child. This individual, Jung, like other humans, slowly emerges into consciousness from the earliest immersion in the surroundings of touch, light, sound, smell and, finally, thought. The associations are recounted as spiralling steps away from the visceral, inarticulate self to the logical, verbal self, and on to the consequent division of the self at the stage of abstraction. The effort and the natural cycle are toward reintegration on another level; the process is the impetus. Vico refers to another agenda in unfolding of the mind aligned to natural development of the student.

Vico's childhood description in his story of himself

In Vico's schema, the movement is alike in conceptual terms about how the mind operates. The child's imaginative mind moves away from authenticity of significance located in the external marking the child's appearance to itself. The adult person, Vico, merges with the fable of his personality; he grows into it. A person develops into a particular psycho-biological type but is also influenced by contingency (which is to say by those things that happen unexpectedly). And, then, on the next level, Vico widens the progression out from the individual to the historical laws of humankind, from the mythic and poetic lives of earliest humans, to the heroic and then to the ironic and alienated human life of his present day, straining to re-grasp its roots. This progression is replicated, he says, in each individual.

Vico tells us that he was born in a propitious year. In fact, we learn, it is not the actual year of his birth; he alters it to incorporate the number 7 which we are told by Verene was significant for Vico who'd actually been born two years earlier. In this way, Vico attains rebirth, in heroic alignment with the imaginary creature of ideal eternal history, Saturn, by means of a catastrophic incident. He is transformed (or else he comes into what he was meant to be – it's problematic) in terms of this heroic imaginal figure into a person characterised in several ways; he is sagacious, intellectual, philosophical and melancholic. He'd fallen off a ladder onto his head and cracked it as a young boy. Doctors thought he'd either become an imbecile or a genius, he was told by his mother. No fool, but as a result, he became a cranky genius. He enters the ranks of heroic figures in a barbaric world. More of this later.

Joyce dramatises the interiors of children and shows their inchoate imaginings, inarticulate and, yet, paradoxically capable of instantiating significance very like the early human race Vico imagines. Jung would not disagree with this analysis of a pre-mythopoetic world. Chaos, like the underworld of the mothers he talks about in referring to Goethe's *Faust,* is a creative place where worlds and meanings are born. And, further, for Vico and Jung, humans are born in time symbolically manifesting exemplary character-figures, especially extraordinary humans.

In his *Vita* Vico does not replicate a childish style, but he exemplifies his poetical key in a chronology of intellectual development. Verene explains the course of Vico's intellectual analysis in reference to the *Vita*'s agenda. The prose discourse aligns itself to the axiomatic development of the mind. Children functioned in their imaginations first (like primitives): he sets this out in

The New Science in a series of axioms. He presents it from this point of view as a philosopher indirectly and objectively might do, in the *Vita.* Here are the axioms are set out in *The New Science* (hereinafter *NS*).

> Axiom XLVIII: the nature of children is such that by the ideas and names associated with the first men, women and things they have known, they afterwards apprehend and name all the men, women and things which have any resemblance or relation to the first . . . children . . . not being able to form intelligible class-concepts of things had a natural need to create poetic characters, that is imaginative class-concepts or universals, by reducing them as to certain models or ideal portraits all the particular species which resembled them.
>
> (Vico 1948, 1730/44: para 206)

Children express themselves in nouns and leave verbs to be inferred. For, as he explains later in *The New Science* (1948, 1730/44: para 453), 'nouns awaken ideas which leave firm traces; particles, signifying modifications, do the same; but verbs signify motions, which involve the past and future, which are measured from the indivisible present, which even philosophers find very hard to understand'.

The autobiographical form was very new to Vico, and he referred to Augustine's *Confessions* while working it out. Autobiographies/biographies were also sources of popular entertainment which absorbed the rhetorical community: mores in form of common places, maxims, fable and other generic forms of popular culture (song, puppet shows). When I talk below specifically about Jung's memoir, I will examine how that deep aspect of the form took its place in his work. Vico's *Vita* operates as a guide to pedagogic principles (perhaps like Rousseau's *Confessions* or *Emile* written almost contemporaneously) based on demonstrating an intellectual life in the midst of 'real' event.

Vico's *Vita* came about in response to a commission from an aristocrat who asked for an intellectual self-portrait for pedagogic purposes. (In fact, Vico was the only one of the three asked who completed it.) In the *Vita* Vico's purpose is to show how character is integrally involved through necessity to communicate, in the poetics of an era, and in the 'eternal history' in which each individual exemplifies the development of all humans.

Talking in the third person, he not only assumes the mantle of a philosopher, but he takes on the 'impersonal' or neutral stance that he finds convincing from Plato's Socratic dialogues. Dialectical exchanges move in on the interlocutor's 'personal' prejudice and confusions in an impersonal way; they are an autonomous force field. He seeks distance in order to elucidate the universal human elements in the growth of the boy's intellect in Naples; Vico's own.

Attention to a universal curriculum corresponding to development of the student underlies the structure: he famously proclaims he learned this by personal experience; he is an auto-didact because of that fall in his father's bookstore. He'd had to stay home.

Learning by himself allowed him freedom to pursue his education in a natural way. In the child's mind stories and fables are what is first essential to learning (earlier rhetoricians, principally Quintilian, set this out in their handbooks). He gathers up the maxims of common sense in his community, and instinctively he eventually notices similarities which lead to the cognitive movement of abstraction. The student, Vico, is integrated into the conventions of his community to become a civic individual. He assesses a society constructed by recognition of similarities rather than an aggregation of differences which would result from an 'average' society of 'conceitful' individuals.

These pedants note superfluous oddities which leads them to decadence and excess. Vico's criticisms of prevailing Cartesian and Port Royal ways had a mix of patriotism, but he felt it was disastrous for young students, since it narrowed their purview. Suarez's handbook on rhetoric was taught in school and Vico rebelled against it despite excelling in his lessons. His favourite authors instead were Plato, Lucretius and Grotius.

In the *Vita,* he describes coming to write his philosophical works, occasional speeches for the state as movements into a more mature stage. Although Vico's observations in *The New Science* and elsewhere were objectively reasoned, he would claim later (he wrote four drafts, editing them down each time to accommodate a diminishing budget), his ironic stance gave him a 'neutral' way to talk of the laws. Plausibility and certitude were the goals. The hypocrisy of rulers, of the rich in instances of legal suits, of civil structures that defied natural human character: these were among many events he discussed in texts on law. He was very enthusiastic about teaching the young, and insisted on poetry being used to feed the imagination in the first years. It is where they lived, how and where they first perceived the world.

As a student he read the banned poet Lucretius, for example, and learned the first ideas about giants as concrete reality, early creatures derived from natural law and history without reference to a prime causer found in an overseeing god. (Hence Lucretius' works being placed on Roman Catholic Church Index.)

In his *Vita* Vico explores the ways that etymology generates meanings in reference to his book on the ancient wisdom of the Italians; the history of a word includes a residue of associations from its origins. Setting out to revitalise these ancient words used in the present brings our primordial capacities as creators alive. This concept amounts to an alteration in what history is. It is not that elements of event or of his personality or others' traits cause things to happen. Events are discovered to come into their own autonomously. Events work in a sequence to be discovered by argumentative intent.

Words, concepts and meanings are traced back to a repository of interconnected images buried in the 'collective unconscious' (to use Jung's phrase) within the individual. Predispositions to action among these allusions amount to negotiated solutions to living in the world as it is given to us. (In some ways, I'd claim, and what I am here extrapolating from Vico's work is a related, early formulation of Jung's ideas of synchronicity.) Finding similarities, using *topics* and etymology, elicits a recurrence in a present contingent movement of eternal time. The discourse harbours our unfolding future.

Jung's *MDR* presents his project of memoir-writing as problematic; like we all do, he experiences a compelling drive to tease out the meaning of himself. His life is a fable representing a particular trajectory.

> The meaning of my existence is that life has addressed a question to me. Or, conversely, I myself am a question which is addressed to the world, and I must communicate my answer, for otherwise I am dependent upon the world's answer.
>
> (Jung 1989/1961: 294)

'Reality' is the given. In Jungian terms, reality is a 'complex'. This equivocal perception of the real as it is given to us makes an enquiry into its nature indeed a rhetorical project. The 'given' presents itself as an anomaly. The 'given', the 'real', imply meanings-to-be-discovered rather than givens of incontrovertible significance.

Einstein wrote to a friend: 'we expect that the real is not given to us, but is put to us by way of a riddle', and this attitude has been a precept of the new physics which intrigued Jung. It is here where Jung's enquiries meet with the new science which recognises that science too is a negotiated agreement within a community.

The elements of Bitzer's formula of exigency functions in Jung's text in specific ways justifying his use of enactment – to disguise, to divert – in a way close to what I'd claim is Vico's *vera narrativa*. It is a form of self-justification; my prose style replicates my wholly fabulist self-presentation, Jung says to us. Jung's Gnostic book, *Septum Sermones ad Mortuos* is his attempt to create a genuine direct expression, a *vera narrativa* – a 'showing forth'.

Enactment as device

In the chapter 'On Life after Death' in *MDR*, Jung talks about the psyche itself as the site of constructive contention. Fragments of figure and image collide with each other to influence personal meanings in the psyche.

Jung's book attempts to grasp the psyche's typical 'deviant' behaviour (Bitzer 1968): 'The psyche appears as the *disturbance* of a probable mode of behaviour postulated by one or other . . . method' (Jung CW8 19134: 93).

It's to be taken with a grain of salt (*cum grano salis*) since common sense intentions may well figure into what such disturbances are, and how they may be regarded. His mind is the site of a mass of images which

> keep him from getting lost in personal retrospection. Many old people become too involved in their reconstruction of past events. They remain imprisoned . . . but if it is reflective . . . it can be a *reculer pour mieux sauter.* I try to see the line which leads through my life into the world.
>
> (Jung 1989/1961: 320)

Exploiting natural impulses that generate rhetorical expressions and embody them is what 'showing forth' or enactment is. There are many instances of this in Jung's work, and before I look at the shape of the text as a whole, and explore other themes of constraints on the self-presentation, I will expand on this general theme.

Devices of enactment

Jung characteristically uses internal dialogue as a device of disclosure. This strategy operates on several levels. It dramatises meaning in stories, establishing voices to enact the meaning. These voices can disagree or agree with each other. Internal dialogue, like dialogue between two interlocutors, most easily of all dialogue seems to us to be able to anticipate the next question or answer; there should be no surprises because there is one sensibility in control. In Jung's internal ruminations, however, there are often surprises. (In fact, despite our expectations, most internal dialogue does include surprises, for the speaker and for us who overhear it.)

This device engages us most deeply, by bringing us into the exchange. We take sides. By implication, in this way, Jung gains our involuntary adherence to his notion of the instability of ideas, whether we take one side or the other.

Bringing internal dialogue into play adds a sense of sincerity to the discourse. Since nineteenth-century romantic times, it is axiomatic that self-deliberation is honest. How could you lie to yourself deliberately? (Of course you may make a mistake and lie to yourself, but that is not your intention.) As Perelman and Olbrechts-Tyteca articulate it, 'the secrecy of self-deliberation seems to guarantee its value and sincerity' (1969: 41).

Jung warns us in the 'Prologue' that he prioritises internal experience which unravels in a gradual way, showing a sustained tenor of experience. We are drawn in closely to follow the drive of some unconscious inner direction. Why move from Pueblo Indians to Africans; why discuss internal disturbances just after he breaks from Freud. Querulous and sarcastic when he discusses other psychological systems, he is begrudging in allowing any strengths they might have. (Tones in the *MDR* are like music in films; they alert us to how he wants us to feel without stating it outright.) Longinus, the rhetorician closest to poets and much admired by Vico, advises us that 'dispersal' is the most effective persuasive technique; another device, I'd suggest of enactment: 'Inventive skill and the proper order and disposition of material are not manifested in a good touch here and there, but reveal themselves by slow degrees as they run through the whole texture of the composition' (Longinus 1969: 54).

Shotter alludes to the topical arts in this regard in a discussion of Vico's work. It suggests, as we experience in the hybrid form of *MDR,* with its combinations of dreams, personal anecdote and styles,' a struggle between different genres of writing', 'and the form-producing ideologies that is the "imaginary worlds" they embody. . . . the study of writers' practices rather than their content, can be expected to extend to a study of *tone* in which they write' (Shotter 1993: 63).

Jung's secret manikin is another example of how he accomplishes this 'showing forth'. The manikin is a symbol of a secret, and it is also the secret itself, with its scrolls of writings whose content Jung can no longer remember. It both *is* and is *representative of* a 'quality of eternity in his childhood'.

Jung is frightened when he thinks back to it even as an older man, when he returns in his mind to his early home. He is nearly sucked back into the fears still attached to what were other emblems of secrecy for him as a child like the site of a fire he tended for days. These symbols have maintained their potency (Jung 1989/1961: 20–2). Mysteries such as this one need to be solved in order to ensure his personal sense of security. Triggered by this fear, he searches natural history to unravel the earth's secrets. One of those elements is the human psyche. He conveys this anxiety to us.

Another form of enactment is creating deliberate similarity of style, an undercover suggestion. When he tells us his dreams, he sets the *mis en scène* in full detail before us. In the same tone, with the same amount of naturalistic detail, specifying colour and shapes, he tells us his real-life travels too. In this way, Jung brings the psychic event of the dream or vision, and the external event in his travels to mind with equal presence. And giving us the full detail has another effect. It brings both dream events and travels to life with great, persuasive immediacy.

Qualities of each transfer to the other: 'objective' authenticity is traded to the dream, and implications of feeling-toned significance attach to the travels. The dream event is as real as the events on his travels. And, further, the events in his travels are blown up into mythic proportions by the very detail he uses. They become both commentaries and amplifications of each other.

He manages during his trip to Africa, in his guise as a wise old shaman (which he deliberately evokes) to quieten down an increasingly riotous late-night dancing ritual after a good hunt; we see the gyrating figures, and the big whip he waves to call them to order. The enactment in this case is located in the construction of similar style.

Ernesto Grassi insists such tactic is *true rhetorical speech*; non-conceptual, moving and 'indicative'. It functions not only persuasively, appealing to reason and logic, but instrumentally, as metaphor is central. He is referring to Vico's *vera narrativa*, which I suggest Jung is deploying here.

> immediately a 'showing' – and for this reason 'figurative' or 'imaginative' and thus in the original sense 'theoretical' [*theorin* – i.e. to see] . . . the speech transfers [*metaphorein*] a signification; in this way the speech which realises this showing 'leads before the eyes' [*phainesthai*] a significance.
>
> (Grassi 1980: 20)

In transferring 'significance' from deeply established primordial sense, that links to the community, the event makes 'visible' or 'shows' listeners a quality that is not otherwise rationally deducible. Startling and unsettling modes of narrative are designed by Jung even unconsciously or by Vico consciously to reconnect us with original meanings.

Reconnection to vitality of meaning can be achieved by the arrangement of phrases and words or by using effective emotional ploys. The feeling-tone involves a passion of discourse conveyed to create renewed impact: Vico's axiom XV in *NS* refers to Homer's 'sublime poetic sentences', 'which must be expressions of true passions, or in virtue of a burning imagination must make themselves truly felt by us, and they must therefore be individuated in those who feel them' (Vico 1948,1730/44: para 825).

Jung aims to provoke readers to seek out active meanings in *MDR* despite what may be the reader's first, instinctive and standard approach to its study. Psychologically, Shotter points out, we are attempting to engage with 'already-set events' in which we are not involved. These events, in this case the presentation of events in a life, are set within a single framework (the autobiographical form).

> the single framework functions as a 'structured container' for all such events [thereby offering a] stable order created according to what our compulsion is: a single coherent order; we must doubt this though to grasp the nature of the third, sensuous involved kind of knowing.
>
> (Shotter 1993: 56–7)

To arouse sensual engagement requires specific skill in evoking the 'deviant' event. Rieff distinguishes Jung's use of events in memory; we note his appreciation of how Jung seeks to engage with sensuality in form of feeling-tone to bring events to mind: Jung, he says, was concerned to reverse aspects of language. He was disappointed by

> a loss of plasticity, of potential responses which, through neglect, have been allowed to slip into unconsciousness. In the unconscious (not in reason) there is a reservoir of strength from which man ought to draw to meet the demands of the day. He must learn to see that what once was true may be true again . . . nothing old in the world of ideas is incapable of becoming novel.
>
> (Rieff 1979: 200)

To accomplish the 'showing forth' to best effect means to arouse connections to the occasion to revitalise its presence; combinations of 'appropriate' words and images, startling and engaging. Seeing the connections in order to approach an argument aimed at revitalising elements of passion and significance make it persuasive in Jung's outlook. Not imposing logical 'self-evident' sequences of rational discussion . . .

Part 2 *MDR* – analysing its organisation and significance

To show better how the author(s) of *MDR* render the text as a call to reconsider how a life signifies, and to persuade us that this is so for us, I will explore *MDR*'s rhetorical devices in the framework of Bitzer's model. We will encounter themes of enactment in this analysis too. Enactment works as consequence and as potentiality in Jung's rhetoric.

Bitzer sets out three central components of the equivocal (or rhetorical) event. Anomalous status is achieved either by design or by natural circumstance. (In Hauser's terminology, the rhetorical situation is always 'deviance'.)

Here are Bitzer's definitions. These are paraphrases for the most part of discussion from his classic essay 'The Rhetorical Situation' (1968: 1–14).

1 Exigency – imperfection marked by urgency; a controlling incongruity that functions as an organisational principle: it specifies the audience to be addressed and the change to be effected;
2 Constraint(s) – made up of persons, objects and relations which are part of the situation because they have the power to constrain decision and action needed – when the rhetor enters the situation, his/her discourse not only harnesses constraints given by situation but provides additional important constraints – for example his/her personal character, his/her logical proofs, and style;
3 Audience – people mediating change, even when a person engages himself or ideal mind as audience.

Referring to Aristotle's *Rhetoric,* the two main groups of constraint are (a) those constructed by the rhetor (Aristotle called these 'artistic proofs'), and (b) those 'natural' constraints – documents, testimonials, etc.

MDR's authors, C. G. Jung and Aniela Jaffé, intentionally shape *MDR* as a 'rhetorical situation'. Exploration of the psyche is the focus of a 'situation' and exigency is created by need to transform as healthful exercise for all, and as moral obligation for him. The purpose of creating exigency, and analysing constraints and audience effect is to best calculate persuasion.

Controlled by autonomous complexes, intervening compulsively, the psyche is itself a rhetorical site.

Exigency

Naturally, it is not unprecedented that a life story be shaped as a rhetorical text. In the eighteenth century, Vico's autobiography reveals his philosophy of knowing the self in history and shapes the form of the *Vita.* Contemporary celebrity autobiographies are designed to promote a commercial image, for example. Augustine's *Confessions* is a prayer which hopes to lead up to prayer.

Vico changed his birth date and so it is a heroic event, celestially marked, creating exigency. And to underscore his isolated heroic posture, he underplays his experiences as a tutor in Vatolla early in his career. His posture for best effect was as outsider, whom no one understood. Arguing that Vico's philosophy of history dictated its form, Verene analyses each chapter and line to demonstrate how the intellect of the individual correlates to the axiomatic play of the history of the species. Vico refers to Augustine's life story, which he uses to demonstrate a life full of the beneficial and cataclysmic effect of God's grace. His great friendships that end in a suicide in one case, turn Augustine toward God and to his destiny as a preacher.

As I have been pointing out, Jung confirms his own theories about personality and individuation in *MDR*. His memoirs seek to effect curative change in his readers. Therefore, in itself, first of all, *MDR* provokes its own exigency. Its claims are unsettling and provoke thought. Anomalies of the memoir accomplish this too: for example, the lack of external detail thwarts our expectations of the memoir form and we are forced to consider why this is so.

But Jung's volume responds to various exigencies, fulfilling other aspects of Bitzer's definition. In fact, in an extended discussion about exigency in autobiography, Gregg finds it a common feature: 'to study human activity as *rhetorical* activity is to inquire into the actual and potential functions of principled symbolic inducement' (Gregg 1984: 131). That this gap in concrete detail overturns formal expectation is one important feature of *MDR*. But it goes deeper than that.

Like all autobiography, Jung's *MDR* is a sample of epideictic rhetoric. Epideictic affirms community values, assigning praise and blame to the actions of individuals or groups, particularly the individual who is the subject of the piece of writing or oration.

As a writer/rhetorician, Jung is dedicated to incorporate what he expects will be readers' assessments of his work. And, so, he expects that prioritising subjective, vague experience in a memoir will meet with resistance. Accordingly, simply by not meeting expectation, it will seem that he is overturning community values. But, he wants us to realise, although we may not immediately see it, the values he proposes are the most important values. And further, we will discover in ourselves that we have always known this.

Paradoxically and stealthily, despite disparities, therefore, he confirms community values. This is the conventional role epideictic discourse takes –

funeral orations, political speeches in support of a new action, occasional speeches or epistles marking a community event, etc. are samples of what the epideictic genre includes. And such orations, including funeral orations may, like Anthony's speech in Shakespeare's *Julius Caesar,* rouse its listeners to action.

Perelman sets a high priority on epideictic rhetoric, critiquing Aristotle's (and Vico's) placement of deliberative rhetoric as the pre-eminent form: 'Epideictic rhetoric is central to discourse because its role is to intensify adherence to values, adherence without which discourses that aim at provoking action cannot find the lever to move or to inspire their listeners' (Perelman 1982: 201).

The impact of *ethotic* concerns on the text can be seen clearly in a text that Angus Gowland critiques. He discusses the flamboyant autobiographical text that most dramatically embodies its message: Burton's *Anatomy of Melancholy.*

Gowland reminds us that *ethos* (rhetorical response to community values) and *pathé* (the emotional, expressive rhetorical function designed to arouse) impacts in paradoxical ways on *logos* (the objective reasoned text). As epideictic discourse, the autobiographical form is most susceptible to *personal* judgement. The rhetor deliberately shields herself, passes judgements and chooses (or not) to overturn conventional expectations.

Gowland analyses Burton's parody of the form, demonstrating how he turns epideictic inside out. Burton displays the melancholic mode of thought, and its subversion of community. Revival of Aristotle's *Rhetoric* at the time Burton was working influenced him, we are told. Gowland reminds us that Aristotle insists that *explication* in this mode is persuasion *by whatever means* to achieve assent. (*Rhetoric* 1.9.1–15 and 28–9). Burton took Aristotle up on it. In this case, *ethos* lies in the discourse, rather than in the character of the speaker. The discourse reacts to community values of sanity; Burton turns the prose inside out, and upside down reflecting the melancholic disposition. 'Epideictic discourses, then, must include a process of self-fashioning . . . simultaneously and coincidentally with the figurative audience as an ethical subject' (Gowland 2001: 21).

Jung's secrets and his allusive, evasive writing are appropriate to the social mores of early twentieth-century bourgeois Switzerland that he conveys. Both Burton and Jung were reacting in real life to personal attack. Burton's career was at a crossroads. In the case of *Anatomy of Melancholy* the 'showing forth' is done figuratively in the person of the subject of the autobiography itself. The narrative displays its author's madness, arbitrary emotion and focus.

Jung had recently had a painful experience absorbing the critical, barbed personal reactions to *Answer to Job.* In *Job*, as I discussed earlier, Jung used *pathé* and direct personal argument to argue its controversial case. This strategy appears uncompromising in the emotive field of religion. He drew fire. Taking on a collaborator and avoiding self-disclosure in *MDR* were solutions. Personal issues with sexual fidelity, accusations of anti-Semitism and collaboration with German government were demoralising.

In his book *Plotting a Cure,* J. Miller also discusses Burton's topsy-turvy motivation in writing *Anatomy of Melancholy*. The validation of the collective resides in this case, he says too, in the personal *ethos.* Burton engages in personal mythmaking. Mythmaking necessarily shares in the *ethos* of the community. Autobiography is shaped to 'show forth' as an *exempla* for the community. The personal, the communal and, Jung says, the archaic primordial images meet up. Jung took recourse in traditional guarded self-revelation.

He demonstrates in the person of the boy and of the man commenting on him, and on the older traveller, the explorer of the unconscious, in his focus on dream and mythic drive, how those underlying and sometimes secret drives shape a life. Focusing on internal motivational figures and dreams can better explain a life, and better fulfil the narrative of a life's significance. These devices are appropriate to the genuine, covert and secret *ethos* of the society too. Sarcasm and irony frequently highlight the non-disclosures.

Of necessity, his work operates within *constraints* imposed by its *audience(s)*, as well as *functioning through discourse to bring about change*, the other essential element in Bitzer's definition.

Before exploring how audience is involved in shaping Jung's work, or what he thought that audience was, I want to explore the types of constraints operating on *MDR.*

Constraints are the themes but they also function as devices compulsively forming the text. Like Jung's buried manikin, they are both emblematic and instrumental. Formal constraints include its shape as the literary genre of autobiography, fulfilling reader expectations; there are mythic formulae too that Jung brings into play. Then there are themes which reveal contingent constraints of life: secrets – fears and untold events; and plausible or otherwise real-time relevant associations. In summary both genre and personal requirements make up the constraints on the text.

Constraints

Constraints: literary device

One major constraint is the hidden polemic of the genre. Quintilian points out in his *Institutiones oratoriae* (Quintilian II.iv, 2–3 cited in Verene 1981: 85) that of course narration of facts is, in itself, a rhetorical act. It depends on the devices of *eloquence* for significance. Narration gives coherence to a life story. Additionally, the pragmatic intention of the narrator impacts on how a narrative is shaped.

Formal, genre constraints are important but those familial constraints are too, like a family objecting to the inclusion of mistresses, or a desire to play down unpopular political affiliations.

The older Jung selects events in the younger Jung's life, and by doing so, comments on their significance. Events are included when they provide the opportunity for revelation of personal myth. Those are the important events. The subject of the narration is also the agent acting out the life, and he has the life-curve of a hero. In Jung's case, the figure of melancholic, wise old Saturn informs his heroic manoeuvres, similar to Vico's self-conception. We will return to this point later.

The polemical aspect of autobiography is universal, and Jung relies on our expectations as readers of memoirs, that we will permit a biased selection of event. We know that self-narratives are biased. In this case, as with all others, the memoir argues Jung's view of life. He typically uses amplification, association, paradox and strategic manipulation of the language, throughout the memoir. These elements will be specifically explored below.

Starobinski makes a distinction about autobiographical narration that seems on first hearing contradictory: such narration is 'discursive narrative' rather than portraiture. It presents arguments that are pointedly about the author's purpose in the telling of event.

We sense strains on the material whenever Jung reaches back to gloss earlier activities. This is 'deviant'. Our sense of the truth of the account is disturbed and these glosses on the text are a 'kind of obstacle to the fidelity of the exact happening' (Starobinski 1980: 76).

The older Jung's commentary/interpretation makes us suspicious. However, at the same time, a perfect stylistic and theoretical fit of the actuality of the past, to the truth of the present recollection, gives us a sense of contrivance, or manipulation. But contrivance is what Jung promised us; we are reading self-confessed transparent 'fable'.

Naturally, also, the identity of the older Jung, telling us the story, with the younger Jung, is constantly affirmed. By adding a theoretical curve – the individual emerging from unconsciousness into consciousness and then integrating into an awareness of the larger, collective unconscious – another fabulist dimension is added. But, he argues, this is what a life story should be.

Jung looks back on his earlier writings, and comments on them, and revises what he says he did: the private work *Sermones Septum* produced during an anxious time is a case in point. Jung dismissed his earlier writing in response to Buber and others when he was answering their criticisms about *Answer to Job.* But here in *MDR* he highlights its importance due to its authenticity, despite its immaturity. He re-casts his painful experience.

> [I]t is the internal transformation of the individual, and the exemplary character of this transformation – that furnishes a subject for narrative discourse in which 'I' is both subject and object . . . the discursive character of the narrative is justified anew by content not by addressee . . . [it is about] retracing the genesis of present situation . . . antecedents of the moment from which the present discourse stems.
>
> (Jung 1989/1961: 75)

The theme of the memoir is in its retrieval of past event to exemplify present revelation of hidden meaning. And this is not only personal; it has a universal aspect. Frank Manuel comments that Vico does what I propose Jung does here: 'he sees the particular as impregnated with the universal and yet still seeks to recreate the particular in all its uniqueness' (1968: xi).

When Jung and Jaffé omit events that are deemed irrelevant or contradictory, they deliberately hide them. This leads us to an important first theme of *MDR*: *secrets.*

Constraints: secrets

Rhetorically speaking, creating secrets is a personal and/or collective drive toward resolution of anxiety or fear. The formation of secrets is motivated by a desire to reconcile discrepancy. The exigencies of life often require solutions that are in this special category. This solution provokes constructive energies in Jung's work. We realise that in a Jungian life, and in the memoir, secrets are pervasive.

They shape personality, motivating action. Since Jung argues that underlying personality is covert mythology, to tell one's life story is to uncover that secret formation. The integrity of the personality is bound up by hidden patterns.

In the first three chapters of *MDR*, and then later among people in his travels, in his encounters with Freud (to whom he discloses he had lied), with his patients in treatment, and finally, in his arduous tussles with another layer of (what are) involuntary 'secret' repositories of meaning – the unconscious – there are hidden matters.

The boy, Jung, hides his frightening dreams, his illicit associations of meaning – the black-skirted fearful Catholic priests who swallow little children – his manikin and scroll with secret writings. He tends a sacred fire and engages others to help him maintain the ritual fire. These were 'inviolable secret(s) which must never be betrayed, for the safety of my life depended on it. Why that was so I did not ask myself. It was simply so' (Jung 1989/1961: 22).

The child, Jung, constructs 'givens' in this way, underlying motivations for behaviour, stirred up by visceral fear. (Fear is always bodily.) The private 'myths' or 'fables' which he discovers (and manipulates) in his patients for therapeutic reasons, are the unconscious 'complex'. These motivating underlying clusters of emotion influence our every act. Cognition and conatus are filtered through these underground elements; Jung's *MDR* reflects this conviction.

> the patient who comes to us has a story that is not told, and which as a rule no one knows of . . . therapy only begins after the investigation of that wholly personal story. It is the patient's secret, the rock against which he is shattered. If I know his secret story, I have a key to the treatment.
>
> (Jung 1989/1961: 117)

Secrets are fearful 'premonitions of things unknown' and that is because they 'fill life with something impersonal' (ibid.: 117). We must all sense that we live in a world 'which in some respects is mysterious; that things happen . . . which remain inexplicable' (ibid.: 356).

Fear is motivating in Vico too, as it derives from realities of physical confrontations with a mysterious natural world. 'Sensation is the act that underlines or is the first moment of any act of knowing' (Verene 1981: 85). But before moving on to Vico's story of Jove and human fear of thunder, Jung's secrets, driven underground by fear, generate a characteristic manoeuvre.

Early on, the young boy has identity anxieties wondering if he was imagining his rock, or was it that he was imagined by the rock.

> I am sitting on top of this stone and it is underneath. But the stone could also say 'I' and think: 'I am lying here on this slope and he is sitting on top of me.' And the question then arose: 'am I the one who is sitting on the stone, or am I the stone on which *he* is sitting?'
>
> (Jung 1989/1961: 20)

This experience remained with him. Much later in life, he has a dream that poses the same dilemma and fear:

> on the floor in front of the altar, facing me, sat a yogi – in lotus posture, in deep meditation. When I looked at him more closely, I realised that he had my face. I started in profound fright, and awoke with the thought: 'Aha, so he is the one who is meditating me. He has a dream, and I am it.'
>
> (Ibid.: 323)

Associating fear with hidden identity issues bars full self-disclosure. But in the recounting, he formulates the Jungian theme of the overlap of identity and analogy in the processes of psychic life. Feeling-toned symbols are sought out to demonstrate his principles. The archetypal and the personal relate to each other by shifting between what are also concurrent representations and identities. Fears are safely disguised in the manipulations.

Jung proposes that differentiation of the subjective from the impersonal begins inside. And it begins early in the child's psyche. Two voices in one consciousness: the characteristic Jungian multiple unity within one psyche. This experience is familiar to all and it is Jung's common theme.

Vico sources divine inspiration in human fear of thunder; bodily trembling gives means to create Jove whose voice it is.

> Once men are seized by a frightful superstition, they refer to it all they imagine, see, or even do or make . . . they gave the being of animate substance . . . the first men naturally believed that lightning bolts and

> thunderclaps were signs made to them by Jove; whence from *nuo*, to make a sign, came *numen*, divine will, by an idea more than sublime . . . and that such signs were real words, and that nature was the [secret and mysterious] language of Jove.
>
> (Vico 1948,1730/44 : para 379)

Trembling fear of mysterious gods sparks off civilisation and humans develop skills of divination to understand Jove: priests, home marriage and burial all were inspired by these secret communications. As Verene says in *Vico's Science of the Imagination*, 'fear is understood by Vico not as passive, but as an active, formative passion'.

Jung shows us how the boy, Jung, derives meaning by association starting first with bodily sensation of fear. His fears, resolved in one instance by concealing the little man with his scroll of secret words, and his undisclosed dreams of a turd falling on the cathedral, were motivations for actions and for resolution in symbolic image. Fear comes to be translated into cognitive purpose. The images ascend to 'givens' in the boy's experience, and become compulsive touchstones. They attain autonomous force, and seem 'impersonal' beyond control. Jung wonders at this.

In the 'Transformation symbolism in the Mass' Jung asks if we can explain where the collective images come from in any other way but from an impersonal source? 'transubstantiation should be a cause of wonder and a miracle which man can in no wise comprehend. It is a *mysterium* in the sense of a . . . secret that is acted and displayed' (Jung CW11 1954: 250).

Whatever the source, the dream of the cathedral, when he reflects on it, leads Jung to realise astonishing and new things about God and about grace; and his manikin comes to seem a kind of repository of the boy's intuition of the collective unconscious.

> the individual on his lonely path needs a secret that for various reasons he may not or cannot reveal . . . it reinforces him in the isolation of his individual aims. . . . The need for such a secret is so compelling that the individual finds himself involved in ideas and actions for which he is no longer responsible . . . [he becomes] deviant from the collective. Internal oppositions are battled with in secret.
>
> (Jung 1989/1961: 342)

As a young boy, he assumed everyone hides secrets like he does. This is a given of the species. How did he get help from his school fellows to tend the 'sacred' fire? He must have appealed to their innate sense of ritual. Those school fellows must have shared his secret agitation.

In fact, the more things are hidden, from his mother's concealed second personality and illnesses, to his father's unravelling faith, the more certain he is that realities are the opposite of what they appear to be. Polarities come to draw each other along. A 'yes' brings its opposite 'no' along. The anxieties of his young life form into a compulsive formula: 'giving reasons in favour of a thesis is to imply that the thesis is not self-evident and does not compel everyone' (Perelman 1982: 140). The boy's earliest solutions put him on the path to a precept of analytical psychology about union of opposites in this case. He comes to recognise that he is constituted as a 'psychic *process*' (*MDR* 1961: 4). Givens are secretly formulated spontaneously, drawn from deep associations.

Constraints: associations

Lifetime associations are formed based on early sensations – the warmth of the sun and milk, sparkling water, the security of a closed home, the strange odour and look of a fascinating nanny, and, a little older, the exhibits in a natural history museum – these are the child's first meanings. As for cultures, associations embedded in language hem in meanings by providing ready-set links. The individual replicates the processes of the culture in its cultural product.

In *MDR* we find the same pivotal associations and fascinations cropping up beginning early on with discussions of the sun, bridges, water, secret compulsions themselves, and secret myths, occurring again and again. Jung's search for resolution to his terrors inspired creative meanings but it also set up patterns that formed his psychology.

We trace the stages of differentiation in the baby by following how Jung constructs associations. The baby, Jung himself, separates himself out from his surroundings, and begins the early process toward individuation. The voice of the older Jung recollects crucial moments. From the primary and wholly bodily sensations, the baby soon evolves reflective responses. Associations are forged.

For example, after his experience of well-being in the pram in the sunny warmth, he recalls spooning up warm milk and bread: 'The milk has a pleasant taste and a characteristic smell. This was the first time I became aware of the smell of milk. It was the moment when, so to speak, I became conscious of smelling' (Jung 1989/1961: 6).

His aunt points across the water to a place far away – awakening an urge to travel – in fact, also awakening an associated sensation of longing, that he later applies or else recognises in other parts of his life. Emotions, concepts, self are awakened as he interacts with the life around him. He 'recognises' these sensations because they were already there, dormant in him. Other psychologists linked developments to biological sequence, and progress was sequential along a formulaic line rather than allusive by in-born or self-formed associations. The typical comparison would be Freud's scenario of polymorphic early sexuality, fixation on mother, latency and fully developed libido.

Ambiguities are inevitably embedded in the associations, and (with his philological approach) the narrator leads us in directions responding to the older Jung's purposes. Motivations also show a personal and a collective dimension. Following the prose closely we note its drives.

By making connections, in this case by internal associations, relating to the body and to meanings buried in words, as readers, we experience the discourse as organic and inevitable whole. No logical sequence is imposed from outside. We are drawn into accepting contentious associations. If we are in the rhythm of accepting one equivocation, we will accept the next.

For example, Jesus' usual image as benevolent, powerful and *numinous* symbol and/or god-man is denied. The child makes leaps of mental imagery to establish a new association. Jesus is a dreaded 'swallower' – not only does he collect to him the little children, the little chicks, in the song he is sung at bedtime, but men are buried in the ground in order to go to Jesus. The consolatory lullaby about Jesus gathering the little chicks to him becomes attached to the bodies being gathered together to Jesus in their graves. Jesuit priests in their funereal garb, what's more, they are wearing female dress, and they stand over the graves. These are Jesus' priests; sinister associations emerge. Jesus is no longer benevolent.

Years later in 'Transformation symbolism in the Mass' cited above, Jung discusses distinctions between Zosimos' vision and the Mass. Mercurius is a generator, like Christ, a 'vivifying' symbol. Jung complains that there should be a correspondence here between Mercurius and Christ since they are archetypes of the same creationist mould, but he says, 'no'. To compare 'eating' to 'being eaten' is not part of the coordinates characteristic of Christ (he refers to the host in the Catholic mass); it is more likely for the 'devouring dragon', the 'corrosive Mercurius . . . who also eats himself'. Jesus is eaten in his form as host. And that's the distinction. But Jung does not recall or else he feels it is irrelevant now, that Jesus was a swallower when he was a little boy. Here is a sample of overturning an early association.

Jung engages his readers and overturns their expectations with new associations, contrasting new ideas to incontrovertible links, which he has just proposed. Paradox is a useful device in Jung's personal and theoretical world; he frequently uses it to express the veiled meanings that are his metier: 'Paradox does more justice to the *unknowable* that clarity can do, for uniformity of meaning robs the mystery of its darkness and sets it up as something known' (Jung CW11 1958/69: para 12).

Jung's reliance on underlying associations has more than cognitive utility. They are underlying 'givens' or compulsions of the personality. In one instance, later in his career, his patient hears noises, and even though he realises after having physical tests that it is a psychosomatic illness, he must rely on Jung to find a route to break his utter certainty he is ill.

Jung tells him that he has had same experience. It is the unconscious trying to grab his attention through the presence of the noise. It is trying to blot out the overbearing reliance on consciousness the patient suffers from. In this way, the one-sidedness of this man's life asserts itself. Pay attention to that layer of your psyche, the unconscious, and the noise will go away, Jung recommends. By the time we follow him along in such statements, we believe him, and so did the patient who was relieved of his symptom.

But there are pitfalls. If we don't 'buy' the association, Jung is on thin ice. For example, in the opening chapter of *MDR* he says that the atmosphere at home during times of trouble between his parents was 'suffocating'. His fainting spells were due to their oppressive relationship as it spread malevolency into the air at home making it unfit to breathe, says the older Jung.

There is room to question this association. It might have been that he felt 'squashed', for example. Would he then have felt 'physically cramped' instead of fainting from breathlessness? Since Jung wants to assert the symbolic and appropriate nature of his illness through associations, he resorts to the metaphor of airlessness to mean an overwhelming psychic conflict. 'Physically cramped' would not have worked in his model.

The opposite strategy of association is disassociation, also a creative rhetorical technique. Disassociation triggers new ways of perception, and is itself a resolution of anomaly. Like associations, disassociations manifest in argumentation and *techné.*

Jung's recognition of a split inside himself into no. 1 and no. 2 personalities allowed him to negotiate his life choices. His theory about how the psyche functions in accounting for seeming incompatible realities is emblematic of his acceptance of disassociation as a typical manoeuvre. The collective unconscious is drawn to the internal imagery of the archetypal figures, while consciousness is drawn to the social, external world. Each personality speaks in its own language and with its own tones.

Perelman demonstrates how an argument would play out using *disassociation* and it correlates almost precisely. He contrasts it, of course, to *association* which he defines as the formation of *liaisons* that 'allow for the transference to the conclusion of the adherence afforded the premises'. *Disassociation* separates 'elements which language or a recognised tradition have previously tied together' (Perelman 1963: 48–9).

Perelman describes Kant's deployment of a conventional argument of disassociation to create an innovative philosophical solution. Jung presents his underlying proposition about the ways the personality integrates and individuates by compensations of opposites in an analogous way. (In fact, Jung refers to Kant's split between the *phenomenal* and the *noumenal* often where this discussion applies in Perelman's work.)

Kant faced the incompatibility of these two perspectives. One reality is that universal determinism is the method of the natural sciences. The other reality is the world of the moral sciences where free will operates. To accommodate these anomalous realities, Kant separates 'reality' into two: the noumenal, where free will functions, and the phenomenal where determinism operates. He establishes a new 'coherent vision of reality' in this way, rather than simply denying that one or the other exists (Ibid.: 126).

Disassociation strategies enable him to bridge these realities that seem opposite: divide and merge. Demonstrate compensatory relationships. They merge into a greater transcendent significance. But it is first a matter of recognising the separate dimensions. Jung's stages of individuation start with recognition, on the one hand, of the individual self and on the other, the archetypal ideal of a self. Jung deploys the *topos* of appearance vs. reality (which underlies disassociation strategies) to stretch our understanding of individuation to accommodate an essential process.

Famously, Winnicott was not persuaded by Jung's argument about stages of integration. Winnicott does not agree that the split of personalities into no. 1 and no. 2 in Jung's childhood had anything to do with personality inadequacy. He thinks it is a pathological split, 'a picture of childhood schizophrenia' (Winnicott in Papadopoulos 1992: vol 1., 320) that the younger Jung suffered, and his solution was the spark for explanations of analytical psychology.

Constraints: mythic formula

An important collective (and often unconscious) constraint is myth. Jung is always eager to underscore its presence in our lives. Mythic dimensions are closer to the archetypal collective unconscious Jung proposed. Autobiography, i.e. a chronicle of individuation in Jung's formulation, is haunted by a figure embodying the *topos* of passing Time, burnished harvests and destructive fathers whose powers paradoxically generate new life – paraphrasing Vico. This is the figure of 'Saturn' (or 'Chronos') and he underlies the fable of the personality of Carl Jung. We have already noted Saturn's appearance in Vico's *Vita*, and we will see there is more in his poetic history about this figure.

First of all, since individuation and a life story happen over time, *MDR* shares Saturn and his ways as part of what is the backdrop to the autobiographical narration.

Chronos has an ancient history. Aristotle opens his essay on genius with the question: 'Why is it that all men who have become outstanding in philosophy, statesmanship, poetry or the arts are melancholic?' (Aristotle 'Problems connected with Thought, Intelligence and Wisdom', *Problems 2*, book 30, 1). Aristotle refers to the god, Saturn. Any important intellectual's life invites comparison to this elite and cold figure.

There is a long history to this personality type. And its history comes down to present day in image and literature as many scholars recount.

In Vico's poetical chronology of ancient history at the opening of *The New Science*, the age of Saturn was a pivotal period. It came at the end of the reign of gods in the Golden age of Greece. Vico explains the God was *Chronos* to the Greeks, and from that comes the word 'chronology' (Vico 1976/1730/1744: 73). It was the end of the barbaric pre-rational stage of history and the beginning of the heroic age. Law and moral choice were now coming into play.

Pursuing a philological approach, Vico informs us that later in Roman times, the name 'Saturn' derived from 'sati', 'sown fields' – the golden harvest is in. Reference to the agricultural cycle is the beginning of marking time. 'Two-harvests-ago' signifies two years ago. So 'sati' comes to mean Time (ibid.: 73).

The black bile associated with Saturn has accompanying personality and physical difficulties associated to the melancholic humour. In fact, the chronic maladjusted physical state – overheated brains – affects the saturnine personality's dreams. Dreams were more disturbing and powerful (Aristotle, Rhetoric Book 1: 14).

And, in other ways too Saturn is significant for Jung's mythic-referenced work – he is a core alchemical figure, the shadow side of Mercurius, the generator.

Both Jung and Vico personally claimed to have saturnine attributes. In fact, while a heroic backdrop is the pattern of every memoir, the saturnine hero is distinct. Overcoming difficulties, working through to successful life from uneasy beginnings, is a pattern we expect. The saturnine figure has destructive elements along the way, however, and cold, rational conclusions to his quest. Repeated chaotic, dark and disturbed events punctuate the story. In the end, rationalised scenarios overcome destruction. Both psychologist and philosopher's self-narrated life stories 'sublimate' these qualities, and thereby shape the narrative trajectory. Here I use the concept from Marshall's discussion of rhetorical fruition in the schema of Vico's idea of civic life.

Jung will not accept that he can be the 'old wise man'; he feels uncomfortable because he feels he just looks on:

> A man once dipped a hatful of water from a stream. What did that amount to? I am not that stream. I am at the stream, but I do nothing. Other people are at the same stream, but most of them find they have to do something with it. I do nothing. I never think that I am the one who must see to it that cherries grow on stalks. I stand and behold, admiring what nature can do.
>
> (Jung 1989/1961: 355)

Hillman provides commentary on Saturn's attributes in his essay on the god. 'Melancholy, anxiety, paranoia, anality, and obsessive memory ruminations reflect this archetype', Hillman says (1970: 147). He consigns this figure to archetypal status; Vico includes him in the imaginative heroes of history, a giant. He highlights the perennial rage for order in the saturnine personality. And destruction is simultaneous with rebirth. Seeing the processes behind representations and personalities was his special gift, Jung thought.

The melancholy quest moves ever-further inward and toward isolation. In their darkest moments, both Vico and Jung suffered the negative side of Saturn.

Jung points out his own early signs of self-destruction, which emerged again when he plunged headlong into his unconscious. As a child, his willingness to let the fearful Cathedral dream play itself out is a sign of a willingness to let it all go.

Apart from his significant near-fall, there were his fainting spells, his withdrawal from studies after a knock on the head. This near-fall summons up another mythical figure, Osiris. The simultaneity of death and rebirth is invoked here.

Recalling fears of water and dismemberment, or death, Jung recounts an event on the river near him as a child, where dead bodies were often found along its banks. He nearly became one of those bodies later, still a boy, when he almost tripped off a dangerous high bridge. The older Jung concurs with his mother that his act might have been a suicidal urge. (Were there other such events in his life?)

By defining the near-slip as potential self-obliteration, Jung presages the ritual of dismemberment, self destruction followed by self-re-collection in the individuation process. Individuation requires differentiation of the self first from the comprehensive collective unconscious as a step towards self-knowledge. The destructive urges of Saturn morph into creativity of the reborn god, Osiris.

Later on in the memoirs, Jung not only achieves isolation, but in retreating into himself, he recognises the natural and familiar creature he is.

> The more uncertain I have felt about myself, the more there has grown up in me a feeling of kinship with all things. In fact it seems to me as if that alienation which so long separated me from the world has become transferred into my own inner world, and has revealed to me an unexpected familiarity with myself.
>
> (Jung 1989/1961: 359)

Jung's creative illness, which is similar to Saturn's trajectory (he swallows his children, obliterating the future, but leaves out the most potent, Zeus, who creates a new world), generates a future. It traces a fall and a rise against overwhelming odds. He tells us of his long period of sinking into his psyche: talking aloud to Philomen, the anima, and other figures inside himself – familiar by way of the primal mythopoetic world we share. The 'frenzy' from which he was born anew, gave Jung tools to empathise with and analyse his patients' illnesses.

Not only, in retrospect, does he position this event in his life as having creative outcome, but it also serves as a bid for validation in the community. It contributes to his mythologizing about himself. He measures the painful depths, but also the success of his 'illness' by its application to his patients. So he claims it was a 'creative illness'. Paradoxically, then, he was not really 'ill' – it was a creative manoeuvre.

Jung instinctively altered events in his life to coincide with the shape of the melancholic hero's life. He left people out; he changed dates, qualified meanings. These obfuscations served to highlight the principles of his personality that correspond to the hero's quest. After all, it is the revelation of his mythic personality that is the important point of the book. It is how the individuation process took him on this quest that coincides with the formula of the heroic journey. On the basis of these mythopoetic forms, Jung develops his science.

As Einstein, writing his autobiographical notes published a decade before Jung's, said of scientific theories: we work out a theory and then find its consistencies with fact. Over their dinners together presumably talking about the new science of physics, and Jung's ideas of personality, they seem to have come to some agreements. Science is a rhetorical process first of all. In the same way, recounting the facts of a life is rhetorical as well. 'A correct proposition borrows its "truth" from the truth-value of a system to which it belongs' (Einstein 1949: 13).

In this case, the scientific system is an idea about what an autobiography is about: individuation. We know within ourselves the heroic narrative structure of a life story. We constantly tell it to ourselves about our self.

Audiences

Much referenced in Jungian discussions (see Jones, Rowland, Gray, Bishop, Tacey, etc.), Bakhtin's theories have much to say about audience participation in the rhetorical triad. To put it crudely, anticipated responses from an audience are fully integrated into the content of the communication. The audience in this formula exerts constraints on the message and on its exigencies. Bakhtin acknowledged the instinctive unthinking part this plays in communication: 'We learn to cast our speech into generic forms, and when hearing others' speech, we guess its genre from the very first words' (Bakhtin 1981: 79).

Bakhtin's 'super-addressee', for whom arguments are formulated, participates in formulating the proposition (or message): 'Responsive understanding is a fundamental force, one that participates in the formulations of discourse, and it is moreover an *active* understanding, one that discourse senses as resistance or support enriching the discourse' (ibid.: 88).

Individuation is the process by which the deep mythic self interacts creatively with the personal self. In respects I would like to explore, this mythic form is the 'super-addressee' of Jung's *MDR.* The fable he creates of himself is differentiated from the personal self, and co-existent with it. Meanings swing back and forth between them. The aspects of the Jungian self and the mythic Jung 'speak' to each other, balancing each other and transferring meaning. They also coincide with each other. Merging these two dimensions is the concretized 'universal' aspect of the psyche. We learn this reading *MDR.*

Vico's theories, like classical rhetoricians, particularly Cicero's, acknowledges the essential participation of an audience. Although it is not as radical a statement as Bakhtin's (who goes so far as to say that the audience is a co-author of the speech or written discourse – see Tindale 2004: 103), it leads us in that direction. '[I]n the art of oratory the relationship between speaker and listeners is of the essence. It is in tune with the opinions of the audience that we have to arrange our speech' (Vico 1990/1709: 15).

We gather from Jung's text that he projects an audience he assumes are reasonable people, persuaded by cogent and objective presentation of fact, but this audience are also people with 'deviant' inner psyches. Perelman and Olbrechts-Tyteca in *The New Rhetoric* call this construction the 'universal audience', as explored in the opening chapters of this book.

This projection of reasonableness takes us in; it persuades Jung's readers that they are reasonable. As rational people, accustomed to real fact, he expects his audience will want to resist his description of autobiography as 'fable'. Believing, as a matter of cultural convention, that incontrovertible fact does exist, and that it needs no disguising, they would feel that 'fable' is the wrong word to describe the facts of a man's life. Jung deals with the issue immediately but it is also the major theme of the whole of *MDR*.

Defining *fact* as 'myth' or 'fable' undermines what the word means in common parlance. To argue this point, Jung takes a two-pronged approach. Analysis of the 'Synchronicity' essay and 'Flying Saucers' and much other work of Jung's reveals that it revolves on this double approach.

First he redefines how the facts of a life should be set out and confirms his readers' belief, i.e. that there is a correspondence between external reality and internal perception. External reality is most often thought to have autonomous existence. Jung points out that external reality is utterly dependent on internal processes. In fact reality is a psychic phenomenon. He had a fellow traveller in this persuasion whose experience with virtual realities allowed him to agree.

In *Autobiographical Notes* (1959) Einstein places realism among the pre-rational springs of human behaviour, 'those springs that we often conceive of not just as the source of creativity, but also as the source of deep satisfaction in creative endeavours' (cited in Fine 1986: 109).

Arthur Fine explores Einstein's 'motivational realism'; the 'propositional attitude' we might say in psychological terms. It is an expression of faith in the access of reason to reality. He cites Einstein's letter to a colleague:

> I have no better expression than the term 'religious' for this trust [*Vertrauen*] in the rational character of reality and in its being accessible, at least to some extent, to human reason. Where this feeling is absent, science degenerates into senseless [*gestlose*] empiricism.
>
> (Ibid.: 110)

And, secondly, Jung uses tactics that are in accord with rhetorical and teleological explanations. The fable comes first. The fable shapes the facts of the narrative, and transfers to facts a feeling of cohesion. And then, in his writings, Jung transforms psychic fact into the realm of rational discourse where a 'universal audience' accesses it.

Perelman and Olbrechts-Tyteca tell us that the nature of this audience is 'always a more or less systematized construction'. 'Everyone constitutes the universal audience from what he knows of his fellow men, in such a way as to transcend the few oppositions he is aware of' (1969: 31).

Jung adopts unusual means to present this more comprehensive 'reality' the audience buys into. He tampers with formal generic expectation; he attributes equal importance to dreams, to Pueblo Indians' perceptions and to shamanism, for example, presenting them not only as scientific evidence, but also as objective and reasonable evidence. He uses methods that scientific discourse does not use: dialogues, fables and mythic figures – i.e. in all the ways that communication is conducted, including objective discourse. He insists on including the irrational and the figural, which is, in fact, what is usual human experience of the world.

Perelman and Olbrechts-Tyteca raise an issue, however, that Jung strains to overcome. They site Pascal's distinction between 'convincing' and 'persuading' (ibid.: 35). A rational audience simply needs self-evident truths set out to be brought along. This is the act of 'convincing'. 'Persuasion' involves other compelling and sometimes irrational means to bring its audience along. Jung wants to appear to be 'convincing' while he is busy 'persuading'. He is sharing a new kind of proof in science. 'Persuasive' devices have transparently entered the field of science where they were not 'needed' in the past since *fact* was supposed to be 'convincingly' self-evident.

The *ethos* of scientific discourse was high status in Jung's time, and it still is now (although less so in recent years). Alan Gross contests that since the advent of physics (particularly Einstein's innovations about what proof is), things have changed. Jung was convinced.

> This absolutist view of scientific truth now has an alternative, a sophisticated relativism in which truth depends not on conformity to a substratum of reality, but on agreement among significant persons . . . since all truth is inter-subjective, science like all persuasive discourse, must convince us of the truth of its claims.
>
> (Gross 1990: 20)

Status and authority are traditionally brought to bear in persuasion. Jung's readers are aware of who he is in the world. His career is established as a scientist who has dared to set himself up as an innovative healer of personality disorders. Yet, at the same time, he has regenerated interest in Gnosticism, in alchemy, in religion and spirituality, and upset ideas about how to explore the human psyche. Although his work is based on empirical evidence, the underpinnings of his discipline rest on arguments built on the reports of unstable psyches – his patients – analogy, arcane mystical writings, and a belief in irrational precepts.

We read his memoirs to find out how his personality developed, and to try to assess how healthy his psyche is. He writes anticipating that interest, and at the same time, shows a new way of integrating experience that applies to the new man. We will now look at *MDR*, its final composition and in a brief overview at least begin to show how it enacts the individuation process.

In the process of writing *MDR,* Jung discloses through his own life, that we are coincidentally growing personally and also growing to a simultaneous discovery of a kind of supra-self, more comprehensive than we imagine, and which is already *there*. We experience this as recollection. Vico's path takes him to philosophical dimension of an 'impersonal' classic self; Jung's rhetorical path – his psyche – travels through the individuation process and provides a mythical bridge between this fabulist self and the personal self. I'd propose he arrives at a creature who is 'universal'. *MDR* is another bridge to meaning, providing its own exigency.

1. 'Prologue' – first years, school years, student years

The opening prologue and three chapters show the young boy's budding fundamental associations, the beginnings of differentiations of consciousness from unconsciousness, and the beginnings of the development of the *persona.*

In the baby, bodily sensations predominate: the sun theme begins here at the start, and is picked up throughout book; bodies of water; milk and warmth appear again and again. He starts to reflect on these sensations and associate them to feelings. Later the sun is fundamental to the Pueblo Indians core meaning and contribution to world well-being. He finds sun myths in his alchemical studies, etc.

Reflections on his experience lead him farther on. He notes the distinction of a nanny and of an aunt from his mother – and he appreciates the fascination of that difference. The anima figure recurs throughout *MDR* coming into her own in his chapter on The Tower and the material on confronting the unconscious with her help.

He goes underground in his dreams; he witnesses death, and cannot resist inspecting the natural phenomenon of a bloody death. He endlessly draws war pictures like young boys around the world. Bridges are transitions both to new meanings and to death. The nanny, whose alien, and at the same time, familiar smell and touch come to embody the *anima*, the bridge to larger meanings in Jung's later psychic life. She saves him from his fall on the bridge. She looked after him when his mother was away.

His dreams are frightening and oblige him to find resolution. Here begins his quest to solve the mysteries of irrational nature. He explores the religion of his parents and of the community and finds them lacking. *Jesus* is more complex than he has been told – he learns this by being overcome with feelings and images in dreams that he cannot control. Swallowing comes to be associated with Jesus, and it is sinister. (Saturn swallows his children, attempting to thwart time.)

His secret dreams and his manikin, and ritual acts are prevalent at this time of his life, and overwhelm the no. 2 personality – the interior darker parts of his psyche induce him to begin withdrawing into fainting fits, away from school, spending hours sitting on his rock, writing secret messages. Being among his schoolfellows isolates him.

The stylistics of this first section is declared right at the opening. We are importuned to read differently to follow the shape of this discourse. And the discourse embodies the method.

We are tipped off metaphorically: 'connections' between the 'islands of memory' we will be reading, are 'afloat in a sea of vagueness, each by itself, *apparently* with no connection between them' (Jung 1961: 4).

That 'apparently' implies questionable associations to be explored; potentialities of meaning. Just as we relax, confident in the prose, pleased by the images, niggles appear. Distinctions between appearance and reality are a theme. Disassociation techniques, mentioned earlier, prevail. He alerts us not to be complacent about what we think 'causes' the connections.

Immediately, then, Jung begins by itemising these 'hazy' memories in detail – is this a redefinition of 'vagueness'? To detail vagueness is a contradiction. In fact, the memories are surprisingly exhaustive sensual experiences despite their having happened such a long time ago. Jung invokes the 'greater is lesser' paradox, a sub-*topos* of the appearance/reality pairing. Harries refers to Augustine's discussion of Paul in an appropriate example:

> 'as poor yet being rich, having nothing yet possessing all this . . . as, then, these oppositions of contraries lend beauty to the language, so the beauty of the course of this world is achieved by the opposition of contraries . . . arranged by eloquence, as it were, not by things.' Augustine's *contrapasso* would present discourse that implies opposition of things that are similar and vice versa: things that are apparently opposite embedded in discourse implying similarity.
>
> (Harries 2004: 37)

Jung explores this double-feint on persuasion frequently. Techniques of disassociation apply here. Harries' comments on divine desire versus human longing in commentary on *Noli me tangere* explore similar opposition: in this scenario Mary Magdelene and Christ meet after his rise from the dead. They are also primal themes, and great detail brings immediacy along with it.

Like images that float to the surface of a lake, and become increasingly vivid, memories float up and sharpen in our psyche. Desire and longing merge from religious dimensions to human aspects.

The earliest memory is warmth in the sun, well-being. Colours are brilliant. The landscape and the lake 'glisten' because of the sun beaming through the branches. This presages the way reality and the unconscious awareness of nature seep into our consciousness. The sun, the source of this increased vivacity, enlivens the particular landscape and lake, and gives them significance as satisfaction for the boy.

He'd been sleeping, and, now the baby is 'awakened' to find these sensations. Is it that he did not previously know of them?

This early sense-orientated memory relates to another sensual experience: warm (again) milk – which he also notices he can smell. He is also aware of being in a specific part of the house – in the western wing (away from the sun?) – appropriately he is in the dining room. And far from being an un-noted all-absorbing sensual experience (as milk for an infant baby seems to be), this is a sensation that is consciously recognised. Senses are separated out by the 'I's' perception of them. Reflection brings consciousness emergent from unconsciousness.

Shifting ground, but still it is the same warm and lovely summer evening, this new 'I' is called away to look at the distance: where the Alps (with the continuity of the sun and the glow and the vivid colour he already recognises) not only lure him away, but suggest to him other places. He is accumulating images and ideas that are moving him on to the next phase of life. He is led to a social world of other children he longs to join.

The order of unfolding consciousness is carefully organised by Jung. The reading experience is of sensual, poetic prose slowly emerging into cooler discourse. The themes are reflected in the style. The transformation of the figural and sensual style into something more objective, both carries and serves to make the meaning. As Gross would say the discourse has both 'probative' and 'heuristic' purpose. It shows the argument, and states it.

He processes his parent's unhappiness both psychically and physically – he overcomes his fixated fainting behaviour when he overhears his father talking about it. He is moving into an awareness of his persona, a social construct he develops to adapt to the world.

And, indeed, the next chapter is 'School'. His *persona* develops in a fabulist direction as 'Father Abraham'. And he learns to accommodate the social mores of the community. He conceals his interior personality at this time. The balance is running the other way. The discourse is settling into a stream of objective talk – no more interruptions of personal complaints. Although there are still flashes of recognition in his relations with his mother of the no. 1 personality they share, the dialogue between no. 1 and no. 2 personalities and the need to integrate them are in abeyance.

Now the social personality prevails. The adolescent, young fellow, Jung, in the memoir recognises the satisfactions to be obtained in the world, his secret longing to solve mysteries of natural science leads him to make choices after school, and he begins his career.

2. Psychiatric activities

The attraction for Jung of psychiatry is that it combines ways of accommodating the interior with the objective scientific and medical world. He also begins to realise that he has different approaches to patients than his peers. He is now fully in the thrall of the no. 2 personality, and looks at the irrational in the psyche with scientific distance. But intimations of no. 1 and what it means to him and to his patients break through. He realises that he must approach patients within the language of their own interior personalities if he is to communicate with them. He still remembers that we all have secrets.

His dialogues are with other figures, his patients, rather than interior, self-contained descriptions of what the younger boy had perceived.

3. Freud

Groping in the world's literature after his own experiments had left him dissatisfied; he looks for techniques that will examine his ideas effectively. This leads him to Freud. Theories about dreams, the 'road to the unconscious', have international standing by now, and Jung hopes to test and to incorporate these ideas. But already there are resistances to Freud.

Dreams are less reductive with wider significance than Freud allows. The unconscious is a more creative organ in Jung's mind than simply what it seems in Freud's scheme, which is that it is a kind of repository of individual repressions. Freud's technique tackles neurotic behaviour, which is only a secondary solution to personal fears. Freud does not recognise broader, deeper significances.

In order to preserve his place at Freud's side, even as he begins to allow the no. 1 personality to enter back into his work, he lies to Freud about their differences. He suppresses his ideas about the libido for as long as he is able to. His therapeutic exchanges with patients embody a *responsive–reactive rhetorical style* that Billig discusses. He anticipates what his patients will bring to him, and seeks identification with them to communicate. Their commonality derives from the shared collective unconscious. 'I maintained that psychiatry, in the broadest sense, is a dialogue between the sick psyche and the psyche of the doctor, which is presumed to be normal' (Jung 1989/1961: 112).

Freud's disengaged approach is a very different technique, valuable with some patients but not with all. When the break comes with Freud, his suppressed inner figures erupt and overcome him. His psyche seeks a balance: his prolonged attachment to Freud had involved him in international endeavours that over balanced his *persona* – his no. 1 personality was suppressed beyond endurance. Plunging deep into his no. 1 personality now touched the other extreme.

4. Confrontation with the unconscious

His breakdown steeps him in the terrifying experience of figures pushing up from the unconscious, as he perceives it. Taking this step into the unconscious, he eschews the Ego. He is prepared to give himself up as agent, to merge passively with archetypal figures he encounters – as Jung describes the sacrificial Christ figure does – the archetypal Self (Jung CW11 'Transformation symbolism in the Mass').

He describes his technique now as giving interpretations up to 'chance' after his move away from Freudian technique. As in his personal experience . . .

> The interpretations seemed to follow of their own accord from the patients' replies and associations. I avoided all theoretical points of view and simply helped the patients to understand the dream-images by themselves, without application of rules and theories.
>
> (Jung 1989/1961: 170)

Splits of consciousness abound, rendered into pieces by confrontations with unconscious – we're getting deeper in with him. Dreams are fragmented – and the individuation process reaches its turning point at rock bottom submersion in the unconscious. He writes his *Septes Sermones* as with another voice, bombastic, an eternal voice, *vera narrativa*, the nominative imperative, inferred by the grandiose style. He has given himself up to the active agent of his own will. The ego is overcome by archetypal figures with his permission, and a kind of disembodied, passive formal style of a universal 'given', a fable emerges.

The universal form speaks through the individual. Vico's primal peoples used a natural form of meaning in *vera narrativa* that is the recurrence of primal original speech in the era of a new barbarism. It irrupts from the *gente* as from 'the simplicity of children, truthful by nature, [and] the first fables could not feign anything false' (Vico 1948,1730/44: para 408); he recalls us to remember Aesop, its prime progenitor. 'The first poets attributed to bodies the being of animate substances, with capacities measured by their own, namely sense and passion and in this way made fables of them' (Vico 1948,1730/44: para 404).

Words and their composition embody and reflect the collective unconscious given their shared nature. Another way to put it is that primordial images haunt words, and they can carry us away into new thoughts and meanings under their own volition. We have already pointed out that Jung's philological approach offers guidance into new meanings. But additionally, metaphors and implicated meanings buried in words and phrases have their own life: '[I]n order to arrive at the more universal and more fundamental language of mythology . . . [giving] us access to the primordial imagery that underlie all thinking and have a considerable influence even on scientific ideas' (Jung 1989/1961: 289).

Hypotheses about what must be – fables – are buttressed by 'fact', validating theory. Noting this process, Jung instinctively engages with the process in analytical psychology. Next he concentrates on the work that he undertook following his descent into his psyche, and his realisation of a break into a new direction.

5. The work and 'The Tower'

He discovers alchemy – a useful heuristic that, again, he strains to elevate to direct and symbolic identification with human psychological experience. He begins by using the mode of his personality no. 2 looking for objective, quantitative evidence in history. As he puts it, he seeks historical pre-figuration of his inner experiences.

Without his discovery of alchemy he could not have substantiated his ideas. Yet, also, given the orientation of alchemical presuppositions, it meant he was susceptible already. Alchemy combines collective symbol and interior projections. Jung uses this body of work as a personal bridge to a deeper integration of his own multiple aspects. At the same time, he demonstrates that the edifice of alchemy offers the world evidence of the ubiquity of the integration of the collective unconscious and the personal.

His lists of associated words in the body of alchemical work, which he tracks forward and back into history achieves another effect. He creates equivocations by selecting sometimes suppressed, original, meanings of words. And also, the catechising lists, with their string of connectives, give us subliminally the sense of the unity of all things.

Since they are shown to connect, they must share ground linking them together, we ascertain. Jung's copiousness aims at achieving that sensation of unity rather than conveying a sense of chaos which otherwise such profusion might imply.

Briefly, in 'The Tower'chapter, he shows the concrete construction of a place where the integration of unconscious and the consciousness in one man, Jung, can be accomplished. The tower is a personal place, on his own land, and now he seeks models in the world.

6. 'Travels'

Having confronted the unconscious personally and on homeland, Jung develops his enquiry further to other turf on his travels.

A sidenote here; I resist naming 'homeland' in the previous paragraph. We can imagine, giving the timing implied here, that it must be Switzerland, in the German region he resided in. But it seems to me that I must comply with the spirit of his memoir and not mention specific places or times. Early on he has mentioned the issue of the canton-style democracy the Swiss government adopts, and he refers to his military service elsewhere. But apart from the specifics in this chapter where he is extensively focused on universality, and so he must talk about localised characteristic, there is little geographical detail throughout.

He not only seeks substantiation of his theories out in the external world, but he looks at how people he calls 'primitives' function at a greater level of participation with the unconscious. These are people who are not only Other in terms of geographical location but also in terms of how they conceive elements in the world.

The paradox of seeking progression among 'primitives' is not lost on us, or on Jung. He plays on ironies in his discourse. His travels are not to the Western cities of New York or Washington DC, for example, in the United States. No, he heads for the Pueblo Indians. He seeks medicine men and shamans, and explores religious practices in communities of India or Africa. Christianity is put in its place among these religions. He focuses with high regard on what are commonly thought to be backward and uncivilised features. To prove his point, he will find a healthier mode of living, a higher integration of the individual, among these uncivilised communities. He must appear to find it sincerely, not deceiving us – he must be surprised with what he finds, or we suspect he's planting ideas. Surprise will indicate an authentic reaction, after all.

The approach he takes in seeking out incongruities – the irrational and the unspoken – is a posture of disingenuity. These are incongruities for civilised, rational man, but plausible aspects of life for these communities. This stance underlies how he tells us about his journeys. In fact, he is discovering what he really already knows is there, and what fits his agenda. His attitude implies the sincerity of this discovery. But he seeks to undermine our sense of being manipulated.

'Primitives' are people more immersed in the unconscious, who operate at a 'primordial' level. The 'vestiges of the primitive' are pieces of psychic experience that will not disappear in time – so there is no intention to say that 'primitivism' is a 'backward' notion. These elements will always be with us.

> The primitive mind is marked by a high degree of dissociability, which expresses itself in the fact, for instance, that primitives assume the existence of several souls . . . besides an immense number of gods and spirits, who are not just talked about as with us, but are very often highly impressive psychic experiences.
>
> (Jung CW8 1960/69: 104)

He makes the first big discovery about what foreign-ness is. In these other places, he notes, they regard Europeans from another perspective. He learns this by sitting in Arab coffee houses, observing the gestures of the people around him. The smells of the land are different, and reek of ancient times.

He is entering the realm of visceral and gestural communication. The air of the waters in North Africa is shady and redolent of ancient fruits and primordial homosexual relationships.

> The dragonman [telling me of the prevalence of homosexuality] could have no notion of the thoughts which struck me like a flash of lightning . . . I felt cast back many centuries to an infinitely more naïve world of adolescents who were preparing . . . to emerge from their original state of twilight consciousness.
>
> (Ibid.: 104)

He strips away Western consciousness, in order to open the path to communication with people in direct touch with the primordial collective. The opening pages of this section enact a cleansing ritual.

Having come to these conclusions, later in the chapter, he is ready to take on the Pueblo Indians' assertion of the universal importance of their solar greeting ritual each morning. At the core of their communal existence are secrets that sustain the cohesion of their lives. As with his own and his patients' lives, secrets are pervasive and essential. 'The air was filled with secrets known to all the communicants [but inaccessible to whites] . . . not a mystification but a vital mystery whose betrayal might bring about the downfall of the community as well as the individual' (ibid.: 239).

Jung sets out the imaginary dialogue he had with them: we see how both interlocutors attempt to tolerate the other's viewpoint.

> If I had hit on something essential, he remained silent or gave an evasive reply, but with all the signs of profound emotion . . . as I sat with Ochwiay Biano on the roof, the blazing sun rising higher and higher, he said, pointing to the sun, 'is not he who moves there our father? How can anyone say differently? How can there be another god? Nothing can be without the sun.' . . . I asked him whether he did not think the sun might be a fiery ball shaped by an invisible god. My question did not even arouse astonishment let alone anger . . . [my question] merely left him cold. 'You think then that what you do in your religion benefits the whole world?' [I asked] . . . He replied with great agitation, 'Of course. If we did not do it, what would become of the world . . . we are the people who live in the roof of the world.'
>
> (Ibid.: 251)

They giggle at his incredulity about their power to control the sun's risings and settings. Jung's voice reflects our surprise and awe at their arrogance. Jung and the Pueblo Indian communicate not only the substance of each other's realities, but also the mutual sense of otherness they share. The dialogue form makes this exchange familiar to us and brings it home.

Jung's rhetorical choice here might have been to show the ritual worship of the sun as completely alien to us, attempting to communicate solely its otherness. But he wants to display its *familiar* otherness – in fact, the unexpected familiarity of the self that he will arrive at in the last sentences of *MDR.*

He finds universal elements in each of the other communities he visits – a moral sense in India based on unconscious elements; a relationship to the anomalies in nature in African communities; and in Ravenna the images on the cathedral walls that also stirred Yeats and Nietzsche, moved Jung to think about the impact of past spirituality on the integrated conscious/unconscious psyches of the present.

Having found substantiation of the presence of the unconscious in the world, and sometimes in forms that are even very similar to what he'd found in his home, he moves inward to find reflections there.

Vico's historical insight that other (and earlier) societies had truly alien habits, values and epistemological processes that we could only hope to try to engage with is reflected in Jung's take on the places he visited. They investigate the same attitude to the world.

7. *'Visions' and 'On life after death'*

In these sections, which I can only paraphrase hastily, Jung discovers the pull toward death that is an element of serious illness. It is a less agitated experience than his confrontation with figures of the unconscious earlier in his life he notes. He sinks into the unconscious and finds visions of collective significance. It is a reformulation of the unconsciousness of the baby.

The later chapters ('Late thoughts' and 'Retrospect') focus on an exploration of the larger Self; here in this section, we see the phenomenon of sinking into the unconscious from the individual self's perspective. The glimmering vagueness of colours and places on the globe he sees as if below him, replicate the experience of the sights in fragments and diffuse shapes he'd seen as a baby. He is floating in a sea of sensation again. The temptation to release himself into it is overwhelming.

Earlier in the book, he'd referred to the collectivity of the dead, an insight he'd elaborated in *Septum sermons*: 'the soul "vanishing", this means it has withdrawn into the unconscious or into the land of the dead . . . [its] animation . . . gives visible form to the ancestral traces, the collective content' (Jung CW8 1960/69: 183).

He speculates about life after death as a psychic longing that must be respected. He weaves in a sense of credulity to his imaginative grasp of those psychic demands in the collective. (The tone he uses in this section is the same he uses when he writes about UFOs in his essays on synchronicity. It is a mix of ironical compliance. He adduces different levels of psychic sophistication to this belief. Proposing, in the same hypothetical way as Abélard's 'propositional attitudes' (and like Einstein, the scientist's 'motivational realism') does, that there is life after death, Jung explores the belief.

8. 'Late thoughts' and 'Retrospect'

In these chapters, he's come to see that meaning is not only personal but is an 'endeavour of cosmology'. Words and meaning are goals of a personal project, just as they are bridges in themselves as a process of attaining goals. Drawing on Biblical references, he describes the cosmological figure of individuation – sketching in how the emanations of God's intuition and concepts fell to earth in the guise of 'bad' angels. This is history from 'the other side' – attributions to God of human traits. The embodiment of these intuitions and concepts is in the human race. These figures underlie human motivations (the angels brought 'inflation' to humankind in the guise of the over-weaning ego of the tyrants of our time) and Jung now focuses on those mythic stories as they inform human history. He has moved into full-blown epic mode.

Now contingent dates and events can take their place in the cosmology – the merger of the unconscious with the conscious is revealed to be a secondary phenomenon. In the full hortatory voice of a preacher, in these sections, Jung sets out his view of the movement of history, which has us in its clutches because we do not know the Self. If we did, we'd understand the nature of the relationship between good and evil, because we would discover it in ourselves.

In his article contrasting Vico and Jung, Verene discusses the self that Vico reveals as an historical type. The self appears over against a moment in the flux of history – related to the divine by analogy and created by language. Vico's intention in writing his book about himself is an *exemplum* of Vico's concept of how the individual 'fits' into history along the lines of principles set out in *The New Science.* It is an idea of self-knowledge that is akin to Jung's purposes in his autobiography. In his earlier book on Vico's *Vita*, Verene sets out the philosopher's conclusions about the individual in history:

> This interlocking of the particular and the universal is characteristic of self-knowledge because such knowledge is not simply the 'knowledge' a subject uniquely has of its own existence (of its own psychological state), nor is self-knowledge simply a knowledge of the object, independent of the self's activity of knowing. Self-knowledge occurs within the unique speech of an individual knower, but what is revealed in this speech is what is true of the speaker's universal human condition.
>
> (Verene 2002: 207)

The unexpected familiarity of the self reflects on a universal condition of dissonance that is negotiated and resolved.

11

CONCLUDING REMARKS

Rhetorical analysis exposes the plausible 'truths' – hidden or unknown by the writer – and analysis has been applied to both Jung and to Vico in these pages – both of whom are adepts, and trained by reference to the Greek and Roman classics in the arts of persuasion.

Kenneth Burke suggested in his work (especially essays in *Philosophy of Literary Form*) that we set out a page of themes, and trace how they work with each other in examining a writer's work. By doing this exercise, we will begin to see her preoccupations and how they are resolved in the ways in which she persuades her audience what those solutions are. Watching how Jung makes associations, and what his presumptions are in attempting to set out his ideas, and to persuade readers or listeners that he is right, tips us off to his presumptions and preoccupations. And I have attempted to explore within his immediate circumstances and also in past associations.

Vico and Jung's aims are different, and this naturally has impact on their discourse. Jung's project was to heal, but in this investigation, we reveal goals he may not have suspected he had. Vico's *techné* has been useful as a guideline to the rhetoric of a writer who shares a belief in the primary faculty of imagination. But Vico had no sense of an inner self; of course he experienced interiority but it was not relevant and he did not recognise it.

The purpose has been to show how rhetorical principle operates in these theoretician's ideas and practice. Vico has often been called an idealist because his aim is to persuade his audience of an 'impersonal' ideal collective who transcend the day-to-day deviations of history. But his 'impersonal' goal, targeted at engaging dialectically with poetical logic, arrives at the *classic*, a concrete eternal conclusion.

Jung's conclusions, as I have been pointing out, aim to reach a 'universal' audience – assembled to meet an exigency, for the moment, and to suit the occasion which refers to collective motifs that have primal force. Closer to the 'personal', its participation in the collective motif weaves individual strands together, recognising all – so the 'universal' can shift to suit. But because it is concrete, it avoids a vague relativism.

We arrived at a paradoxical and, I think, shared sense of what 'fact' is – it's a plausible 'truth' and it is related to fiction since it proves variable given assumptions about the situation, and the posture of the speaker or writer telling it to us. Its force in making change is what is relevant, not its idealised truth. Jung makes comments that suggest he has come to similar conclusion: 'there exists a [second] psychic system of a collective, universal, and impersonal nature which is identical in all individuals' (Jung CW9: para 89).

'Universal' and 'impersonal' are synonymous in this context. The 'impersonal' is reference to the disinterested autonomous force, while 'universal' contains multiple points of view and interest. He sensed they were both part of what the collective is. As a scientist, he concludes that evidence demonstrates that the archetypes of collective unconscious and complexes that underlie our individual lives are 'real' and pivotal in psychic participation in coping with the 'external world'.

> the collective unconscious is a part of the psyche which can be negatively distinguished from a personal unconscious by the fact that it does not, like the latter, owe its existence to personal experience and consequently is not a personal acquisition . . . whereas the personal unconscious consists of the most part of *complexes,* the content of the collective unconscious is made up essentially of *archetypes* . . .
>
> (Ibid.: para 95)

I will leave the final word to Jung.

REFERENCES

Agosta, L. 2010. 'Heidegger's 1924 clearing of the affects using Aristotle's *Rhetoric, Book II*', in *Philosophy Today* (Winter), pp. 333–45.

Arieti, S. 1979. 'Vico and modern psychiatry', in *Vico and Contemporary Thought*, ed. G. Tagliacozzo, pp. 81– 94 (Atlantic Highlands, NJ: Humanities Press).

Aristotle. 1937. *Problems II*, Book XXX, 1, trans. H. Rackham, Loeb edition (Cambridge, MA: Harvard University Press).

——. 1954. *Rhetoric*, trans. W R. Roberts and *Poetics* trans. I. Bywater (New York: Modern Library).

——. 2004. *Topics*, trans. W. A. Pickard-Cambridge (Montana: Kessinger Press).

Auerbach, E. 1946. *Mimesis*, trans. W. Trask, 1953 (Princeton, NJ: Princeton University Press).

——. 1965. *Literary Language and its Public in Late Latin Antiquity and in the Middle Ages* (London: Routledge).

——. 1973. *Scenes from Drama of European Literature* (Gloucester, MA: Peter Smith Publishers).

Augustine. 1995. *De doctrina Christiana*, trans. R. P. H. Green (Oxford: Oxford University Press).

——. 1992. *The Confessions*, trans. and commentary James J. O'Donnell (Oxford: Clarendon Press).

Bakhtin, M. M. 1981. *Speech Genres and Other Late Essays*, trans. Vern W. McGee, ed. C. Emerson and M. Holquist 1986 (Austin, TX: University of Texas Press).

Barzilai, S. 1991. 'Borders of language: Kristeva's critique of Lacan', in *PMLA*, 106:2 (March), pp. 294–305.

Battistini, A. 1985. 'Autobiography', in *Cultura e meridionale a letteratura italiana: I modelli narrative dell'eta moderna Naples La Degnità della Retorica: Studi du G B Vico* (1975), pp. 145–90 (Pacini).

——. 2002. 'Ariadne and the Minotaur: The cultural role of a philosophy of rhetoric', in *Festschrift for Donald Philip Verene, Philosophy and Culture*. trans. George A. Trone (www.pdcnet.org [accessed on 17 April 2009]).

Baumlin, J. and T. F. Baumlin. 1989. 'Psyche/Logos: Mapping the terrains of minds and rhetoric', in *College English*, 51:3 (March), pp. 245–61.

Baumlin, J., T. F. Baumlin and G. Jensen. 2004. *Post-Jungian Criticism: theory and practice* (Albany, NY: State University of New York Press).

Benveniste, E. 1966. *Problems in General Linguistics*, trans. M. Meek (Coral Gables, FL: University of Miami Press).

Berlin, I. 1976. *Three Critics of the Enlightenment: Vico, Hamann, Herder* (London: Hogarth Press).
——. 1978. 'Review "*Corsi e ricorsi*"', in *Journal of Modern History*, 50:3 (September), pp. 480–9.
Billig, M. 1987. *Arguing and Thinking – a rhetorical approach to social psychology* (Cambridge: Cambridge University Press).
——. 1997. 'The dialogic unconscious: psychoanalysis, discursive psychology and the nature of repression', in *British Journal of Social Psychology*, p. 36, pp. 139–59.
——. 1998. 'Dialogic repression and the Oedipus complex: reinterpreting the little Hans case', in *Culture and Psychology*, 4:1 (March), pp. 11–47.
——. 1998. 'Rhetoric and the unconscious', in *Argumentation*, 12: pp. 199–216.
——. 2000. 'Freud's different versions of forgetting "signorelli": rhetoric and repression', in *International Journal of Psycho-analysis*, 81 (part 3), pp. 483–98.
Bishop, P. 1995. *The Dionysian Self: C. G. Jung's reception of Frederich Nietzsche* (Berlin: de Gruyter).
——. (ed.). 1999. *Jung in Contexts* (London: Routledge).
——. 1999. *Jung's Answer to Job* (London: Brunner/Routledge).
——. 2000. *Synchronicity and Intellectual Intuition in Kant, Swedenborg, and Jung* (London: E. Mellen Press).
Bitzer, L. 1959. 'Aristotle's enthymeme revisited', in *Quarterly Journal of Speech*, 45, pp. 400–12.
——.1968. 'The rhetorical situation', in *Philosophy and Rhetoric,* 1, pp. 1–14.
Bonevac, D. 1991. 'Review of Cocchiarella's *Logical Investigations of Predication Theory and the Problem of Universals*' (Naples 1986), in *Nous*, 25:2 (April 1991), pp. 221–230.
Booth, W. C. 1961. *The Rhetoric of Fiction* (Chicago, IL: University of Chicago Press).
——. 2004. *The Rhetoric of Rhetoric* (Oxford: Blackwell).
Bowie, M. 1987. *Freud, Proust and Lacan* (Cambridge, MA: Cambridge University Press).
——. 1991. *Lacan* (Cambridge, MA: Harvard University Press).
Boyd R. 1979. 'Metaphor and theory change: what is "metaphor" a metaphor for?', in *Metaphor and Thought*, ed. A. Ortony, pp. 356–407 (Cambridge, MA: Cambridge University Press).
Buber, M. 1988. *Eclipse of God* (Atlantic Heights, NJ: Humanities Press International).
Burke, K. 1950. *A Rhetoric of Motives* (Princeton NJ: Prentice Hall).
——. 1961. *Rhetoric of Religion* (Boston, MA: Beacon Press).
——. 1967. *Philosophy of Literary Form* (Baton Rouge, LA: Louisiana State).
——. 1969. *Grammar of Motives* (Berkeley, CA: University of California).
Burke, P. 1985. *Vico* (Oxford: Oxford University Press).
Cambray, J. 2001. 'Enactments and Amplification', in *Journal of Analytical Psychology*, 46, pp. 275–303.
Campbell, J. 1971. *Hero with a Thousand Faces* (Princeton, NJ: Princeton University Press)
Cassirer, E. 1946. *Language and Myth* (New York: Dover).
——. 1951. *Philosophy of the Enlightenment*, trans. F. C. Koelin and J. P. Pettegrove (Princeton, NJ and Oxford: Princeton University Press and Oxford University Press).
——. 1968. *Philosophy of Symbolic Forms*: Myth vol. 3, ed. J. M. Krois and D. P. Verene 1968 (Princeton, NJ: Princeton University Press).

Catana, L. 1999. *Vico and Literary Mannerism: a study in the early Vico and his idea of rhetoric and ingenuity*, Emory Vico Studies (London: Peter Lang Publishers).

Cherwitz, R. A. and J. W. Hikins 1999. 'Rhetorical perspectivism', in *Contemporary Rhetorical Theory*, eds J. L. Lucaites, C. M. Condit and S. Caudill, pp. 249–66 (London: Guilford Press).

Cicero. 2004. *De inventione*. trans. C. D. Yonge (Whitefish, MT: Kessinger Publishing).

——. 2004. *Topica*. trans. Tobias Reinhardt, Oxford Classical Monographs (Oxford: Oxford University Press).

——. 1946. *In Catilinam*. trans. L. E. Lord, Loeb Classics (Cambridge, MA: Cambridge University Press).

Cocchiarella, N. B. 1986. 'Conceptualism, ramified logic, and nominalised predicates', in *Topoi*, 5, pp. 75–87 (Dordrecht: D. Reidel Publishing Co).

Colish, M. 1968. *Mirror of Language: a study in the medieval theory of knowledge* (New Haven, CT: Yale University Press).

Conley, T. 1984. 'Enthymeme in perspective', in *Quarterly Journal of Speech*, 70:2, pp. 168–87 (London: Routledge).

Croce, B. 1913. *The Philosophy of Giambattista Vico*, trans. Collingwood (London: Howard Latimer Publishers).

Crosswhite, J. 1989. 'Universality in rhetoric: Perelman's universal audience', in *Philosophy and Rhetoric*, 22:3, pp. 157–73.

Crowley, S. and D. Hawhee. 1999. *Ancient Rhetorics for Contemporary Students* (London: Allyn and Bacon).

Culler, J. 1997. *Literary theory* (Oxford: Oxford University Press).

Curtius, E. R. 1953. *European Literature and the Latin Middle Ages* (Princeton, NJ: Princeton University Press).

Danesi, M. 1993. *Vico, Metaphor and the Origin of Language* (Indianapolis: Indiana University Press).

——. 2002. 'Abstract concept formation as metaphysical layering', in *Studies in Communication, Sciences* 2:1, pp. 1–22.

De Man, P. 1979. *Allegories of Reading: figural language in Rousseau, Nietzsche, Rilke and Proust* (New Haven, CT: Yale University Press).

De Romilly, J. 1975. *Magic and Rhetoric in Ancient Greece* (Cambridge, MA: Harvard University Press).

Dempster, D. J. 1989. 'Exemplification and the cognitive value of art', in *Philosophy and Phenomenological Research*, 49:3, pp. 393–412.

Derrida, J. 1987. *The Post Card*, trans. A. Bass (Chicago, IL: University of Chicago Press).

Descartes, R. 1620. *Discours de la méthode*, Penguin Classics, 1999 (London: Penguin).

Dilthey, W. 1985. *Poetry and Experience*, ed. R. Makkreel and F. Rodi, vol. 5, *Selected Works* (Princeton, NJ: Princeton University Press).

Dixon, P. 1971. *Rhetoric* (London: Methuen).

Dourley, J. P. 1994. 'In the shadow of the monotheisms: Jung's conversations with Buber and White', in *Jung and the Monotheisms*, ed. J. Ryce-Menuhin, pp. 135–47 (London: Guild of Pastoral Psychology).

Dubois, J., F. Edeline, J.-M. Klinkenberg, P. Minguet, F Pire and H. Trinon (Group µ). 1970. *A General Rhetoric*, trans. P. B. Burrell and E. Slotkin, revised 1981. Centre for Poetic Studies, University of Liege (Baltimore, MD: Johns Hopkins University Press).

Dyck, J. 1989. 'Rhetoric and psychoanalysis', in *Rhetorical Society Quarterly*, 19:2 (Spring), pp. 95–104.
Einstein, A. 2007. *Autobiographical Notes*, ed. P. Schilpp, 2007 (Boston, MA: Open Court Press).
Ellenberger, H. 1970. *Discovery of the Unconscious: the history and evolution of dynamic psychiatry* (New York: Basic Books).
Ellman, R. 1984. *James Joyce* (Oxford: Oxford University Press).
Entralgo, P. L. 1970. *The Therapy of the Word in Classical Antiquity*, trans. L. J. Rather and J. M. Sharp (New Haven, CT: Yale University Press).
Erasmus, D. 1999. *On Copia of Words and Ideas*, trans. D. King and D. Rix (Marquette University Press).
Fahnestock, J. 1998. *Rhetorical Figures in Science* (Oxford: Oxford University Press).
——. 2000. 'Aristotle and theories of figuration', in *Rereading Aristotle,* ed. A. G. Gross and A. E. Walzer (Carbondale, IL: Southern Illinois University Press).
Fáj, A. 1987. 'Vico's basic law of history in *Finnegans Wake*', in *Vico and Joyce,* ed. D. P. Verene, pp. 20–31 (Stony Book, NY: State University of New York Press).
Farias, V. 1987. *Heidegger and Nazism*, ed. J. Margolis and T. Rockmore (Philadelphia PA: Temple University Press).
Felman, S. 1975. 'Madness and philosophy of literature's reason', in *Yale French Studies*, 52, pp. 206–28.
Fine, A. 1986. *The Shaky Game: Einstein realism and quantum theory* (Chicago, IL: University of Chicago Press).
Fisher, W. R. 1987. 'Technical logic, rhetorical logic, and narrative rationality', in *Argumentation*, 1:1, pp. 3–21.
Forrester, J. 1980. *Language and the Origins of Psychoanalysis* (London: Macmillan).
Fortenbaugh, W. 1975. *Aristotle on Emotion* (London: Duckworth).
Frascari, M. 1990. 'A new angel/angle in architectural research: the ideas of demonstration', in *Journal of Architectural Education*, 44:1 (November), pp. 11–19.
Frentz, T. S. 2006. 'Memory, myth, and rhetoric in Plato's Phaedrus', in *Rhetoric Society Quarterly*, 36:3 (Summer), pp. 243–63.
Freud, S. 1900. *Interpretation of Dreams*, reprint Penguin, 1986 (London: Penguin).
——. 1906. 'Psychoanalysis and establishment of the facts in legal proceedings', in *Standard Edition of Complete Psychological Works of Sigmund Freud*, vol. 9, pp. 97–114, trans. J Strachey (London: Hogarth Press).
——. 1913. 'Two lies told by children', in *Standard Edition of Complete Psychological Works of Sigmund Freud*, vol. 12, pp. 303–10.
——.1919. 'The Uncanny', in *Standard Edition of Complete Psychological Works of Sigmund Freud*, vol. 17, pp. 217–52.
——. 1925. 'Negation', in *Standard Edition of Complete Psychological Works of Sigmund Freud*, vol. 19, pp. 235–9.
Frye, N. 1957. *The Anatomy of Criticism* (Princeton, NJ: Princeton University Press).
——. 1987. 'Cycle and Apocalypse in *Finnegans Wake*', in *Vico and Joyce*, ed. D. P. Verene, pp. 3–19 (Albany, NY: State University of New York Press).
Furbini, M. 1946. *Stile e Umanita di Giambattista Vico* (Bari: Laterza).
Garin, E. 1983. *Astrology in the Renaissance*, 1961 (Copenhagen: GEC GAD Publishers).
Gaukroger, S. 1997. *Descartes* (Oxford: Oxford University Press).
Gelley, A. 1966. 'Ernst Robert Curtius: topology and critical method', in *MLN*, 81:5 (December), pp. 579–94.

Gennette, G. 1982. *Figures of Literary Discourse*, trans. A. Sheridan (1982) (Oxford: Blackwell).
Gergen, K. J. and M. Gergen. 1986. 'Narrative form and the construction of psychological science', in *Narrative psychology*, ed. T. R. Sarbin (New York: Praeger).
Giegerich, W., 1999. *The Soul's Logical Life* (Berlin: Peter Lang).
Gill, C. 1984. 'The ethos/pathos distinction in rhetorical and literary criticism', in *The Classical Quarterly* New series, 34:1, pp. 149–66.
Goetsch, Jr., J. R. 1995. *Vico's Axioms* (New Haven, CT: Yale University Press).
Goodman, N. 1952. 'Sense and Certainty', in *The Philosophical Review* 61:2 (April), pp. 160–7.
——. 1976. *Language of Art* (Indianapolis, IN: Hackett Publishers).
——. 1978. *Ways of Worldmaking* (London: Harvester).
Goss, A. G. 1990. *The Rhetoric of Science* (Cambridge, MA: Harvard University Press).
Gowland, A. 2001. 'Rhetorical structure and function in *The Anatomy of Melancholy*', in *Rhetorica*, 19:1, pp. 1–48.
Grassi, E. 1980. *Rhetoric as philosophy* (Philadelphia, PA: Pennsylvania State University Press).
——. 1990. 'Vico e Ovid: il problema della preminenza della metafora', in *Vico in Italia e in Germania: letture e prospetive*, ed. G. Cacciatore and G. Cantillo (Naples).
——. 1994. *Primordial Metaphor* (Binghampton, NY: Medieval & Renaissance Texts & Studies in collaboration with the Italian Academy).
Gregg, R. B. 1984. *Symbolic Inducement and Knowing, a study in the foundations of rhetoric* (Columbia, SC: University of South Carolina Press).
Grendler, P. F. 1989. *Schooling in Renaissance Italy* (Baltimore, MD: Johns Hopkins University Press).
Gross, A. 2002. *Chaim Perelman* (Albany, NY: State University of New York Press).
Gross, A. C. 2005. 'Presence as Argument in the public sphere', in *Rhetoric Society Quarterly,* 35 (Spring), pp. 5–21.
Gross, D. M. 1996. 'Metaphor and definition in Vico's *New Science*', in *Rhetorica* 14:4 (Autumn), pp. 359–81.
——. 2001. 'Early Modern Emotion and the Economy of Scarcity', in *Philosophy and Rhetoric*, 34:4, pp. 308–21.
——. 2006. *The Secret History of Emotion* (Chicago, IL: University of Chicago Press).
Gunn, J. 2005. *Modern occult rhetoric* (Tuscaloosa, AL: University of Alabama Press).
Hauser, Gerard A. 1986. *Introduction to Rhetorical Theory* (Long Grove, IL: Waveland Press).
Hermans, H. J. and H. J. G. Kempen. 1993. *Dialogical Self* (Boston, MA: Academic Press/Elsevier).
Hillman, J. 1960. *Emotions* (London: Routledge).
——. 1964. *Suicide and the Soul* (New Orleans, LA: Spring Publications).
——. 1975. *Loose Ends* (New Orleans, LA: Spring Publications).
——. 1983. *Archetypal Psychology* (New Orleans, LA: Spring Publications).
—— and K. Kerényi. 1990. *Oedipus Variations* (New Orleans, LA: Spring Publications).
——. 1992. *Re-visioning Psychology*, reissue edition (29 Feb 1992) (New York: Harper Perennial).
——. 1994. *Healing Fiction* (New Orleans, LA: Spring Publications).
——. 1997. *Myth of Analysis* (Chicago, IL: Northwestern University Press).

Hobbes, C. 2002. *Rhetoric on the margins of modernity: Vico, Condillac, Monboddo* (Carbondale, IL: Southern Illinois Press).

Hogenson, G. B. 2005. 'The self, the symbol and synchronicity; virtual realities and the emergence of the psyche', in *Journal of Analytical Psychology*, 50:3 (June), pp. 271–84.

Horace. 1969. 'The Art of Poetry', in *Classical Literary Criticism*, trans. T. S. Dusch (London: Penguin).

Hubback, J. 1973. 'The uses and abuses of analogy', in *Journal of Analytical Psychology*, 18, pp. 91–104.

Ijsseling, S. 1976. *Rhetoric and Philosophy in Conflict: an historical survey*, trans. Dunphy (The Hague: Nijhoff).

Jaffé, S. 1980. 'Freud as rhetorician: *Elocutio* and the dream-work', in *Rhetorik: Ein internationals jahrbuch*, pp. 42–69.

Jakobson, R. 1985. 'Verbal communication' and 'On aphasic disorder from a linguistic angle', in *Selected Writings VII: Contributions to comparative mythology. Studies in linguistics and philology 1972–1982*, ed. S. Rudy, pp. 81–2; pp. 128–41 (Gravenhage: Mouton Publishers).

James, S. 1997. *Passion and Action: the emotions in 17th century philosophy* (London: Oxford University Press).

James, W. 1907. *Pragmatism* (London: Longmans).

——. 1902. *Varieties of Religious Experience*, 1997 (New York: Simon and Schuster).

Jameson, F. 1977. 'Imaginary and symbolic in Lacan: Marxism, psychoanalytic criticism and the problem of subject', in *Yale French Studies* no. 55/56, Literature and Psychoanalysis. The Question of Reading: Otherwise, pp. 338–95.

——. 2007. *Archaeologies of the Future: The Desire Called Utopia and Other Science Fictions* (London: Verso Books).

Jardine, L. 1974. *Francis Bacon, Discovery and the Art of Discourse* (Cambridge: Cambridge University Press).

Johnson, B. 1977. 'The frame of reference: Poe, Lacan, Derrida', in *Yale French Studies*, no. 55/56, Literature and Psychoanalysis. The Question of Reading: Otherwise, pp. 457–505.

——. 2003. 'Allegory and psychoanalysis', in *Journal of African American History*, 88:1 (Winter), pp. 6–70.

Joyce, J. 1916. *Portrait of the Artist as a Young Man*, 1992 (London: Paladin).

——. 1939. *Finnegans Wake* (1999/1939) (London: Penguin).

Jung, C. G. 1960. *The Collected Works* ed. Sir Herbert Read, RFC Hull (London: Routledge Kegan Paul).

——. 1967. *VII Sermones mortuos* (London: Stuart and Watkins).

——. 1968. *Analytical Psychology: The Tavistock Lectures* (New York: Pantheon).

——. 1989/1961. *Memories, Dreams, Reflections* (New York: Vintage).

Kahn, J. with H. Solomon. 1975. *Job's Illness: Loss, Grief and Integration, A Psychological Interpretation* (Oxford: Pergamon).

Kalshed, D. 1996. *The Inner World of Trauma* (London: Brunner Routledge).

Kelley, D. 1969. 'Vico, law and history', in *Giambattista Vico: an international symposium*, ed. G. Tagliacozzo, pp. 601–11 (Baltimore, MD: Johns Hopkins University).

Kennedy, G. A. 1983. *Greek Rhetoric under Christian Emperors* (Princeton, NJ: Princeton University Press).

——. 1998. *Comparative Rhetoric; an historical and cross cultural introduction* (London: Oxford University Press).

——. 2003. 'Some recent controversies in study of late Greek rhetoric', in *American Journal of Philology*, pp. 295–301 (Baltimore, MD: Johns Hopkins University Press).

Kerrigan, W. 1991. *Psychiatry and the Humanities* 6 (New Haven, CT: Yale University Press).

Kerrigan, W. and J. H. Smith (eds). 1984. *Taking Chances: Derrida, psychoanalysis and literature* (Baltimore, MD: Johns Hopkins University Press).

King, P. 2004. 'Peter Abelard', *The Stanford Encyclopedia of Philosophy* (Fall 2004 Edition), Edward N. Zalta (ed.), at http://plato.stanford.edu/archives/fall2004/entries/abelard/ (accessed April 2007).

Klossowski, P. 2005. *Nietzsche and the Vicious Circle* (New York: Continuum).

Kovecses, Z. and G. Radden. 1998. 'Metonymy: developing a cognitivist view', in *Cognitive Linguistics* (includes *Cognitive Linguistic Bibliography*), 9:1, pp. 37–78.

Kristeva, J. 1983. 'Within the microcosm of "the talking cure"', in *Interpreting Lacan*, trans. T. Gora and M. Waller, ed. J. H. Smith, pp. 33–48 (New Haven, CT: William Kerrigan Yale University Press).

Kugler, P. 1982. *The Alchemy of Discourse* (Philadelphia, PA: Bucknell University Press).

——. 2005. *Raids on the Unthinkable* (New Orleans, LA: Spring Journal).

Kuhn, T. 1962. *The Structures of Scientific Revolutions* (Chicago, IL: University of Chicago Press).

——. 1979. 'Metaphor in science', in *Metaphor and Thought*, ed. A. Ortony, pp. 408–19 (Cambridge: Cambridge University Press).

Lacan, J. 1977. *Four Fundamental Concepts of Psycho-analysis* (London: Hogarth Press).

——. 1981. *The Language of the Self: the function of language in psychoanalysis.* trans. and notes by A. Wilden (Baltimore, MD: Johns Hopkins University Press).

——. 2002. *Ecrits*, trans. B. Fink (New York: W. W. Norton).

Lachterman, D. R. 1983.'Descartes and the philosophy of history', in *Independent Journal of Philosophy*, 4, pp. 31–46 (Oxford: Oxford Univesity Press).

——. 1985. 'Mathematics and nominalism in Vico's *Liber metaphysicus*', in *Sachkommentaur zu Giambattista Vico 'Liber metaphysicus*', ed. S. Otto and H. Viechtbauer (Berlin: Willhelm Fink Verlag).

——. 1989. *The Ethics of Geometry* (London: Routledge (London).

Lakoff, G. and M. Johnson. 1980. *Metaphors We Live by* (Chicago, IL: University of Chicago Press).

Lammers, A. C. 1994. *In God's Shadow: the collaboration of Victor White and C G Jung* (Mahwah, NJ: Paulist Press).

Lanham, R. 1991. *Handlist of Rhetorical Terms* (Berkeley, CA: University of California).

Lear, J. 1988. *Aristotle, the Desire to Understand* (Cambridge: Cambridge University Press).

——. 1998. *Open Minded: working out the logic of the soul* (Cambridge, MA: Harvard University Press).

——. 1992. *Love and its Place in Nature* (London: Faber & Faber).

——. 2005. *Freud* (London: Routledge).

Leff, M. 1983. 'The topics of argumentative invention in Latin rhetorical theory from Cicero to Boethius', in *Rhetorica*, 1:1 (Spring), pp. 23–44 (Irvine, CA: University of California).

——. 1993. 'Uses of Aristotle's *Rhetoric* in contemporary American scholarship', in *Argumentation*, 7, pp. 313–27.

——. 1996. 'Commonplaces and argumentation in Cicero and Quintilian', in *Argumentation*, 10, pp. 445–52.

——. 2000. 'Rhetoric and dialectic in the 21st century', in *Argumentation*, 14, pp. 241–54.

——. 2003. 'Tradition and agency in Humanistic rhetoric', in *Philosophy and Rhetoric*, 36:2, pp. 135–47.

Lenz, M. 2005. 'Peculiar perfection: Peter Abelard on propositional attitudes', in *Journal of the History of Philosophy*, 43:4, pp. 377–86.

Littleford, M. S. and J. R. Whitt. 1988. *Giambattista Vico, post-mechanical thought and contemporary psychology* (London: Peter Lang).

Longinus. 1969. 'On the sublime', in *Classical Literary Criticism*, trans. T. S. Dusch (London: Penguin).

Mack, P. 2011. *A History of Renaissance Rhetoric, 1380–1620* (Oxford: Oxford University Press).

Mahony, P. 1977. 'Toward a formalist approach to dreams', in *International Review of Psycho-Analysis*, 4, pp. 83–98.

——. 1987a. *Freud as a Writer* (New Haven, CT: Yale University Press).

——. 1987b. *Psychoanalysis and Discourse* (London: Tavistock).

Main, R. 2000. 'Religion, science and synchronicity', in *Harvest*, 46:2, pp. 25–36.

Makkreel, R. A. 1975. *Dilthey: Philosopher of the human studies* (Princeton, NJ: Princeton University Press).

Mali, J. 1997. *The Rehabilitation of Myth* (Cambridge: Cambridge University Press).

Manuel, F. 1959. *The Eighteenth Century Confronts the Gods* (Boston, MA: Harvard University Press).

——. 1968. *Reflections on Philosophy of History by Herder*, introduction Manuel Frank, trans. T. O. Churchill (Chicago, IL: University of Chicago Press).

Marshall, D. L. 2010. *Vico and the Transformation of Rhetoric in Early Modern Europe* (Cambridge, MA and Cambridge: Cambridge University Press).

Mathien, T. and D. G. Wright (eds). 2006. *Autobiography as Philosophy: the philosophical uses of self-presentation* (London: Routledge).

Mazlish, B. 1996. *The Riddle of History* (New York: Harper and Row).

McClure, G. 1991. *Sorrow and Consolation in Italian Humanism* (Princeton, NJ: Princeton University Press).

McKeon R. 1966. 'Philosophy and the development of scientific methods', in *Journal of the History of Ideas*, 27:1 (January–March), pp. 3–22.

Mogenson, G. 2005. *A Most Accursed Religion: when a trauma becomes God* (New Orleans, LA: Spring Publications).

Mooney, M. 1985. *Vico and the Tradition of Rhetoric* (Princeton, NJ: Princeton University Press).

Muller, J. P. and W. J. Richardson (eds). 1988. *The Purloined Poe: Lacan, Derrida, and psychoanalytic reading* (Baltimore, MD: Johns Hopkins Press).

Myerson, G. 1984. *Rhetoric, Reason and Society* (London: Sage Publications).

Natali, C. 1994. 'La retorica di Aristotle negli studi europei piu recenti', in *Peripatetic Rhetoric after Aristotle*, ed. W. Fortenbaugh, pp. 365–82, Rutgers Classical Studies vol. 6 (New Brunswick, NJ: Transaction).

Nelson Jr, Lowry. 1961. *Baroque Lyric Poetry* (New Haven, CT: Yale University Press).

Neumann, E. 1982. *The Origins and History of Consciousness* (London: Routledge Kegan Paul).

Niccolini, F. 1927. *Giambattista Vico nella vita domestica: la moglie, I figli, la casa* (Milan: Edizioni Osanna Venosa).

Nichols, M. F. 1987. 'Aristotle's defence of rhetoric', in *The Journal of Politics*, 49:3 (August), pp. 657–77.

Nietzsche, F. 1979. 'On the pathos of truth' (1873); 'On truth and lies in a nonmoral sense' (1873); 'The philosopher as cultural physician' (1873) from *Philosophy and Truth: Selections from Nietzsche's Notebooks of the early 1870's*, ed. D. Breazeale (Atlantic Hieghts, NJ: Humanities Press).

Nussbaum, M. 1994. *Therapy of Desire* (Princeton, NJ: Princeton University Press).

——. 2001. *Upheavals of Thought* (Boston, MA: Cambridge University Press).

Ogden, C. K. and I. A. Richards. 1923. *The Meaning of Meaning* (London: Kegan Paul).

Ong, W. J. 1958. *Ramus: Method and the Decay of Dialogue from the Art of Discourse to the Art of Reason* (Cambridge, MA: Harvard University Press).

——. 1982. *Orality and Literacy* (London: Methuen).

Papadopoulos, R. 1984. 'Jung and the concept of the Other', in *Critical Assessments* (London: Routledge).

Papadopoulos, R. and G. S. Saayman (eds). 1984. *Jung in Modern Perspective* (London: Wildwood House).

Parkes, G. 1994. *Composing the Soul: The Reaches of Nietzsche's Psychology* (Chicago, IL: University of Chicago Press).

Perelman, C. 1963. *Idea of Justice and the Problem of Argument* , trans. J. Petrie (London: Routledge Kegan Paul).

——. 1982. *The Realm of Rhetoric* (Notre Dame, IN: University of Notre Dame Press).

Perelman, C. and L. Olbrechts-Tyteca. 1969. *The New Rhetoric: A Treatise on Argumentation,* trans. J. Wilkinson and P. Weaver (Notre Dame, IN: University of Notre Dame Press).

Pettegrew, L. 1977. 'Psychoanalytic theory: a neglected rhetorical dimension', in *Philosophy and Rhetoric*, 10 (Winter), pp. 46–59.

Pietikainen, P. 1999. *C. G. Jung and the Psychology of Symbolic Forms* (Norway: Academia Scientarum Fennica).

Pietropaolo, D. 1987. 'Vico and literary history', in *Vico and Joyce*, ed. D. P. Verene, pp. 100–9 (Albany, NY: SUNY Press).

——. 2000. 'Scrissela da filosofo: The Life of Giambattista Vico Written by himself', in *Autobiography as Philosophy*, ed. T. Mathien and D. G. Wright, pp. 109–19 (London: Routledge).

Pirelli, L. J. 1989. *A Rhetoric of Science: Inventing Scientific Discourse* (Columbia, SC: South Carolina Press).

Plato. 1959. *Gorgias*, revised edition with commentary E. R. Dodds.

——. 1994. *Symposium*, trans. Dover reprint (New York, USA).

——. 2008. *Timaeus and Critias*, trans. T. J. Johansen, Penguin Classics (London: Penguin).

——. 2012. *Cratylus*, trans. Penguin (London, UK).

Polkinghorne D. E. 1989. *Narrative, Knowing and the Human Sciences* (Albany NY: State University of New York Press).

Pritchard, J. B. 1950. *Ancient Near Eastern Texts* (Princeton, NJ: Princeton University Press).
Proust, M. 1999. *The Captive* (*In Search of Lost Time*, vol. 5) (Penguin, Modern Library).
Putnam, H. 1979. 'Reflections of Goodman's Ways of Worldmaking', in *Journal of Philosophy,* 76:11, pp. 603–18.
Quintilian. 2001. *Orator's Education*, trans. D. A. Rusell, Loeb Classical Library, vols 1–12 (Boston, MA: Harvard University Press).
Reiff, P. 1959. *Freud: The Mind of the Moralist.* (New York: Viking Press).
Richards, I. A. and C. Ogden. 1923. *The Meaning of Meaning*. International Library of Psychology, Philosophy and Scientific Method/Routledge reissue (London: Routledge).
Ricoeur, P. 1970. *Freud and Philosophy* (New Haven, CT: Yale University Press).
——. 1975.*The Rules of Metaphor* (Toronto: University of Toronto Press).
——. 1978. 'Psychoanalysis, physics and the mind–body problem", in *The Annual of Psychoanalysis*, pp. 336–42.
——. 1995. *Figuring the Sacred: Religion, Narrative, and Imagination*, trans. D. Pellauer (Minneapolis, MIN: Fortress Press).
Rorher, T. C. 1999. 'When metaphors bewitch, analogies illustrate, and logic fails: controversies over the use of metaphoric reasoning in philosophy and science' (DPhil thesis, University of Oregon).
Rowland, S. 1999. *C. G. Jung and Literary Theory* (London: Macmillan).
——. 2005.*Jung as a Writer* (London: Routledge).
—— (ed.). 2008. *Psyche and Imagination* (London: Routledge).
Said, E. 1985. *Beginnings* (New York: Columbia University Press).
Samuels, A. 1984.*Jung and Post-Jungians* (London: Routledge Kegan Paul).
—— with A. Plaut. 1986. *Critical Dictionary of Jungian Analysis* (London: Routledge Kegan Paul).
Schaeffer, J. 1990. *Sensus Communis: Vico, Rhetoric and the Limits of Relativism* (Columbia, NC: Duke University Press).
Schaeffer J. and P. Eubanks. 2004. 'A dialogue between traditional and cognitive rhetoric: readings in figuration', in *Rhetoric Society Quarterly*, 34:2 (Spring), pp. 53–70.
Schafer, R. 1976. *A New Language for Psychoanalysis* (New Haven, CT: Yale University Press).
Scult, A. 1999. 'Aristotle's Rhetoric as ontology: a Heideggerian reading', in *Philosophy and Rhetoric*, 32:2, pp. 146–59.
Shamandasani, S. 2003.*Jung and the Making of Modern Science* (Cambridge: Cambridge University Press).
——. 2004. 'Psychologies as ontology-making practices', in *William James and the Varieties of Religious Experience*, ed. J. Carrette (London: Routledge).
Sherwood, M. 1969. *The Logic of Explanation in Psychoanalysis* (Boston, MA: Academic Press, Harvard Medical School).
Shotter, J. 1993. *Conversational Realities: Constructing Life through Language* (Indianapolis, IN: Sage Publications).
Sloane, T. 1997. *On the Contrary: The Protocol of Traditional Rhetoric* (Georgetown: Catholic University Press).
Solmsen F. 1938. 'Aristotle and Cicero on the orator's playing upon the feelings, in *Classical Philology*, 33:4 (October), pp. 390–404.

Sorel, G. 1950. *Letter to Daniel Halévy* (1907) from *Reflections on Violence* (1908), trans. T. E. Hulme and J. Roth, pp. 26–56 (New York: Collier).
——. 1908. *Studies de Vico* in *Speculum*, 34:1 (January), pp. 76–89.
Spence, D. 1982. *Narrative Truth and Historical Truth: Meaning and Interpretation in Psychoanalysis* (New York: Norton).
——. 1994. *Rhetorical Voice of Psychoanalysis: Displacement of Evidence by Theory* (Cambridge, MA: Harvard University Press).
Spitzer, L. 1948. *Linguistics and Literary History* (Princeton, NJ: Princeton University Press)
Sprinker, M. 1980. 'Fictions of the self: the end of autobiography', in *Autobiography: Essays Theoretical and Critical*, ed. J. Olney (Princeton. NJ: Princeton University Press).
Stanley, J. and C. From. 1976. *Georges Sorel* (Oxford: Oxford University Press).
Starobinski, J. 1970. 'Le style de l'autobiographie', in *Poetique* no. 3, pp. 257–64.
——. 1975. 'The inside and the outside', in *Hudson Review*, 28:3 (Autumn), pp. 333–51.
Stern, C. and W. Stern. 1907. *Recollection, Testimony and Lying in Early Childhood* , trans. J. Lamiell, 1999, Washington, DC: American Psychological Association).
Stocks, J. L. 1933. 'The composition of Aristotle's logical works', in *The Classical Quarterly*, 27:2 (April), pp. 115–24.
Struever, N. 1974. 'Classical investigations', in *New Literary History*, 5:3, pp. 515–26.
——. 1983. 'Fables of power', in *Representations*, 4 (Autumn), pp. 108–27.
——. 2005. 'The impersonal in Vico: "the classical endures because it is impersonal" in Il corpo e le sue facolta G. B. Vico, a cura di G. Cacciatore, V. Gessa Kurotschka, E. Nuzzo, M. Sanna e A. Scognamiglio in ' Laboratorio dell'ISPF' at www.ispf.cur.it/ispf-lab)II (accessed 31 July 2011).
Tell, D. 1996. 'Gorgias: Sophist and artist', in *Rhetoric Society Quarterly*, 35 (Summer), p. 242.
Thomas, D. 1993., 'Burke, Nietzsche, Lacan: three perspectives on the rhetoric of order", in *Quarterly Journal of Speech* 79, pp. 336–55.
Tindale, C. W. 2004. *Rhetorical Argumentation* (New York: Sage Publications).
Todorov, T. 1982. *Theories of the Symbol*, trans. C. Porter (Paris: du Sueil).
Toulmin, S. 1949. 'The logical status of psychoanalysis', in *Analysis*, pp. 23–9.
——. 1958. *The Uses of Argument* (Cambridge: Cambridge University Press).
Uitti, K. D. 1969. *Linguistics and Literary Theory* (New York: Norton).
Vaihinger, H. 1935. *The Philosophy of 'as if'*, trans. C. K. Ogden (London: Kegan Paul).
Verene, D. P. 1976. 'Vico's science of imaginative universals and the philosophy of symbolic forms', in *Giambattista Vico's Science of Humanity*, ed. G. Tagliacozzo and D. P. Verene (Atlantic Heights, NJ: Humanities Press).
——. 1981. *Vico's Science of the Imagination* (New York: Cornell University Press).
—— (ed.). 1987. *Vico and Joyce* (Albany, NY: State University of New York Press).
——. 1991. *The New Art of Autobiography: An Essay on the Life of Giambattista Vico, written by himself* (Oxford: Oxford University Press).
——. 1997. 'Freud's consulting room archaeology and Vico's principles of humanity: a communication', in *British Journal of Psychotherapy*, 13:4, pp. 499–505.
——. 2002. 'Coincidence, historical repetition and self-knowledge: Jung, Vico and Joyce', in *Journal of Analytical Psychology*, 47:3 (July), pp. 459–78.

Vickers, B. 1988. *In Defence of Rhetoric* (Oxford: Oxford University Press).
Vico, G. 1993. *On Humanistic Education: Six Inaugural Orations 1699–1707*, trans. G. A. Pinton and A. W. Shippee (New York: Cornell University Press).
——. 1709. *On Study Methods of our Times*, trans. E. Gianturco and B. Merrill, 1965 (Indianapolis).
——. 1711. *On the Most Ancient Wisdom of the Italians*, trans. L. Palmer, 1988 (New York: Cornell University Press).
——. 1711–41. *The Art of Rhetoric*, trans. and ed. G. A. Pinton and A. Q. Shippee, 1984 (Amsterdam: Rodopi).
——. 1725–31. *Autobiography*, trans. M. Fisch and T. G. Bergin, 1944, revised 1963 (New York: Cornell University Press).
——. 1730/1744. *The New Science, 2nd edn*, trans. M. Fisch and T. Bergin, 1948 (New York: Cornell University Press).
Wardy, R. 1996. *The Birth of Rhetoric* (London: Routledge).
Warnick, B. 2000. 'Topics', in *Rereading Aristotle*, ed. A. G. Gross and A. E. Walzer (Carbondale, IL: Southern Illinois University Press).
Wellek, R. 1962. 'Auerbach's debt to Vico', in *Lettere italiane*, 53, pp. 1–22.
White, H. 1974. *Metahistory* (Baltimore, MD: Johns Hopkins University Press).
——. 1978. *Tropics of Discourse* (Baltimore, MD: Johns Hopkins University Press).
Whitmont, E. 1961. 'The magical dimension in transference and counter-transference', in *Current Trends in Analytical Psychology*, pp. 182 ff.
Wilden, A. 1973. 'On Lacan, psychoanalysis, language and communication', in *Contemporary Psychoanalysis*, 9, pp. 445–70.
Wilshire, B. 1997. 'The breathtaking intimacy of the material world: William James's last thoughts', in *Cambridge Companion to William James*, ed R. Putnam, pp. 103–24.
Wind, E. 1980. *Pagan Mysteries in the Renaissance* (Oxford: Oxford University Press).
Winnicott, D. 1992. 'Review of *Memories, Dreams, Reflections*', in *Critical Assessments: Jung and his method in Contexts*, ed. R. Papadopoulos, pp. 315–22 (London: Routledge).
Witzenmann, W. 1935. *Politischer aktivismus und sozialer mythos: Giambattista Vico und die Lehre des faschismus*, Neue deutsche Forshungen, Bd 15 pp. 160 ff. (Berlin Germany).
Yates, F. 1969. *Giordano Bruno and the Hermetic Tradition* (London: Routledge).
——. 1969. *The Art of Memory* (London: Penguin).

INDEX

abduction 14
Abélard 7, 40, 52, 57, 61–2, 64–6, 74, 99, 203
Abraham 159–60
abstraction 12–13, 63–4, 146, 162
accuracy 55, 104, 123
action 37
acuity 48, 51
Adam and Eve 164
addressees *see* audience
Adler, G. 67
adverbs 8, 20, 64
Africa 117, 175–6, 201–3
afterlife 38, 203–4
Agricola, R. 45
agriculture 190
Aion 157
alchemy 30, 33, 36, 76–81, 190, 200
Alchemy of Discourse 25
aliens 86
allegory 11, 122
ambiguity 27, 98
amplification 14, 27, 31, 33–4, 98–100, 104; Jung/Vico affinities 107–8
analogy 22, 27, 90, 92, 94–5
analytical psychology 2, 16, 189
Anatomy of Criticism 84, 115
Anatomy of Melancholy 180–1
anger 149, 151, 153–6, 163, 165
anima 34, 38, 79, 195
animals 3–4, 21
anomalies 87, 179
Answer to Job 67, 149, 151–3, 156–7, 159–60, 162–6, 180, 182
antinomies 165
Antisthenes 62
aphasia 94
Aphrodite 135
Apollo 10, 109, 162
appearance/reality 37–8, 43, 75, 189
appropriateness *see decorum*
Archaeologies of the Future 87
archaic 85, 98, 106, 110, 113, 124, 201; Jung/Vico affinities 114–19
archetypal psychology 10, 26, 34, 109, 124
archetypes 4–6, 13, 206; Jung/Vico affinities 106–9, 113; of meaning 37–8
Archetypes and the collective unconscious 37, 51
Arguing and Thinking 147
argumentation 2, 16, 19–20, 24, 26, 69; dream as argument 30–1
Arieti, S. 106, 113
aristocracy 80
Aristotle 4–5, 7, 19, 37, 39–42, 45–8, 52, 55, 89–91, 122, 128, 135, 138, 143, 149–51, 153–6, 160, 162, 178, 180, 189
arousal 100
arrangement *see* dispositio
Ars poetica 139
ars topica 7
art 50, 58–9, 83
Art of Rhetoric 8, 148
artifice 50
associations 37, 126–30, 132–5, 137–40, 142, 144–8, 205; memoirs 186–9

assumptions 13, 30
astrology 36
audience 5–6, 29; memoirs 178, 181, 192–5; *pathé* 152, 154–6; tensions 20, 22–3; topical invention 37, 50
Auerbach, E. 3, 55, 104, 120–2, 162
Augustine 10, 14–15, 122, 155, 168, 172, 179, 196
authenticity 123, 139
author 23–4
authority 42, 49–50, 52–3
Autobiographical Notes (Einstein) 193
autobiography 6, 9–10, 37, 117, 168–9, 172, 177, 180–1, 189–92 *see also Memories, Dreams, Reflections*
Autobiography (Vico) 3, 5, 9, 71, 118, 155, 168, 171–3, 179, 189

baby 186, 195, 197, 203
Bacon, F. 71, 118
Badiou, A. 83
Bakhtin, M.M. 192–3
Baroque prose 2
Barthès, R. 23, 37
Baudrillard, J. 69
Baynes, H. 8
becoming more oneself 10 *see also* self-discovery
Benjamin, W. 2, 8, 58, 67
Bergin, T.G. 8
Bible 152, 156, 162–3, 204
bile 5, 155, 190
Billig, M. 20–1, 147, 198
Bishop, P. 159, 163–4
Bitzer, L. 15, 47, 150, 174, 178–9, 181
black bile 5, 190
blame *see* epideictic rhetoric
Blass, A. 8
Bloch, E. 156
body 92
Boethius 41
Bologna 75
Booth, W. 5, 16, 21, 23
borrowing 90
Brown, N.O. 22
Buber, M. 158, 182
burial 11
Burke, K. 7, 23, 70, 205
Burton, R. 180–1

Cadmus 79–80
Caesar 48
canons of rhetoric 23, 37, 39
Capital 3
Carotenuto, A. 26
case studies 17
categories 144–7
catharsis 154
Catholicism 32, 34, 66, 92, 165, 185, 187
causality 19, 85
centaur 59
certainty 11–12, 16, 24, 43, 46, 101–2, 120–1
children 5, 138, 168–73, 186–7; comparison to 'primitives' 63, 114–18; illegitimate 151; Jung's childhood 176, 189, 191, 195–7; lies 132, 139
chreia 52
Christ *see* Jesus
Christianity 32, 34, 67, 79–80, 82, 92, 152–3, 157, 163–5, 199, 201
chronology 189
Chronos *see* Saturn
church 32–3, 92, 96, 122
Cicero 3, 7, 15n2, 29, 41–2, 47, 49–51, 100, 120, 129, 131, 136, 155, 161, 192
Clark University 139–40
Clarke, A.C. 86
clear and distinct ideas 53–4
Cocchiarella, N.B. 62, 65
cognition: pre-eminence of imagination 106, 109–14, 116; role of emotion 153, 155, 157
cognitivism 99
coincidence 44, 124–5
collective 34; individual's relation to 4–7
collective unconscious 24, 38, 81–3, 173, 206; Jung/Vico affinities 106, 110, 113; topics/common sense 41–2
common sense 6, 24, 41, 43, 55, 106, 120–1, 136, 142

Communion 67
complexes 118, 127–30, 140, 144–5, 147–8, 174, 206; 'truth' 135–8
conceptualism 65
conclusion phase *see lysis*
concreteness 63–4
Confessions (Augustine) 14, 168, 172, 179
configi 70
coniunctiones 30
conjecture 130–1, 133
Connecticut Yankee in King Arthur's Court 84
Conrad, J. 155
consciousness, origins of 115
constellations 129
constraints 178, 181–3; associations 186–9; mythic formula 189–92; secrets 183–6
containment 76–9
contexts 93
Conversational Realities 21
convincing, vs. persuading 194
copiousness 24, 26, 31, 50, 98–100, 107
corsi 124, 167
cosmology 204
courtroom 129–35
creativity 191 *see also* imagination
creeds 103
criminals 127, 130–1, 141, 144
Croll, M.W. 2
Crowley, A. 17
Crowley, S. 42
culmination phase *see peripeteia*
culture 7, 113, 120
currency 142
Curtius, E.R. 16, 30, 53, 106–7, 119
cyclicality 124–5

Danesi, M. 106, 109–10, 115
Daphne 10, 109
Darwin, C. 115
death 191, 203–4
decorum 14, 36, 122
deduction 39, 47, 52, 101
definition 161–2
Deleuze, G. 2
deliberative rhetoric 37, 126, 180
Delusion and Dream 18
demonstration 46–7 *see also* proof
Dempster, D.J. 59
Derrida, J. 8, 23, 37, 72–4
Descartes, R. 35, 39, 41, 49, 52–4, 72, 101, 136–7, 155, 173
desire 97
determinism 188
development phase 29–31
dialect 146
dialectic 23–4, 27, 37, 41, 144, 172; dialectical invention 39
dialogism 20, 22
Dilthey, W. 3, 120–1
Diogenes 64
disassociation 188–9
discernment 125
Discours 53–4
dismemberment 78
dispersal 175
dispositio 15, 37, 76, 122, 139–41
disturbances 174
divinity 153
divisio 30–1
divisions of rhetoric 37
Dora case 17
dormant metaphor 92
Dourley, J.P. 158–9
dramatic structure 29, 31–3
dreams 14, 37, 79, 96–9, 103–5, 121; memoirs 176, 183–5, 190, 195–6, 198; rhetorical stance 29–33; space travel 83
drives 5, 150
Dupin 71–3

Eastern rhetoric 37
Ecclesiastes 69
Ecrits 71
education 121–2, 146–7, 172–3
effigy 70–1
Ego 199
Egyptians 11, 123
Eighteenth Century Confronts the Gods 115
Einstein, A. 22, 99, 103, 192–3
elenchus 144
Ellenberger, H. 127

elocutio 41, 54, 137, 142; vs. *logos* 135–6
eloquence 26, 35–6, 54, 181
emotion 149–51, 153–7, 159–63
empiricism 101–3
enactment 167–9, 174–6
Encomium on Helen 54
English 22; translations 8
Enigma of Bologna 71, 75–8, 80–2, 85, 98
Enlightenment 24, 135
Enneads 122
enthymeme 7, 40, 42, 46–8, 95, 148
Entralgo, P.L. 7, 22
epideictic rhetoric 37, 179–80
epiphora 90–1
epistemology 39, 59, 85, 107
epistolary 10
epitaph 75–8
Erasmus 99–100
Eros and Pathos 26
errors 55
Estés, C.P. 26
eternal history 172
ethos 39–40, 136, 167, 180–1
etymologies 14–15, 54–6, 69–70, 99–101, 104, 143, 161, 173–4; Jung/Vico affinities 107, 119–22; *rhetorica* 35
Europe 135
European Literature and the Latin Middle Ages 30, 53, 107
event 83
evidence 30, 101–3, 126, 130, 143, 193–4
evil 80, 152–3, 155–6, 159, 164–5
exemplification 58–60
exemplum 27
exigency 178–9
expectation 179
experience 103, 143
experiment 7, 126–7, 139, 145–7
expositio 29–31, 37, 120
expression, and translation 8
extraversion 64, 66
Ezekiel 165

fable 10–11, 14, 54, 56, 120, 141–3, 182, 193, 199; Cadmus 79–81
fact 55, 79, 88, 99, 101–3, 128, 193–4, 206
facticity 103, 163
Fahnestock, J. 19, 22, 95, 136, 141, 144
faith 152
fallacious argument 47
family 109
fantasia 7, 55–6, 105
fantasy 54, 66–7, 84, 86–7, 96–7
Faust 171
fear 45, 183–5
feeling 151, 162
feigning 70–1
feminine 32–4, 164–5 *see also* anima
fiction 71–5, 81, 169
figural language 16–21, 24, 26–7, 39–40, 88–95
Figural rhetoric in science 141
Fine, A. 22, 193
Finnegans Wake 3, 124, 167
fluency 35–6, 50, 53, 139
flying saucers 38, 67, 81–7, 104, 203
foreign-ness 201
forensics 30, 37, 128–35; inadequacies 146–8; techniques 139–46; truth complex 135–8
Fortenbaugh, W. 22, 153–4
France, A. 61
Frascari, M. 36
free will 96
Freud, S. 8, 31–2, 37, 50, 67, 72, 93–4, 96–8, 113, 126–8, 132, 134, 138, 186, 198; science tensions 16–20, 22–4
Freud as a Writer 23
Frisch, M. 8
Frye, N. 3, 84, 115
funeral orations 180

genealogy 109
genera *see* universals
Genesis 159–60
Gennette, G. 69
genre 82, 84, 181, 192
gente 7, 24, 121, 199
German 8, 138
Giegerich, W. 115, 116, 120

given 174, 183, 185–7
God 5, 96–7, 101, 150–3, 156–60, 162–6, 179, 204
goddesses 135
godlikeness 161–2
gods 5, 117–18, 123, 137, 201–2 *see also* Saturn
Goethe, J.W. 3, 171
good/evil 80
Goodman, N. 57–63
Gorgias 20, 47, 54, 69
Goss, A. 141
Gowland, A. 180
grammar 37
Grassi, E. 3, 12, 55, 112, 116, 176–7
Greek 35
Greeks 3, 22, 38, 53, 135, 189
Gregg, R.B. 179
Grendler, P.F. 100
Gross, A. 22, 161, 163, 194
Gross, D.M. 91–2, 150–1, 154–5
Grotius, H. 173
Guardian 18
guilt 130–5, 139, 141, 143
Gunn, J. 17–18, 21

Habermas, J. 5, 18
hallucinations 82
Harries, 196
harvest 190
Hauser, G.A. 43, 45
Hawhee, D. 42
healing *see* therapy
Healing Fiction 108, 118
Hebrews 5
Heidegger, M. 3, 12, 150
heimlich 8
Hercules 4
hermaphrodite 34, 78
hermeneutics 1, 9 *see also* interpretation
Hermes 11, 109
Hermes Trismegisthus 123
heroism 190, 192
Hill, R.F.C. 75
Hillman, J. 1–2, 3, 4, 10, 26, 34, 106, 108–9, 115, 118–20, 122–4, 157–8, 162, 190
historians 70
history 25, 109, 204; alternative 84; of consciousness 115; Descartes' attitude to 49; ideal eternal 3; Vico's laws of 105
hoax 71–2, 77–8, 98
Holy Spirit 163
Homer 38, 50, 123, 162, 177
Homeric times 7, 22
homosexuality 202
Horatio 42, 49, 51, 139
Hubbard, L.R. 17
human nature 11–12
human rights 150
humanism 1, 104
humanity 152, 163–4, 204
humours 5, 155, 190
hybrid texts 2, 82, 86
hysteria 17

I Ching 124–5
identification 7, 23
identity 11
ideology 57
Iliad 38, 154, 162
imagination 12–13, 40, 54, 75, 115–16, 121; pre-eminence in cognition 109–14
imaginative universals 4, 10, 12–13; Jung/Vico affinities 106–12
imitation 70–1, 89, 104 *see also Mimesis*
impersonal 4, 6, 9–10, 37, 151, 154, 172, 205–6; audience 29
incarnation 164
incontrovertability 24–7
India 201
Indians *see* Native Americans
indignation 151, 153
individual 12, 29, 112–13; nominalism 58, 62–5; relation to collective 4–7; Vico's schema 9
individuation 10, 13, 113–14, 124–5, 167–70, 189, 191–2, 195
inference 7, 40, 42
inherence 62
insinuato 160, 164
instincts 5, 150
Institutiones oratoriae 35, 181

intellectual universals 6, 110
intelligible universals 4, 11, 13
intentionality 45; author's intentions 23–4
interior, personal 9, 110, 126, 198, 205
internal dialogue 175
interpretation: of dreams 29–33, 37, 99, 121; and translation 8; trauma of 73 *see also* hermeneutics
Interpretation of Dreams 17
introversion 64, 66
inventio 7, 36–7, 39, 41–2, 46, 98–100, 114, 136, 144–5, 148
Ion 8
irony 44, 88
irrationality 5–6, 40, 153
Isocrates 14, 129
Italian 8
Italy 119

Jacobi, M. 3
Jaffé, A. 168, 178, 183
Jaffé, S. 8, 37
Jakobson, R. 90, 94
James, W. 83, 97–9, 102–3, 131–2, 137
Jameson, F. 87
Jesus 14, 67, 122, 153, 163–5, 187, 195–6, 199
Job 67, 149, 151–3, 156–7, 159–60, 162–6, 180, 182
Johnson, B. 72–3
Johnson, M. 91–2, 95
Johnson, N. 22
Jove 25, 184–5
Joyce, J. 1–3, 74, 124–5, 167–71
Judas 96–7
judgment 45, 59, 75, 180; *Answer to Job* 161–5
juridical rhetoric *see* forensics

kairos 42
Kalsched, D. 118
Kant, I. 188
Kellery, D.R. 121
Kennedy, G. 3–4, 37
Kirby, J. 91
knowledge: of self 204 *see also* epistemology
Kovecses, Z. 93
Kugler, P. 25–6, 95
Kuhn, T. 16, 58

Lacan, J. 22–3, 69–74, 81, 87, 90, 93–5, 97–8
Lakoff, G. 91–2, 95
Langer, S. 21
language 80, 93; and culture 7; etymologies 69–70, 119–21; figural 16–21, 24, 26–7; translations 8–9
Lanham, R. 30, 44
Latin 35–6, 70–1, 79, 104
law 151, 161; written vs. natural 161
Leff, M. 24
letters, Jung's 29
libido 50, 91, 96, 198
lies 132, 139
Literary Language in Late Latin Antiquity 120, 122
literary theory 3, 82
logic 2, 11, 17, 19–21, 41, 45, 47; topical/poetic 7
logos 39, 53–4, 128, 137, 180; vs. *elocutio* 135–6
Longinus 3, 42, 49, 51, 122, 166, 175
Loose Ends 108
Lucretius 173
Luther, M. 57, 62, 67
lysis 29, 31

magic 22, 36, 141–2
Mahony, P.J. 8–9, 22–4
Maier, M. 78
mandalas 123
manikin 176, 185
Manuel, F. 115, 183
Marshall, D. 3
Marx, K. 3, 156
Mass 185, 187
mathematics 135, 137
meaning 32, 119, 177, 204; archetype of 37–8; making of 11; transfer of 14; and translation 8–9
mechanistic language 20
medieval philosophy 41, 65–6

Meditations 49
Memories, Dreams, Reflections 8, 63, 167–70, 174–83, 186–7, 189, 192–3; confrontation with unconscious 199; Late thoughts/Retrospect 204; prologue 195–7; psychiatry/Freud 198; travels 200–3; Visions/life after death 203; work/Tower 200
memory 7, 37, 40, 126, 196–7
mental illness 116–18
Mercurius 187, 190
message 37
messiah 152–3
Metahistory 115
Metamorphosis (Ovid) 12
metaphor 12–14, 88–95, 97, 104; Jung/Vico affinities 120, 124; psychological types 58, 60–1; in science 22; topical invention 44, 55; and translation 8
metonymy 22, 44, 78, 88, 90, 93–5, 97
Middle Ages 75, 83, 100
middle term 48
Miller, J. 181
Mimesis 104, 120, 162 *see also* imitation
Modern Occult Rhetoric 17
modernism 82
Mogenson, G. 157, 165
monstrosity 151
motivation 19–20, 130–1, 133, 149
Mussolini, B. 112
Mysterium coniunctiones 75, 85
myth 107–8, 123–5; -making 106, 116; mythic formula 189–92; mythopoetics 6, 9, 11, 115
Myth of Analysis 108, 118

naming 4
nanny 195
narratio 14, 121, 142–3
narrative 17, 26–7, 55, 120, 181–2; Jung's rhetorical stance 30 *see also vera narrativa*
NASA 86
Native Americans 106, 117, 175, 193, 195, 201–2
natural law 161, 173
natural proof 48, 128
naturalness 50
nature 11–12
Nazis 3, 52
necessity 106
Negri, A. 152–3, 156
neo-Platonism 14–15, 71, 107–8; Jung/Vico affinities 122–5
Neumann, E. 116
New Language for Psychoanalysis 20
New Rhetoric 5, 47, 102, 193
New Science 3–5, 38, 44, 63, 71, 80, 82, 88–9, 111, 117, 172, 189; on becoming 10; imaginative universals 12; translators of 8
Nietzsche, F. 8, 97
nominalism 7, 12, 57–63, 65–6
North Africa 202
notatio 139–40, 143
nothing 69–72, 74–5, 79–80
noumena 188
nouns 8, 117, 172
numinosity 32–4, 79, 82, 187
nurse theft case 133, 139
Nussbaum, M. 157–8, 161

objectivity 6, 148, 163
objet petit a 87
occult 17–18, 87
Odyssey 38
Oedipal complex 31, 73, 98
Oegger, A. 96–7
Olbrechts-Tyteca, L. 5–6, 24, 47, 50, 90, 95, 102, 160–1, 175, 193–4
Old Testament 152, 159, 162–3
On the wisdom of the ancient Italians 49, 70, 119
Ong, W.J. 24, 45–6
ontology 39, 59, 115
opposites 45–6, 61, 66; union of 67, 78, 80
Oratoriae 30
Origen 62
ornamentation 16–19, 24, 26, 42, 51, 135
Osiris 78, 191
Ovid 12

pain 152–3, 156–7, 165

paintings 83
parables 14, 66–7, 122
Paraclete 164–5
paradox 27, 67, 75–8, 80–1, 87, 165, 187
paraphrase 9, 98–101, 104–5
Pascal, B. 193
passion 5, 150, 153–6, 160–1, 163; extremities 165–6
pathé 149, 155, 180
pathology 118, 146
pathos 39–40, 156
patriotism 162
Peirce, C.S. 137
Peithos 135–6
Perelman, C. 5–6, 15, 24, 41, 47, 50, 90, 92, 94–5, 99, 102, 122, 160–1, 175, 180, 188, 193–4
peripeteia see reversal
Persians 123
persona 197–8
personal 4–6, 9–10, 37, 112, 157–8, 206 *see also* individual
personality 9–10, 57, 67, 189; types 4, 61, 64
persuasion 36–7, 39–40, 46–7, 50, 160; vs. convincing 194
persuasiveness 149
phallus 97
phenomena and noumena 188
philology 190; Jung/Vico affinities 107, 119–21 *see also* etymology
philosophy 135; development of 11, 24; inclinations 57
phylogeny 115
physics 81, 85, 174, 192, 194
pineal gland 155
Plato 3, 8, 17, 22, 36, 39, 47, 62, 135, 144, 172–3 *see also* neo-Platonists
Platonism 70
ploche 141
Plotinus 122–3
Plotting a Cure 181
Plutarch 50
Poe, E.A. 22, 71–3, 98
poesis 4, 36, 39, 120, 167
poetic logic 7, 25, 43–4, 54, 88, 136
poetic universals 11, 109
Poetics 4, 52, 89, 154
poetry 70, 115; Platonic ban 22 *see also* figurative language
polemic 165, 181–2
Port Royal 173
Portrait of the Artist as a Young Man 168–70
postmodernists 2
pragmatism 137
precedence 60
precursor 123
predication 45, 59–60, 62–4, 95, 146
premises 13, 30
presentation 139
primal scene 31
primal time 6
primitives *see* archaic
Prince and the Pauper 84
probabilistic approach 7, 12, 14, 47
projection 82, 106, 113–14
pronunciato 37
proof 14, 19–20, 24, 30, 37, 39–41, 77, 101–2; forensics 128; methods of 129–35
property 11
prose 2
protagonists 29
Protagoras 20, 144
Protestantism 32, 34
Proust, M. 126
psychoanalysis 2; tensions with science 16–24
Psychoanalysis and Discourse 9, 23
Psychological Types 7, 40, 57, 67, 75, 129, 131, 149
Psychology and Alchemy 29, 33
Psychology and Religion 99
public 6
Pueblo 106, 117, 175, 193, 195, 201–2
Purloined Letter 71–4, 98
Putnam, H. 57, 59–60
Pythagoras 135

Quine, W. 57, 63
Quintilian 100, 136, 173, 181

Radden, G. 93
Raids on the Unthinkable 25

Rama 86
Ramus, P. 135–6
rationality 39, 85, 193
Ravenna 203
realism 12, 57, 62, 65, 193
reality 38, 40, 52, 58–9, 85–7, 93, 163, 174, 193–4; fantasy 66; Kantian 188
Realm of Rhetoric 122
reasonableness 193
reference 91
relativism 58–9, 194, 205
religion 32–3, 40, 66, 96, 99, 102–3, 158–9; memoirs 180, 185, 195–6, 201–2
Renaissance 3, 41, 135
repetition 141; compulsion 72–3
representation 58–61, 86–7
Republic 22
result phase 29
reversal 29, 31–3, 142
Rhetoric of animals 4
Rhetoric (Aristotle) 4, 7, 14, 19, 39, 42, 52, 89–90, 122, 128, 138, 149–50, 154, 178, 180
Rhetoric of Rhetoric 16
Rhetoric of Science 141
Rhetorical Situation 15
Rhetorical Voice of Psychoanalysis 18
Richards, I.A. 95
Ricoeur, P. 1, 8, 19–21, 57, 60–1, 63–4, 88–91, 95
ricorsi 3, 15n1, 124, 167
riddle 71, 76–8
Rieff, P. 177
ritual 202–3
romance 84–5, 87
Romans 3
romanticism 93
Rowland, S. 111–12
Rules of Metaphor 89
rumours 82, 104

Said, E. 3
salvation 164
Sartre, J.-P. 6
Satan 164
Saturn 171, 182, 189–91
Saussure, F. 94
savages 116–17
scarab 44–5
Schaeffer, J. 55, 99
schizophrenia 118, 189
scholastics 65–6, 101
school 197
science 85–6, 101–2, 142–5, 161, 174, 188, 192–4; Jung's mode of enquiry 1–2; scientific method 126–8; tensions with psychoanalysis/rhetoric 16–22, 24, 28
science fiction 84, 86–7
Scientology 17
Scult, A. 150
secrets 183–6, 202
self 9–10, 192, 195, 199, 203; discovery 10, 124–5; -knowledge 204
semiology 23
semiotics 67, 71
sensation 126, 146, 197
sensualism 57, 67
sensus communis see common sense
sermon 66, 152–3, 155–6
Sermons to the Dead 67, 174, 182, 199, 203
setting forth 30
Shafer, R. 20–1
Shakespeare, W. 48, 180
Shotter, J. 21–2, 176–7
showing forth 174–6, 178, 180
signification 93–4
Silvia Rhetoricus 144
similitude 120
Simulacrum and Simulation 69
sincerity 160
situation 178
Sloane, T. 24
sociology 21
Socrates 144
Sodom and Gomorrah 159
solution phase 29
sophists 20–1
soul 122–5
species 44–5, 56, 65, 91
Spence, D. 18, 20–1, 26
spontaneity 49–51, 53, 139
Starobinski, J. 182
stars 83

stasis theory 129–35
statement of place 29
Stern, W. 127, 132, 139
Stoics 41
Strachey, J. 22–3
structuralism 23, 69, 94
Structure of Scientific Revolutions 16
Struever, N. 6, 27, 36, 55, 136
style 1–2, 23, 58; low/middle/high 14–15, 122
Suarez, F. 173
subjectivity 5–6; of motivation 19
sublime 14
sun 195, 197, 202–3
swallowing 187, 191, 196
Swann's Way 126
Switzerland 29, 138, 180, 200
syllogism 39–40, 42, 46–8, 95, 148
symbolism 67, 98, 162–3
Symbols of Transformation 50, 96
synchronicity 44–5, 85, 124, 203
synechdoche 44, 66, 88, 90

talking cure 7–8, 16
Tavistock 142, 145
techné 36, 39
techniques 27
tension 29, 31, 34
Terry Lectures 103
Tertullian 64
testimony 52, 99, 101, 139
Thebes 80
theft 133–4, 139
theology 157–9, 164–5
therapy 23, 26–7, 110, 118
thinking/thought 39
throwness 150
Thucydides 8
thunder 184
Tibetan Book of the Dead 37
time and space 4, 6
time travel 84, 86
topical invention 24–5, 35, 39, 42–3
topical logic 7, 41, 43–6; medieval 65
topics 3, 14–15, 41–3, 45, 54, 100, 137–8
Topics (Aristotle) 39, 41–2
Topics (Cicero) 41
topos 30, 123
Totem and Taboo 94
Toulmin, S. 2, 18–21
Tower 195, 200
tragedy 154
transference 8
translation 8–10, 22–3, 75
transubstantiation 185
trauma 157
travels of Jung 200–3
tree 79
trellace 3
triad 37
trivium 37
tropes 44, 55, 60, 66, 88–9, 95
truth 7, 16, 79, 88, 101–2, 120, 192; forensics 128–9, 132, 136, 144; psychological types 58, 67; simulacrum 69; topical invention 40–1, 43, 46, 48, 52
turning point *see peripeteia*
Twain, M. 84, 86

UFOs 38, 67, 81–7, 104, 203
Ulysses 4
Ulysses 74, 125, 168
uncanny 8
unconscious 93–5, 98, 104, 121, 206; fantasy 74, 79; Jung's confrontation with 199; memoirs 198, 203; science 22–3, 26
universal audience 5–6, 143, 158, 193–4
universals 4–6, 10–13, 44–5, 56, 65, 91, 154, 157–8, 205–6; ontological 64–6 *see also* imaginative universals; intellectual universals
univocality 4, 11
Upanishads 37
USA 106, 117
Utopian literature 84–6

vagueness 196
value judgment 161
Varieties of Religious Experience 98–9
vera narrativa 4, 55, 115, 120, 174, 176, 199
verbs 20, 63–4, 117, 172

Verene, D.P. 44, 54–6, 106, 108, 110, 112, 114–15, 116, 124–5, 171, 179, 185, 204
Vickers, B. 24, 55, 114
visionaries 83–4, 103–5
visual attitude 123
Vita see Autobigraphy (Vico)
Volkerpsychologie 113

Wardy, R. 24
warmth 63, 186, 195, 197
Warnick, B. 24
warrants 2, 7, 14, 19
Ways of Worldmaking 58
Weber, S. 8
Weimer, W.B. 7, 22, 40, 42
West 36–7; consciousness 202
White, H. 115
Wilden, A. 72
will 50–1
Winnicott, D. 189
wisdom 43
Women who run with wolves 26
word association *see* associations
words *see* etymology
Wotan 82
writer *see* author
Wundt, W. 7, 106, 113, 126

Yahweh 151–3, 157, 159–60, 162–5

Zeno 9, 104
Zurich 142
Zwingli, H. 67